The Philosophy of Management Research

The field of management research is often regarded as a science discipline. As such, management researchers face similar methodological problems as their counterparts in other science disciplines. There are at least two ways that philosophy is connected with management research: ontological and epistemological. Researchers' ontological and epistemological stances affect the methods they consider legitimate in carrying out empirical research, and determine what they regard as a valid contribution to theory.

Despite an increasing number of scattered philosophy-based discussions of research methodology, there has not been a book that provides a systematic and comprehensive treatment of the subject. This book addresses this gap in the market and provides new ideas and arguments for guiding management researchers.

Eric W. K. Tsang is the Dallas World Salute Distinguished Professor of Global Strategy at the University of Texas at Dallas. He received his PhD from the University of Cambridge. He is among the top contributors to the philosophical analysis of methodological issues in management research.

Routledge Advances in Management and Business Studies

For a full list of titles in this series, please visit www.routledge.com/series/SE0305

The Philosophy of Management Research

Eric W. K. Tsang

Routledge
Taylor & Francis Group

LONDON AND NEW YORK

First published 2017
by Routledge
2 Park Square, Milton Park, Abingdon, Oxon OX14 4RN

and by Routledge
711 Third Avenue, New York, NY 10017

First issued in paperback 2017

*Routledge is an imprint of the Taylor & Francis Group,
an informa business*

British Library Cataloguing in Publication Data
A catalogue record for this book is available from the British Library

Library of Congress Cataloging-in-Publication Data
Names: Tsang, Eric W. K., author.
Title: The philosophy of management research / by
    Eric W.K. Tsang.
Description: Abingdon, Oxon ; New York, NY : Routledge, 2017. |
    Series: Routledge advances in management and business studies ;
    64 | Includes bibliographical references and index.
Identifiers: LCCN 2016015195 | ISBN 9781138902572 (hardback) |
    ISBN 9781315463216 (ebook)
Subjects: LCSH: Management—Research—Philosophy. |
    Management—Methodology—Philosophy.
Classification: LCC HD30.4 .T79 2017 | DDC 658.0072—dc23
LC record available at https://lccn.loc.gov/2016015195

ISBN 13: 978-0-8153-5076-7 (pbk)
ISBN 13: 978-1-138-90257-2 (hbk)

Typeset in Galliard
by Apex CoVantage, LLC

Contents

Illustrations

Figures

Tables

Preface

This book provides a philosophy-based discussion of some key methodological issues encountered by social scientists, in particular management researchers. It is the outcome of a long journey of getting to know philosophy that began when I was a teenager. Since philosophy is not the usual kind of knowledge that management researchers possess, I was occasionally asked – out of curiosity, I suppose – how I learned the subject. Let me briefly recollect this personal journey here.

I don't have a college degree in philosophy. My knowledge of philosophy accumulated naturally over the years; I started reading philosophy as a hobby when I was a secondary schooler in Hong Kong. I can't recall the title of the first philosophy book I read, but I can vividly remember the mind-altering experience when reading Bertrand Russell's *The Problems of Philosophy* decades ago. The book begins with the question: "Is there any knowledge in the world which is so certain that no reasonable man could doubt it?" To answer that question, Russell challenges a commonsensical view: "I believe that, if any other normal person comes into my room, he will see the same chairs and tables and books and papers as I see, and that the table which I see is the same as the table which I feel pressing against my arm." Then he picks the table as an example to illustrate that our knowledge of it may not be as certain as we may have thought. After reading his razor-sharp analysis of the experience of seeing and touching a table, I began to doubt whether the table in front of me really existed! This was not the kind of arguments found in the normal school subjects – such as Chinese, English, history, geography, physics, chemistry, biology, and mathematics – that I took at that time.

I read mostly Western philosophy. In fact, existentialism and the writings of Albert Camus partly shaped my character during those adolescent years. I continued the hobby when I worked for HSBC. After a long day at work, many of my colleagues would watch a movie, sing karaoke songs, or play mahjong. (In that era – the late 1980s – video games were not yet popular.) For me, I read philosophy as a way of relaxing my mind. My interest in philosophy of science was ignited by Karl Popper's works. Gradually I became one of his numerous admirers, fascinated by his rigor of argument, breadth of knowledge, and defense of liberal democracy. My reading list was also narrowed down to mainly philosophy of science with a focus on critical realism.

Later, I left HSBC and started my current career. When I studied in the doctoral program at the University of Cambridge, I sat in the late Professor Peter Lipton's course in philosophy of science as a means of indulging in my hobby. It was my most favorite course at Cambridge. My dissertation, under the supervision of Professor John Child, was about how Singapore companies learned from their joint venturing experience in China – a topic in the areas of organizational learning and strategic alliances, nothing related to philosophy. In those days, I never dreamed that my knowledge of philosophy could foster my career development.

The first opportunity to use my philosophical knowledge arose when I saw the *Academy of Management Review*'s call for the second special topic forum on theory development in the late 1990s. After reading the papers published in the first (1989) forum, I realized that philosophy could help tackle certain methodological issues. I invited my secondary school classmate, Professor Kai-Man Kwan, to join in. He was an Oxford-trained professional philosopher. Our paper, "Replication and Theory Development in Organizational Science: A Critical Realist Perspective," was accepted by the forum and published in 1999. Subsequently I published a number of philosophy-based papers in not only management journals but also marketing and information technology journals.

After spending some time in this career, I find that the training in research methodology received by management doctoral students is mostly concerned with statistical analysis and that training in logic and philosophy is neglected. There are at least two detrimental consequences. First, rigor of argument is sacrificed. From time to time I come across seriously flawed arguments in not only the term papers of doctoral students but also in manuscripts submitted to journals. Second, certain methodological issues are misunderstood. For example, statistics alone will not be able to explain why replication is or is not needed in our discipline simply because the issue is intimately associated with ontological and epistemological beliefs. Similarly, while generalizing from research findings appears to be a purely statistical problem, it is not – at least according to David Hume.

Contributing my effort to rectifying the situation, since 2011 I have been giving a seminar titled "Why Should Business Researchers Study Logic (and Philosophy)?" in business schools around the world – Australia, Japan, Hong Kong, mainland China, Singapore, and the U.S. While agreeing with my argument that there is a need for business, and not only management, researchers to receive more training in logic and perhaps philosophy as well, some seminar participants reflected that there were few introductory texts on the subject for doctoral seminars or handy references for management researchers. That "complaint" gave rise to this book. It goes without saying that given the general nature of methodological issues, researchers in other social science disciplines will also find the book useful.

I included in this book some of my previous philosophy-based journal papers. I revised and updated these publications to take into account current developments and in response to the comments received in my aforementioned seminar. For example, the chapter on replication is based on my 1999 *Academy of Management Review* paper. The literature on this topic has grown fast during the last decade or so. I kept the classification of replication intact, substantially revised some other parts, and added new materials. I believe the result is a much improved product. I tried to strike a balance between abstract philosophy and practical methodology, pitching the book at a suitably sophisticated level. I excluded pedantic philosophical issues that have few implications for management research. Although the topics in this book have been covered in the literature, readers will find a much stronger philosophical flavor in the treatment here. Yet in-depth knowledge of philosophy is not required for understanding most of the discussions.

I am deeply indebted to my co-authors of the papers included in this book; they are Professors Kai-Man Kwan, Kent Miller, Jochen Runde, and John Williams as well as Dr Florian Ellsaesser. When I worked with Kai-Man and John (another professional philosopher), I was amazed by their sharp minds and skills of formulating rigorous arguments. The collaborations turned out to be fruitful lessons for me. Kent and I share a common interest in philosophy. Our co-authored paper on theory testing, on which chapter 4 is based, took a rather long time to come to fruition. With the benefit of hindsight, this was a blessing for me because I had more opportunities to learn from him the skills of using philosophy to address methodological problems. Finally, Florian and I graduated from the same doctoral program, although more than 10 years apart. He has never pursued an academic career and is currently a successful entrepreneur. Through our collaboration I got to know the meaning of German efficiency. Through Florian, I had an opportunity to work with Jochen, an economist with an enviable amount of philosophical knowledge. I learned from him the skills of lucid reasoning and writing. In short, I was fortunate to have these companions who appeared at different points of my intellectual journey.

I would like to thank the guidance provided by Ms Yongling Lam (editor of Routledge for Business and Economics) and her assistant, Ms Samantha Phua. I can't think of another editor who is more patient, responsive, and helpful in answering my queries, some of which would only come from first-time book authors like me.

Last, but certainly not least, I am grateful for the support from my wife, Heidi, and our sons, Brian and Boris. The time I spent writing this book certainly reduced the time I could spend with them.

Eric W. K. Tsang
Dallas, Texas

Articles

Journal articles partially incorporated into this book

Ellsaesser, F., Tsang, E.W.K. and Runde, J. 2014. Models of causal inference: Imperfect but applicable is better than perfect but inapplicable. *Strategic Management Journal*, 35: 1541–1551.

Kwan, K.-M. and Tsang, E.W.K. 2001. Realism and constructivism in strategy research: A critical realist response to Mir and Watson. *Strategic Management Journal*, 22: 1163–1168.

Miller, K. D. and Tsang, E.W.K. 2011. Testing management theories: Critical realist philosophy and research methods. *Strategic Management Journal*, 32: 139–158.

Tsang, E.W.K. 2006. Behavioral assumptions and theory development: The case of transaction cost economics. *Strategic Management Journal*, 27: 999–1011.

Tsang, E.W.K. 2013. Case study methodology: Causal explanation, contextualization, and theorizing. *Journal of International Management*, 19: 195–202.

Tsang, E.W.K. 2014. Case studies and generalization in information systems research: A critical realist perspective. *Journal of Strategic Information Systems*, 23: 174–186.

Tsang, E.W.K. 2014. Generalizing from research findings: The merits of case studies. *International Journal of Management Reviews*, 16: 369–383.

Tsang, E.W.K. and Ellsaesser, F. 2011. How contrastive explanation facilitates theory building. *Academy of Management Review*, 36: 404–419.

Tsang, E.W.K. and Kwan, K.-M. 1999. Replication and theory development in organizational science: A critical realist perspective. *Academy of Management Review*, 24: 759–780.

Tsang, E.W.K. and Williams, J. N. 2012. Generalization and induction: Misconceptions, clarifications, and a classification of induction. *MIS Quarterly*, 36: 729–748.

1 Philosophy
An under-laborer serving researchers

Economics, psychology, and sociology are commonly regarded as the mother disciplines of management;[1] philosophy is often perceived as a recondite subject remotely related to management.[2] Yet, the fact is that every management researcher subscribes to a certain philosophical perspective consciously or unconsciously.[3] There are at least two ways – ontological and epistemological – that philosophy is connected with management research. Researchers' beliefs about the nature of the phenomena that they investigate reflect their ontological commitment. If ontology is concerned with the entities that constitute reality, their categorization and relations, epistemology is concerned with how researchers acquire, formulate, and justify their knowledge claims. Researchers' ontological commitment often affects their epistemological orientation. Their ontological and epistemological stances together affect the methods they consider legitimate in carrying out empirical research and determine what they regard as a valid contribution to theory.

Students of management research mostly associate research methodology with statistical analysis, without being aware that certain methodological problems are intrinsically philosophical in nature. An apotheosis of such problems is the well-known methodological debate that took place in economics more than half a century ago. Marginal theory in microeconomics assumes that firms maximize profits by equating marginal revenue and marginal cost. However, Lester's (1946) empirical study found that managers did not arrive at their production decisions through consulting schedules or multivariate functions showing marginal cost and marginal revenue. Lester (1946) thus attacked the realism of marginal theory's assumptions. This methodological problem has an ontological dimension because it is about whether or not an assumption corresponds with reality. There is also an epistemological dimension because researchers face the question: is it justifiable to have a theory, such as marginal theory, that has unrealistic assumptions? In response to the debate aroused by Lester's challenge, Friedman (1953: 15) put forward his famous methodological thesis:

> . . . the relevant question to ask about the "assumptions" of a theory is not whether they are descriptively "realistic," for they never are, but whether they are sufficiently good approximations for the purpose in hand. And this

question can be answered by seeing whether the theory works, which means whether it yields sufficiently accurate predictions.

His response attracted rejoinders from not only economists but also philosophers. Instead of settling the original debate, the thesis expanded it to become the most important methodological debate in economics (Mäki 2000).

Although the field of management is short of a similarly prominent debate, a recent heated debate concerning the nature of entrepreneurial opportunities has caught the attention of at least the entrepreneurship segment of the field. In delineating the domain of entrepreneurship research, Shane and Venkataraman's (2000) landmark paper considers the defining feature of entrepreneurial phenomena "the discovery and exploitation of profitable opportunities" (p. 217). The objective existence of entrepreneurial opportunities constitutes the foundation for entrepreneurship as a distinctive subject of study, with the nexus between individuals and opportunities forming the most promising research topic. Their stress on the objectivity of opportunities leads some researchers to deem that the discovery approach is based on a realist ontology (e.g., Alvarez and Barney 2013; Calás et al. 2009; Ireland 2007; Roscoe et al. 2013).

One of the major challenges facing the discovery approach is that opportunities are supposed to exist "out there," somewhat similar to "mountains – exist as objective phenomena just waiting to be discovered and exploited" (Alvarez and Barney 2007: 11). Some researchers attempt to address this ontological conundrum by emphasizing the creative agency of entrepreneurs and argue that "opportunities do not exist until entrepreneurs create them through a process of enactment" (Alvarez et al. 2013: 307). Based on the premises of constructivism, the creation approach proposes that opportunities are socially constructed entities which do not exist independently of the ways entrepreneurs conceive and develop them (Spedale and Watson 2014).

The opposing stances of the discovery and the creation approaches nicely illustrate how a fundamental conceptual issue – the nature of entrepreneurial opportunities – is deeply embedded in philosophy. The issue has far-reaching methodological implications because the two approaches provide different recommendations as to what constitutes a research problem, what theoretical procedures to follow, and how data are analyzed and interpreted. This debate also demonstrates the importance of philosophical training, which is currently neglected by most doctoral programs in management.[4] Contrary to the view of some researchers mentioned earlier, the discovery approach is grounded in empiricism instead of realism, a mistake that can be avoided easily by those who possess a reasonable level of knowledge in philosophy. To clarify the confusions caused by philosophical misunderstandings in the debate, my colleague and I propose the actualization approach, which is truly based on realism (Ramoglou and Tsang 2016).

A major reason for the perception that philosophy is hard to understand is the proliferation of vastly divergent perspectives. It is beyond the scope of this book to discuss them in detail. Rather, the next section briefly compares some major philosophical perspectives that have been discussed by management researchers.

A brief comparison of key philosophical perspectives

Since the 1980s there have been a growing number of articles in the management literature that employ philosophy to tackle methodological problems. The appendix reports a systematic review of 50 such articles published in nine leading management journals during the periods starting from their first issues until the end of 2015. Several popular philosophical perspectives emerge from the review. Table 1.1 summarizes the comparison of these perspectives in terms of ontology, epistemology, and methodology. Although they by no means exhaust the various perspectives that have appeared in the management literature, they provide a

Table 1.1 Comparison of positivism, postmodernism, critical realism, and pragmatism

	Positivism	*Postmodernism*	*Critical realism*	*Pragmatism*
Ontology	Objective reality with causality conceived as a constant conjunction of events	Reality socially constructed through subjective meanings, shared language, and social politics; multiple realities possible	Objective, stratified reality with domains of the real, actual, and empirical consisting of structures, mechanisms, and events	Objective reality, stressing the influence of the inner world of human experience in action
Epistemology	Empirical testing and verification of theories based on a hypothetico-deductive approach, with an aim of discovering law-like relationships that have predictive power	Knowledge produced by particular language games; rejection of metanarratives and acceptance of pluralism and fragmentation	Theoretical explanations retroduced from empirical data for describing the structures and mechanisms that generate the observable events, emphasizing explanation over prediction	Concepts and theories as instruments to solve human problems rather than as representations of reality; truth as an increase in the power to cope with the environment
Methodology	Researcher assumed to be unbiased and value-free; tendency toward using quantitative methods such as surveys, experiments, and analysis of archival data	Involvement of researcher in shaping research results explicitly described in detail; preference for semiotic and deconstructive techniques	Researcher reminded of the need to control for bias; no preference for any specific form of research methods	Researcher as active participant in the process of transformation; preference for mixed research methods

concise overview of the divergent ontological, epistemological, and methodological assumptions that different perspectives may represent.[5]

Positivism

Positivism, also called logical positivism, is a philosophical movement initiated
in the 1920s by the Vienna Circle – a group of philosophers, scientists, and
mathematicians who met periodically for discussions in Vienna from 1922 to
1938. Positivism flourished for about two to three decades and came under
severe attack in the second half of the last century (*Cambridge Dictionary of
Philosophy* 1999). In spite of its demise, positivism is often considered the most
popular philosophical perspective among management researchers as they are
usually trained in using quantitative research methods (Daft and Lewin 1990;
Gephart 2004; Johnson and Duberley 2000).

Positivism assumes the existence of an objective, mind-independent reality
that can be investigated by unbiased and value-free researchers. It adopts
the Humean conception of causality, regarding the constant conjunction of
events as an indicator of a causal relationship. To develop general theories
that consist of law-like relationships among a set of empirically measurable
constructs, positivists follow Hempel's (1965) covering law model of explanation and adopt a hypothetico-deductive approach to empirical research.
Theories are expected to not only explain but also predict phenomena,
reflecting Hempel's (1942: 38) argument for the symmetry between explanation and prediction:

> An explanation . . . is not complete unless it might as well have functioned
> as a prediction; if the final event can be derived from the initial conditions
> and universal hypotheses stated in the explanation, then it might as well
> have been predicted, before it actually happened, on the basis of a knowl-
> edge of the initial conditions and general laws.

The covering law model introduces a *logic* of scientific explanation: the explanandum (i.e., that which is explained) should be logically deducible from a set of
explanans (i.e., that which does the explaining) that include general laws (Douglas
2009).

Establishing a nomothetic body of knowledge usually requires statistical
analysis of large databases. Moreover, generalizability of research results depends,
to a great extent, on sample size. Therefore, positivists often prefer using quantitative methods such as questionnaire surveys, experiments, and analysis of
archival data. A caveat is that positivists do not confine themselves to the use
of quantitative methods. As Phillips (1987: 96) well says, "A positivist, *qua*
positivist, is not committed to any particular research design. There is nothing
in the doctrines of positivism that necessitates a love of statistics or distaste for
case studies." In fact, positivism is a popular perspective underlying case studies
in management (Gephart 2004).

Postmodernism

Postmodernism is a late-twentieth-century intellectual movement in the social sciences, ranging from economics, psychology, and sociology to cultural studies and urban planning (Rosenau 1992). Its influence extends to art, music, architecture, and literature, and it is considered to be one of the greatest challenges to established knowledge in the last century (Wisdom 1987). If the meaning of positivism is frequently misunderstood (see Phillips 2000; Wight 1998), the meaning of postmodernism is even more so as "there is no unified postmodern theory, or even a coherent set of positions" (Best and Kellner 1991: 2). Bearing the risk of over-simplification, I here summarize a few characteristics shared by the more popular postmodernist positions in the management literature such as constructivism and interpretivism.

Potter and López (2001: 4) summarize two key achievements of postmodernism as to promote "a more widespread recognition of the sociological determinants of knowledge" and to challenge "previous naïve notions of intellectual and scientific progress." Instead of assuming an objective reality, postmodernism regards reality as socially constructed via subjective meanings, shared language, and social politics (Berger and Luckmann 1967). While positivism considers that the methods of natural science should form the foundation for social inquiry, postmodernism rejects these methods. Unlike natural science phenomena, which are non-intentional, social science phenomena consist of the subjective meanings attached to the phenomena by their actors (Schutz 1970). It is therefore important to interpret such meanings based on the actors' own subjective frame of reference, resulting in the possibility of multiple realities.

Lyotard (1984) famously states that, simply put, postmodernism can be understood as incredulity toward metanarratives, which refer to grand, large-scale theories and philosophies of the world such as Marxism. Drawing on Wittgenstein's (1958) notion of language games, postmodernism regards knowledge as produced by particular language games in specific contexts and thus accepts pluralism and fragmentation. Instead of assuming researchers to be unbiased and value-free, postmodernism deems that a researcher approaches a phenomenon with a preconceived notion or theory about its nature and, by implication, a possible explanation for it (Kukla 2000). Postmodernism therefore recognizes the role played by researchers in shaping their findings and recommends that researchers' involvement in the whole process be reported in detail. Semiotic and deconstructive techniques are considered particularly useful postmodern research methods (Dickens and Fontana 1994). However, in the spirit of diversity and pluralism, postmodern researchers are open to other techniques and methods (Kilduff and Mehra 1997).

Critical realism

There is a variety of philosophical positions called "realist" (Harré 1986; Putnam 1987). The version discussed here, which is called critical realism, is advocated by Bhaskar (1978) and Harré (1970)[6] and was originally developed as a philosophy of science that attempts to answer the question, "what must reality be like in order to make science possible?" (Danermark et al. 2002). There are two basic philosophical theses: the existence of a reality independent of human perception and cognition, and this reality having its own inherent order (Fay 1996). Critical realism distinguishes between *transitive* objects of knowledge (i.e., scientific concepts, laws, and theories) and *intransitive* objects of knowledge (i.e., the structures and mechanisms associated with the phenomena to which our theories aim to explain) (Bhaskar 1978). The meaning of intransitivity is that these structures and mechanisms exist independently of our knowledge of them.

Structures and mechanisms refer to sets of internally related objects and ways of acting, respectively (Sayer 1992). Objects are internally linked within a structure such that their identities depend on their being in a relationship with the other components of the structure. For example, the supplier–buyer relation presupposes the existence of a purchase agreement, the good or service itself, monetary payment, customer support, warranty, and so forth; together they form a structure. A mechanism describes "a set of interacting parts – an assembly of elements producing an effect not inherent in any one of them" (Hernes 1998: 74). Using the analogy of a watch, Davis and Marquis (2005: 336) succinctly illustrate this abstract concept: "If a regression tells us a relation between two variables – for instance, if you wind a watch it will keep running – mechanisms pry the back off the watch and show *how*."

Structures and mechanisms together *may* generate events that in turn *may* be observed. Structures and mechanisms are real and should be distinguished from the patterns of events they generate. Critical realism distinguishes between three domains of reality: the real, actual, and empirical (Bhaskar 1978). While the empirical domain is made up of events experienced through direct or indirect observation, the actual domain consists of events whether or not they are observed. Lastly, the real domain is where causal mechanisms capable of producing patterns of events reside. The moves from the real to the actual domain and from the actual to the empirical domain depend on the ambient contingent conditions (Outhwaite 1987). That is, the same structure and mechanism may or may not generate any observable events under different circumstances.

Researchers collect data in the empirical domain and attempt to work out the structures and mechanisms in the real domain that can explain the pattern of events represented by the data. To achieve this, they engage in retroduction, a reasoning process intending to identify the properties that must exist in order for the phenomenon of interest to exist and be what it is (Danermark et al. 2002). Recognizing the contingent nature of generating observable events, critical realism emphasizes the explanatory rather than the predictive function of theories, contrary to the symmetrical view of positivism mentioned earlier.

To account for the contingent nature of observable events, critical realism distinguishes between closed and open systems. Bhaskar (1978: 70) defines a closed system as "one in which a constant conjunction of events obtains; i.e. in which an event of type a is invariably accompanied by an event of type b."

Scientific experiments are conducted precisely because of the open character of the world where events are subject to diverse causal variations. The idea of experiments in the natural sciences is to create closed systems by producing the appropriate conditions so that regular sequences of events occur in the empirical domain. Positivists focus on the regular sequences of events generated under controlled experimental conditions based on the Humean conception of causality. On the other hand, realists regard experiments as providing ideal conditions for the study of mechanisms (Pawson and Tilley 1997).

Taking into account the insights of both positivism and postmodernism, critical realism helps us steer a course between the Scylla of crude empiricism and the Charybdis of relativism. Critical realism deems that while researchers are not completely unbiased and value-free, they could conduct fairly impartial investigations if they consciously control their bias. In other words, critical realists reject the relativist view that there are no objective standards for evaluating across different theoretical positions (see Hunt 2003). Finally, there is no preference for any specific form of research methods.

Pragmatism

Pragmatism is a philosophical movement that began in the U.S. around the 1870s. Key figures include Dewey (1988), James (1975), and Peirce (1992) and contemporary philosophers such as Putnam (1995) and Rorty (1989). Pragmatism was formulated by Peirce in the Metaphysical Club in Cambridge, Massachusetts. It represented an attempt to find a way out of the seemingly irresolvable problems associated with metaphysics and epistemology that had haunted the development of science. A typical example of such problems is the famous Hume's problem of induction, which challenges that the use of inductive reasoning is unjustifiable (see Chattopadhyaya 1991 for a detailed explanation). Dewey (1988), for instance, argues that the objective of knowledge creation is not to uncover the real but, rather, to gain the kind of understanding that is necessary for solving problems as they arise. What principally characterizes pragmatism is its emphasis on the practical relations of human beings to their world.

Pragmatism accepts the importance of such processes as researcher interpretation, discursive framing, and social construction without denying that there is a reality which exists independently of the way it is observed or interpreted. Nevertheless, pragmatism stresses the influence of the inner world of human experience in affecting action. Knowledge is regarded as a tool for organizing experience, and concepts serve as rules of action or habits of belief (*Cambridge Dictionary of Philosophy* 1999). Truth is not to do with obtaining a correct "representation of reality in cognition" but is an expression of "an increase of the power to act in relation to an environment" (Joas 1993: 21). Truth is fallible and subject to revision when experience accumulates.

Pragmatism advocates the use of abduction for generating and justifying hypotheses (Peirce 1992). Somewhat similar to retroduction promoted by critical realism, abduction is one form of inference beyond deduction and induction.[7] Abduction is often called inference to the best explanation (see Lipton 1991) and is frequently used, in one form or another, in both everyday and scientific inference. Lacking a specific format, abduction combines reasoning with intuition and requires the researcher to be creative and imaginative in going from an observation to a hypothesis that explains the observation. For example, when we see water drops on a lawn in the morning, we might abduce that it had rained the night before.

As pragmatism abandons the conception of truth as correspondence to reality, hypotheses are validated through their practical consequences. Thus, in contrast to the positivist view of researcher as passive observer, pragmatism stresses the active participation of researchers in restructuring the environment. As Vygotsky (1978: 65) argues, "to study something means to study it in the process of change [in order to] discover its nature, its essence, for it is only in movement that a body shows what it is." Pragmatism rejects traditional dualisms such as mind versus body, facts versus values, and free will versus determinism. Accordingly, instead of engaging in the debate concerning the methodological dualism of qualitative versus quantitative methods, pragmatism chooses a middle position of mixed research methods – combining qualitative and quantitative techniques in a single study – with the objective of incorporating the strengths of both techniques (Johnson and Onwuegbuzie 2004; Maxcy 2003).

Philosophical under-laboring

What role does philosophy play in advancing a substantive discipline such as management? In discussing the relationship between philosophy and science, Locke (1996 [1689]: 3) maintains that philosophy can be "employed as the under-laborer in cleaning a little, and removing some of the rubbish, that lies in the way to knowledge."[8] In other words, philosophy assists substantive research by removing whatever obstacles are deemed to be standing in the way to progress (Bhaskar 1978). More specifically, Lawson (2004) identifies the following three under-laboring functions of philosophy with respect to economics:

1   demystifying – "exposing, criticizing and explaining the unsustainable assumptions, inconsistencies and confusions these may contain" (p. 320),
2   informing – "to help the researchers understand where they stand in the wider field of knowledge-producing activities, and to help make them aware of potentialities they might explore" (pp. 320–321),
3   method-facilitating – "to dissect and better understand the methods which economists or, more generally, scientists do, or could, use, and thereby to refine the methods on offer and/or to clarify their conditions of usage" (p. 321).

While this book focuses on the method-facilitating function, it occasionally clarifies common misconceptions and touches upon the demystifying function as well. Philosophy surely also offers insights to managers for solving problems and guiding actions in their organizations (Jones and ten Bos 2007), but this aspect of philosophical contribution will not be covered here because this book is concerned with management *research*, not managerial *practice*. Nevertheless, given the fact that research informs theory and that theory and practice are mutually interdependent, the methodological issues discussed in this book may subsequently influence managerial practice.

A philosophical perspective represents a worldview, consisting of a set of assumptions and beliefs about the nature of the world and how we interact with and come to know about it. Such assumptions and beliefs are not open to empirical testing in the usual sense of the term. Accordingly, a philosophical perspective is neither verifiable nor falsifiable. It does not follow that the choice of a perspective is a matter of personal taste and that one perspective is as good as others. A perspective can be objectively evaluated with respect to not only internal consistency and rigor of argument but also its effectiveness in serving its under-laboring role.[9] As I have advocated in my previous publications in this domain, I consider critical realism a well-developed worldview and the most effective perspective in tackling the methodological problems faced by management researchers.[10] Accordingly, the following chapters are based on critical realist premises with occasional comparison with other perspectives.

A brief overview

This book consists of eight chapters and one appendix as mentioned earlier. Each of chapters 2 to 6 address a crucial methodological issue often encountered by management researchers. Although these issues are distinct, they are in fact interrelated. For example, the core assumptions of a theory have to be realistic (chapter 3) because management researchers should aim at constructing mechanismic explanations (chapter 2); replicating prior empirical studies (chapter 6) is the most important means of checking whether and how far the findings of these studies are generalizable to other contexts (chapter 5); rigorous theory testing (chapter 4) requires, among other things, replications (chapter 6) and the distinction between different types of assumptions (chapter 3).

A key objective of theory is to explain phenomena. Chapter 2 first covers three major types of explanation: the covering law model, mechanismic explanation, and contrastive explanation. Since researchers may mistakenly think that explanations are necessarily general, the chapter discusses the generality of explanations. Finally it deals with the case where a research finding cannot be explained by any existing theory and thus the explanation is atheoretical. Or, worse still, the finding may not be explained at all, at least at the time it was discovered.

Every theory has assumptions. Chapter 3 discusses the role played by core assumptions in management theories and uses transaction cost economics (TCE) as an illustrative example. Core assumptions often constitute the foundation of the mechanismic explanations of a theory and thus should play a pivotal role in theory development. The chapter distinguishes between assumption-based and assumption-omitted theory testing and shows that empirical research in TCE has been dominated by assumption-omitted testing. To establish a solid foundation for a new theory, management researchers should pay more attention to assumption-based testing.

Management researchers' emphasis on theory building and verification – at the expense of falsification – has led to a proliferation of theories, which in turn gives rise to conceptual and managerial confusion. Chapter 4 identifies the practical and philosophical difficulties associated with testing management theories. It advocates a four-step approach for advancing theory testing that prioritizes identifying and testing for the presence and effects of hypothesized causal mechanisms, rather than solely focusing on correlational methods to jointly test the set of effects composing a theoretical system. The approach helps winnow out weak or false theories through improving the rigor of theory testing.

"Generalization," though a seemingly simple term, has created muddled debates among researchers. In particular, the case study as a key research method has often been criticized for generating results that are less generalizable than those of large-sample, quantitative methods. Chapter 5 clearly defines generalization and induction, proposes a classification of induction, and clarifies some major misconceptions about generalization. It rebuts the view that case studies are weak in generalizability. Case study results may be less generalizable than those of quantitative methods only in the case of within-population generalization. Case studies have merits over quantitative methods in terms of theoretical generalization, identifying disconfirming cases, and providing useful information for assessing the empirical generalizability of results.

Despite repeated calls for more replication research over the past decades, replications have been seldom published in management journals. Chapter 6 examines the reasons for the paucity of replications and argues that, despite claims to the contrary, replication is possible in the social sciences. To facilitate research practice, replications are classified into six types along two dimensions. The chapter then develops a detailed argument for the epistemic significance of replication and proposes a multi-focal pattern of knowledge accumulation to be integrated with the scattered pattern commonly found in management research.

Chapter 7 is different in nature than chapters 2 to 6: it introduces historiography, a method largely neglected by management researchers. Based on the example of the vertical integration between General Motors and Fisher Body in 1926, the chapter argues that historiography enriches theoretical knowledge and may provide "pre-theoretical" contexts for theory testing. A major advantage of historiography over case studies as a research method is that the availability of commonly accessible relics facilitates the replication of an original study. Historiography avoids a key limitation of experiments that research results may not be generalizable to the real world. Historiography also has a clear merit of identifying causal relationships by showing the mechanisms related to the focal event when compared with analysis of archival data. In addition to introducing historiography, this chapter nicely illustrates how the methodological issues covered in chapters 2 to 6 can be used to evaluate a research method.

The concluding chapter discusses the current predicament of the management discipline. On the one hand, many, if not most, management researchers consider the discipline scientific. On the other hand, some of their practices are not in line with the norms of scientific research. It discusses three possible responses to the predicament: stretching the meaning of "science," dropping the science label, and living up to the scientific status that the discipline aims to achieve. To address this predicament, the chapter calls for an open discussion by the whole management research community.

Throughout this book, especially in chapters 3 and 7, TCE is used as the main illustrative example. TCE is a leading organization theory (David and Han 2004) normally covered in organization and management theory, strategic management, or international business courses at the doctoral level. Researchers in organizational behavior should also be familiar with TCE. In short, TCE is likely to be the most well-known theory among management researchers, who are the target readers of this book.

Last but not least, I follow the argumentative tradition of Western philosophy; that is, if I am of the opinion that a view is flawed, I shall frankly and clearly point it out. As Mahoney (1993: 174) well says, "Disagreement does not entail disrespect." My comment should by no means be interpreted as constituting a personal attack on the holder(s) of the view. Rather, it is a necessary step in our collective pursuit of the truth – regardless of how truth is defined – and promotion of sound reasoning. It goes without saying that the comments I make in this book are not necessarily valid. I always welcome others pointing out my mistakes, if any.

Notes

1 I follow the Academy of Management in delineating the domain of the management discipline – as reflected by the Academy's divisions and interest groups – which includes, among others, the more common research streams such as organizational behavior, strategy, international business, and entrepreneurship.

2 As a social science subject, management's weak link with philosophy is in fact more apparent than real. Historically both the social and natural sciences originated from Western philosophy:

> It should not really be surprising that the social sciences and philosophy bear a profound and indissoluble link to one another. Like the natural sciences, each of the social sciences is a discipline that was once part and parcel of philosophy. Indeed, whereas the natural sciences separated themselves from philosophy in the 2,200 yeas from Euclid to Darwin, the social sciences became independent only during the course of the twentieth century.
>
> (Rosenberg 1995: 211)

3 I prefer using the word "perspective" instead of "paradigm" as some management researchers do (e.g., Brannick and Coghlan 2007; Romani et al. 2011) because the latter term has been used indiscriminately in a wide variety of ways – or abused, to be precise. For example, Donaldson (1995) distinguishes between structural contingency, population ecology, institutional, resource dependence, agency, and transaction cost theories. He considers each theory a paradigm and

used the terms "theory" and "paradigm" interchangeably. Moreover, even Kuhn (1962) himself failed to clearly define "paradigm" (Masterman 1970). More importantly, one of Kuhn's (1962) major uses of the term is in the context of one scientific theory (e.g., Newtonian mechanics) being replaced by another (e.g., Einstein's relativity theory) – the so-called scientific revolution. To extend its use to the domain of philosophy is a tenuous attempt. Attaching the label "paradigm" to both, say, Newtonian mechanics and positivism simply lacks academic rigor. The inappropriate use of "paradigm" in management was probably made popular by Burrell and Morgan's (1979) seminal work, *Sociological Paradigms and Organizational Analysis*. Burrell and Morgan (1979: 23) use the term "paradigm" to "emphasise the commonality of perspective which binds the work of a group of theorists together in such a way that they can be regarded as approaching social theory within the bounds of the same problematic." Note that their meaning of paradigm is narrower than that of a philosophical perspective.

4 This view is shared by a well-established management scholar: "with a few rare exceptions, PhD programs do not have a course on the philosophy of science" (Abrahamson 2008: 422).

5 Space limitations do not allow me to provide a more elaborate discussion of the philosophical perspectives. To have a more in-depth understanding of these perspectives, it is essential to know their origins – or even better, the history of Western philosophy. Interested readers may refer to Hunt (2003), who provides a concise and lucid introduction to the history of Western philosphy for beginners. A more motivated reader may read Russell's (1945) landmark work, *A History of Western Philosophy*. For an introduction to the more current developments in philosophy, I would recommend Soames's (2003a, b) two-volume *Philosophical Analysis in the Twentieth Century*.

6 Roy Bhaskar and his teacher at Oxford, Rom Harré, are unquestionably the two most important thinkers in the development of critical realism. Although they hold similar views concerning the critique of positivism and the basic premises of critical realism, they differ in other aspects, such as whether social structures have causal powers (see Harré and Bhaskar 2001). Such differences do not affect the critical realist arguments presented in this book.

7 Pierce used the terms "retroduction" and "abduction" interchangeably (see Burch 2011). Danermark et al. (2002) provide a nuanced distinction between the two.

8 Similar to Locke's under-laborer analogy is Socrates's famous midwife analogy. In a long passage of the *Theaetetus*, Socrates uses the analogy to describe his work as helping people give birth to the wisdom that resides in themselves (Benardete 2006: 1.13–1.14). Applying this analogy to the context of management research, philosophy's function may be regarded as helping people use their wisdom to tackle problems encountered in the research process.

9 Once I received this comment from a journal editor on my philosophy-based submission: "The choice of an ontological stand is necessarily subjective and guided by one's beliefs, so it is impossible to claim that one perspective is better reasoned than others." Contrary to this view, Russell's (1945) *A History of Western Philosophy* beautifully illustrates how a philosophical perspective can be evaluated. After describing a perspective, Russell often provides his critique in terms of how far the perspective is logically consistent (e.g., in his comment on Descartes), whether the philosopher practiced what he preached (e.g., Schopenhauer), and/or what loopholes the perspective contains (e.g., Kant). The following passage succinctly demonstrates his – sometimes bitter – critique:

> John Stuart Mill, in his *Utilitarianism*, offers an argument which is so fallacious that it is hard to understand how he can have thought it valid. He says:

Pleasure is the only thing desired; therefore pleasure is the only thing desirable. He argues that the only things visible are the only things seen, the only things audible are things heard, and similarly the only things desirable are things desired. He does not notice that a thing is "visible" if it *can* be seen, but "desirable" if it *ought* to be desired. Thus "desirable" is a word presupposing an ethical theory; we cannot infer what is desirable from what is desired.

(p. 778)

10 Critical realism is a growing intellectual movement in not only management but also various social science disciplines such as accounting (Modell 2009), economics (Lawson 1997), education (Clegg 2005), geography (Yeung 1997), information systems (Wynn and Williams 2012), marketing (Easton 2002), operations research (Mingers 2006), political science (Patomäki 2003), psychology (Sims-Schouten et al. 2007), social work (Houston 2001), sociology (Steinmetz 1998), and tourism (Downward and Mearman 2004).

It is beyond the scope of this book to compare in detail critical realism with other philosophical perspectives, but there are a few references for interested readers. Sayer (2000: part II) contrasts critical realism with various postmodernist perspectives. Bhaskar (1998: chapter 4) writes a critique of positivism and hermeneutics. Manicas (1987: chapter 12) comments on positivist empiricism. Danermark et al. (2002: chapter 6) argues for the merits of critical realism, as a methodological guide, over positivism (which is associated with quantitative methods), as well as hermeneutics and phenomenology (which are associated with qualitative methods). In strategic management, Mir and Watson (2000, 2001), on one side, and Kwan and Tsang (2001), on the other, debate the merits of constructivism and critical realism.

References

Abrahamson, E. 2008. 22 things I hate: Mini rants on management research. *Journal of Management Inquiry*, 17: 422–425.

Alvarez, S. A. and Barney, J. B. 2007. Discovery and creation: Alternative theories of entrepreneurial action. *Strategic Entrepreneurship Journal*, 1: 11–26.

Alvarez, S. A. and Barney, J. B. 2013. Epistemology, opportunities, and entrepreneurship: Comments on Venkataraman et al. (2012) and Shane (2012). *Academy of Management Review*, 38: 154–157.

Alvarez, S. A., Barney, J. B. and Anderson, P. 2013. Forming and exploiting opportunities: The implications of discovery and creation processes for entrepreneurial and organizational research. *Organization Science*, 24: 301–317.

Benardete, S. 2006. *The being of the beautiful: Plato's Theaetetus, Sophist, and statesman*. Chicago, IL: University of Chicago Press.

Berger, P. L. and Luckmann, T. 1967. *The social construction of reality*. New York: Anchor Books.

Best, S. and Kellner, D. 1991. *Postmodern theory: Critical interrogations*. New York: Guilford Press.

Bhaskar, R. 1978. *A realist theory of science* (2nd ed.). Hassocks, England: Harvester Press.

Bhaskar, R. 1998. *The possibility of naturalism: A philosophical critique of the contemporary human sciences* (3rd ed.). New York: Routledge.

Brannick, T. and Coghlan, D. 2007. In defense of being "native": The case for insider academic research. *Organizational Research Methods*, 10: 59–74.

Burch, R. 2011. Charles Sanders Peirce. Stanford Encyclopedia of Philosophy. <http://plato.stanford.edu/archives/fall2010/entries/peirce>.

Burrell, G. and Morgan, G. 1979. *Sociological paradigms and organizational analysis*. Hants, England: Ashgate.

Calás, M. B., Smircich, L. and Bourne, K. A. 2009. Extending the boundaries: Reframing "entrepreneurship as social change" through feminist perspectives. *Academy of Management Review*, 34: 552–569.

Cambridge dictionary of philosophy (2nd ed.). 1999. Cambridge, England: Cambridge University Press.

Chattopadhyaya, D. P. 1991. *Induction, probability, and skepticism*. Albany, NY: State University of New York Press.

Clegg, S. 2005. Evidence-based practice in educational research: A critical realist critique of systematic review. *British Journal of Sociology of Education*, 26: 415–428.

Daft, R. L. and Lewin, A. Y. 1990. Can organization studies begin to break out of the normal science straitjacket? An editorial essay. *Organization Science*, 1: 1–9.

Danermark, B., Ekström, M., Jakobsen, L. and Karlsson, J. C. 2002. *Explaining society: Critical realism in the social sciences*. London: Routledge.

David, R. J. and Han, S.-K. 2004. A systematic assessment of the empirical support for transaction cost economics. *Strategic Management Journal*, 25: 39–58.

Davis, G. F. and Marquis, C. 2005. Prospects for organization theory in the early twenty-first century: Institutional fields and mechanisms. *Organization Science*, 16: 332–343.

Dewey, J. 1988. *The middle works of John Dewey, Volume 12, 1899–1924: 1920, reconstruction in philosophy and essays (Collected works of John Dewey)*, J. A. Boydston (Ed.). Carbondale, IL: Southern Illinois University Press.

Dickens, D. R. and Fontana, A. 1994. *Postmodernism and social enquiry*. New York: Guilford Press.

Donaldson, L. 1995. *American anti-management theories of organization: A critique of paradigm proliferation*. Cambridge, England: Cambridge University Press.

Douglas, H. E. 2009. Reintroducing prediction to explanation. *Philosophy of Science*, 76: 444–463.

Downward, P. and Mearman, A. 2004. On tourism and hospitality management research: A critical realist proposal. *Tourism and Hospitality Planning and Development*, 1: 107–122.

Easton, G. 2002. Marketing: A critical realist approach. *Journal of Business Research*, 55: 103–109.

Fay, B. 1996. *Contemporary philosophy of social science*. Oxford, England: Blackwell.

Friedman, Milton. 1953. *Essays in positive economics*. Chicago, IL: University of Chicago Press.

Gephart Jr., R. P. 2004. Qualitative research and the *Academy of Management Journal*. *Academy of Management Journal*, 47: 454–462.

Harré, R. 1970. *The principles of scientific thinking*. Chicago, IL: University of Chicago Press.

Harré, R. 1986. *Varieties of realism: A rationale for the natural sciences*. Oxford, England: Basil Blackwell.

Harré, R. and Bhaskar, R. 2001. How to change reality: Story v. structure – a debate between Rom Harré and Roy Bhaskar. In J. López and G. Potter (Eds.), *After postmodernism: An introduction to critical realism*: 22–39. London: Athlone Press.

Hempel, C. G. 1942. The function of general laws in history. *Journal of Philosophy*, 39(2): 35–48.

Hempel, C. G. 1965. *Aspects of scientific explanation*. New York: Free Press.

Hernes, G. 1998. Real virtuality. In P. Hedström and R. Swedberg (Eds.), *Social mechanisms: An analytical approach to social theory*: 74–101. New York: Cambridge University Press.

Houston, S. 2001. Beyond social constructionism: Critical realism and social work. *British Journal of Social Work*, 31: 845–861.

Hunt, S. D. 2003. *Controversy in marketing theory: For reason, realism, truth, and objectivity*. Armonk, NY: M. E. Sharpe.

Ireland, R. D. 2007. Strategy vs. entrepreneurship. *Strategic Entrepreneurship Journal*, 1: 7–10.

James, W. 1975. *Pragmatism*. Cambridge, MA: Harvard University Press.

Joas, H. 1993. *Pragmatism and social theory*. Chicago, IL: University of Chicago Press.

Johnson, P. and Duberley, J. 2000. *Understanding management research: An intro-duction to epistemology*. London: Sage.

Johnson, R. B. and Onwuegbuzie, A. J. 2004. Mixed methods research: A research paradigm whose time has come. *Educational Researcher*, 33: 14–26.

Jones, C. and ten Bos, R. 2007. Introduction. In C. Jones and R. ten Bos (Eds.), *Philosophy and organization*: 1–17. New York: Routledge.

Kilduff, M. and Mehra, A. 1997. Postmodernism and organizational research. *Academy of Management Review*, 22: 453–481.

Kuhn, T. S. 1962. *The structure of scientific revolutions*. Chicago, IL: University of Chicago Press.

Kukla, A. 2000. *Social constructivism and the philosophy of science*. London: Routledge.

Kwan, K.-M. and Tsang, E. W. K. 2001. Realism and constructivism in strategy research: A critical realist response to Mir and Watson. *Strategic Management Journal*, 22: 1163–1168.

Lawson, T. 1997. *Economics and reality*. New York: Routledge.

Lawson, T. 2004. Philosophical under-labouring in the context of modern econom-ics: Aiming at truth and usefulness in the meanest of ways. In J. B. Davis, A. Marciano and J. Runde (Eds.), *The Elgar companion to economics and philosophy*: 317–338. Northampton, MA: Edward Elgar.

Lester, R. A. 1946. Shortcomings of marginal analysis for wage-employment prob-lems. *American Economic Review*, 36: 63–82.

Lipton, P. 1991. *Inference to the best explanation*. London: Routledge.

Locke, J. 1996 [1689]. *An essay concerning human understanding* (abridged and edited by K. P. Winkler). Indianapolis, IN: Hackett Publishing.

Lyotard, J. F. 1984. *The post-modern condition: A report on knowledge*. Minneapolis, MN: University of Minnesota Press.

Mahoney, J. T. 1993. Strategic management and determinism: Sustaining the con-versation. *Journal of Management Studies*, 30: 173–191.

Mäki, U. 2000. Kinds of assumptions and their truth: Shaking an untwisted F-twist. *Kyklos*, 53: 317–336.

Manicas, P. T. 1987. *A history and philosophy of the social sciences*. Oxford, England: Basil Blackwell.

Masterman, M. 1970. The nature of a paradigm. In I. Lakatos and A. Musgrave (Eds.), *Criticism and the growth of knowledge*: 59–89. Cambridge, England: Cam-bridge University Press.

Maxcy, S. J. 2003. Pragmatic threads in mixed methods research in the social sciences: The search for multiple modes of inquiry and the end of the philosophy of formalism. In A. Tashakkori and C. Teddlie (Eds.), *Handbook of mixed methods in social and behavioral research*: 51–89. London: Sage.

Mingers, J. 2006. A critique of statistical modelling in management science from a critical realist perspective: Its role within multimethodology. *Journal of the Operational Research Society*, 57: 202–219.

Mir, R. and Watson, A. 2000. Strategic management and the philosophy of science: The case for a constructivist methodology. *Strategic Management Journal*, 21: 941–953.

Mir, R. and Watson, A. 2001. Critical realism and constructivism in strategy research: Toward a synthesis. *Strategic Management Journal*, 22: 1169–1173.

Modell, S. 2009. In defence of triangulation: A critical realist approach to mixed methods research in management accounting. *Management Accounting Research*, 20: 208–221.

Outhwaite, W. 1987. *New philosophies of social science: Realism, hermeneutics and critical theory*. London: MacMillan.

Patomäki, H. 2003. *After international relations: Critical realism and the (re)construction of world politics*. London: Routledge.

Pawson, R. and Tilley, N. 1997. *Realistic evaluation*. London: Sage.

Peirce, C. S. 1992. *The essential Peirce: Selected philosophical writings, 1893–1913* (edited by N. Houser and C. J. W. Kloesel). Bloomington, IN: Indiana University Press.

Phillips, D. C. 1987. *Philosophy, science, and social inquiry: Contemporary methodological controversies in social science and related applied fields of research*. Oxford, England: Pergamon Press.

Phillips, D. C. 2000. *The expanded social scientist's bestiary: A guide to fabled threats to, and defenses of, naturalistic social science*. Lanham, MD: Rowman and Littlefield Publishers.

Potter, G. and López, J. 2001. After postmodernism: The new millennium. In J. López and G. Potter (Eds.), *After postmodernism: An introduction to critical realism*: 3–16. London: Athlone Press.

Putnam, H. 1987. *The many faces of realism*. La Salle, IL: Open Court.

Putnam, H. 1995. *Pragmatism: An open question*. Malden, MA: Blackwell.

Ramoglou, S. and Tsang, E. W. K. 2016. A realist perspective of entrepreneurship: Opportunities as propensities. *Academy of Management Review*, 41: 410–434.

Romani, L., Primecz, H. and Topçu, K. 2011. Paradigm interplay for theory development: A methodological example with the Kulturstandard method. *Organizational Research Methods*, 14: 432–455.

Rorty, R. 1989. *Contingency, irony and solidarity*. New York: Cambridge University Press.

Roscoe, P., Cruz, A. D. and Howorth, C. 2013. How does an old firm learn new tricks? A material account of entrepreneurial opportunity. *Business History*, 55: 53–72.

Rosenau, P. M. 1992. *Post-modernism and the social sciences: Insights, inroads, and intrusions*. Princeton, NJ: Princeton University Press.

Rosenberg, A. 1995. *Philosophy of social science* (2nd ed.). Boulder, CO: Westview Press.

Russell, B. 1945. *A history of Western philosophy*. New York: Simon and Schuster.

Sayer, A. 1992. *Method in social science: A realist approach* (2nd ed.). London: Routledge.

Sayer, A. 2000. *Realism and social science*. London: Sage.

Schutz, A. 1970. *On phenomenology and social relations*. Chicago, IL: University of Chicago Press.

Shane, S. and Venkataraman, S. 2000. The promise of entrepreneurship as a field of research. *Academy of Management Review*, 25: 217–226.

Sims-Schouten, W., Riley, S. C. and Willig, C. 2007. Critical realism in discourse analysis: A presentation of a systematic method of analysis using women's talk of motherhood, childcare and female employment as an example. *Theory and Psychology*, 17: 101–124.

Soames, S. 2003a. *Philosophical analysis in the twentieth century, Volume 1: The dawn of analysis*. Princeton, NJ: Princeton University Press.

Soames, S. 2003b. *Philosophical analysis in the twentieth century, Volume 2: The age of meaning*. Princeton, NJ: Princeton University Press.

Spedale, S. and Watson, T. J. 2014. The emergence of entrepreneurial action: At the crossroads between institutional logics and individual life-orientation. *International Small Business Journal*, 32: 759–776.

Steinmetz, G. 1998. Critical realism and historical sociology: A review article. *Comparative Study of Society and History*, 40: 170–186.

Vygotsky, L. S. 1978. *Mind in society: The development of higher psychological processes*. Cambridge, MA: Harvard University Press.

Wight, C. 1998. Philosophical geographies: Navigating philosophy in social science. *Philosophy of the Social Sciences*, 28: 552–566.

Wisdom, J. O. 1987. *Challengeability in modern science*. Dorset, England: Blackmore Press.

Wittgenstein, L. 1958. *Philosophical investigations*. Oxford, England: Basil Blackwell.

Wynn Jr., D. and Williams, C. K. 2012. Principles for conducting critical realist case study research in information systems. *MIS Quarterly*, 36: 787–810.

Yeung, H. W.-C. 1997. Critical realism and realist research in human geography: A method or a philosophy in search of a method? *Progress in Human Geography*, 21: 51–74.

2 Explanation
Different ways of answering "why?"

Theories are created to explain phenomena of interest by imposing order on unordered human experiences (Dubin 1978). Although another major function of theory is to predict, thorough explanation constitutes the foundation for such prediction (Salmon 1998). But to understand how theory explains, we first need to understand the nature of explanation. As Sutton and Staw (1995: 374) argue, "Data describe *which* empirical patterns were observed and theory explains *why* empirical patterns were observed or are expected to be observed." In other words, theory explains phenomena by providing an answer to the question "why?" rather than only the question "what?" (Hempel and Oppenheim 1948). Following Lipton (1991), I denote answers to "why" questions as causal explanations. Although explanations need not be causal (Ruben 2012),[1] this chapter focuses on causal explanations, which are central to management research.

For the sake of discussion, causes refer to "events that make their effects occur" (Ruben 2012: 212). I hold a nondeterministic view of causation: simply put, a cause raises the probability of the occurrence of its effect but does not necessarily make the occurrence a certainty (Lewis 1986; Suppes 1984). I adopt a realist perspective of explanation, believing that "some objective relation between the events underlies, or grounds, the explanatory relation between their descriptions" (Kim 1994: 57). The term "causal explanation" consists of two components: causality and explanation. Strawson (1985: 115) draws a realist distinction between the two:

> . . . causality is a natural relation which holds in the natural world between particular events or circumstances . . . But if causality is a relation which holds in the natural world, explanation is a different matter . . . it is not a natural relation in the sense in which we perhaps think of causality as a natural relation. It is an intellectual or rational or intensional relation. It does not hold between things in the natural world, things to which we can assign places and times in nature. It holds between facts or truths.

Note that constructivists would conflate the two. Although Strawson's comment is intended for natural phenomena, it is equally applicable to social phenomena that management researchers study. An observed phenomenon was the outcome of interactions of a set of causes. To explain the phenomenon is to engage in an academic exercise of inferring such causal interactions. The causes and their interactions that actually gave rise to the phenomenon constitute "a natural relation." They are unique in the sense that no other causal interactions led to that phenomenon. In contrast, the explanation of the phenomenon may vary from one researcher to another because it is just "an intellectual or rational or intensional relation" after all.[2]

A good example illustrating Strawson's point is the vertical integration between General Motors and Fisher Body discussed in chapter 7 concerning the merits and limitations of historiography. The integration that took place in 1926 was the outcome of a unique and objective nexus of causal factors operating until the event's occurrence. Klein et al. (1978) were the first to explain the event as a holdup example supporting the transaction cost economics (TCE) arguments. However, their explanation was later challenged by other researchers.

This chapter first discusses the covering law model, which is the best-known account of explanation (Friedman 1974). Then it introduces mechanismic explanation, on which subsequent chapters are based. Unlike the covering law model that is more than half a century old, mechanisms and mechanism-based explanations have attracted substantial attention from both natural and social scientists during the past two decades. To account for the fact that we do not explain events, but only aspects of events (Hempel 1965), the chapter also discusses contrastive explanation, which specifically accommodates this essential characteristic of explanation. Since researchers may mistakenly think that explanations, such as those embedded in theories, are necessarily general, the chapter discusses the generality of explanations. Finally, it deals with the case where a finding cannot be explained by any existing theory and thus the explanation is not theoretical in nature or, worse still, no explanation can be found.

The covering law model

The origin of the model can be traced to Mill (1843), but its prominence grew as the development of neopositivism gathered speed during the middle of the last century. The model has two versions. The first, and more well-known, version is Hempel's (1942) deductive-nomological (D-N) model, which consists of one or more general laws and existential statements stating that certain events occurred. A general law is "a statement of universal conditional form which is capable of being confirmed or disconfirmed by suitable empirical findings" (Hempel 1942: 35), and it is assumed to be deterministic in nature. It states a regularity of the following type: whenever an event of a specified kind C occurs, an event of a specified kind E will occur. The claim that a set of events – say, $C_1, C_2, \ldots, C_n$ – have caused the occurrence of event E amounts to the following D-N explanation that consists of three main steps:

1   a set of general laws stating that if $C_1, C_2, \ldots, C_n$ occur, then E will occur,
2   a set of existential statements confirming the occurrence of $C_1, C_2, \ldots, C_n$,
3   a deduced conclusion stating the occurrence of E.

Steps 1 and 2 are the premises, and Step 3 is the conclusion.

Deterministic general laws that rule out exceptions are uncommon in the social sciences; as Hempel and Oppenheim (1948: 140) admitted, "the regularities invoked cannot be stated with the same generality and precision as in physics or chemistry." Hempel (1965) therefore later retreated to a probabilistic version, which is called the inductive-statistical (I-S) model:

1   a set of general laws stating that if $C_1, C_2, \ldots, C_n$ occur, then the probability is p that E will occur,
2   a set of existential statements confirming the occurrence of $C_1, C_2, \ldots, C_n$,
3   a conclusion stating that E will occur with a probability of p.

On the one hand, the I-S model does not seem to differ effectively from its D-N counterpart in terms of explanation because, in this case, E did occur. On the other hand, when prediction is called for, the I-S model can only suggest the probable occurrence of E when the premises are true whereas the D-N model deduces E's occurrence with certainty.

To explain why, for example, oil prices go up in abnormally cold winters, we need to invoke the law of supply and demand. Note that under the covering law model, explanation and prediction have the same logical structure – or are subject to what is usually called the symmetry thesis (Achinstein 2000). If we have an adequate explanation of a phenomenon, then, in principle, we can predict its occurrence (Gasper 1990). In Hempel's (1942: 38) own words:

> Quite generally, prediction in empirical science consists in deriving a statement about a certain future event (for example, the relative position of the planets to the sun, at a future date) from (1) statements describing certain known (past or present) conditions (for example, the positions and momenta of the planets at a past or present moment), and (2) suitable general laws (for example, the laws of celestial mechanics). Thus, the logical structure of a scientific prediction is the same as that of a scientific explanation . . . While in the case of an explanation, the final event is known to have happened, and its determining conditions have to be sought, the situation is reversed in the case of a prediction: here, the initial conditions are given, and their "effect" – which, in the typical case, has not yet taken place – is to be determined.

Despite its elegance, the symmetry thesis does not always hold even in the natural sciences. For example, geologists can satisfactorily explain earthquakes *after* they have occurred, but fail to predict their occurrence, at least according to the current state of the art. Other than the fact that the covering law model has intrinsic problems such as explanatory irrelevance (see Kitcher 1981),[3] it is more applicable to the natural rather than social sciences as laws or law-like generalizations are less common in the latter (Ruben 1990). In fact, Sayer (1992: 2) goes further to argue that "social science has been singularly unsuccessful in discovering law-like regularities."

Mechanismic explanation

The covering law model is not wholly satisfactory even in the natural sciences because "no event or process is regarded as having been satisfactorily understood unless its actual or possible mechanism has been unveiled" (Bunge 1997: 454). The covering law model is deficient in this respect. In line with the discussion of how structures and mechanisms may generate observable events in chapter 1, a critical realist perspective argues for what Bunge calls "mechanismic explanation," which describes the cogs and wheels of the causal process through which the event was brought about (Hedström and Ylikoski 2010). For social studies, King et al. (1994: 85–86) maintain that "an emphasis on causal mechanisms makes intuitive sense: any coherent account of causality needs to specify how its effects are exerted." Even if we only focus on predictions, as Friedman (1953) did with respect to economic theories, we need to understand the mechanism underlying a theory's predictive power in order to properly make use of the normative implications of the theory. As Hodgson (2004: 404) comments, "A faulty explanation would be likely to lead to faults in corporate strategy and in the design of governance structures."

A causal mechanism (M) is usually conceptualized as opening the black box between inputs (I) and outcomes (O) of a causal process: "Statements of the type 'If I, then O' ($I \rightarrow O$) become 'If I, through M, then O' ($I \rightarrow M \rightarrow O$)" (Falleti and Lynch 2009: 1146). It is not a single *variable* or a set of *variables* but an *account* of the way the events occur (Pawson 1989).[4] Mechanisms facilitate causal inference. On the positive side, the knowledge that M connects I to O supports the inference that I is a cause of O. The negative flip side is that the absence of a plausible mechanism that can be postulated to link I to O provides a sound reason for not hypothesizing a causal relation between I and O (Hedström 2005; Steel 2004). In this case, the problem of confounders, where I and O are caused by a confounder, should be investigated. The problem of confounders remains a difficult challenge in social research, and mechanisms have been proposed as a solution:

> We can best exclude the possibility of a spurious correlation between variables by forming a hypothesis about the mechanisms at work in the circumstances. If we conclude that there is no plausible mechanism linking nicotine stains to lung cancer, then we can also conclude that the observed correlation is spurious.
>
> (Little 1991: 24–25)

In brief, proponents of mechanismic explanation generally hold the view that I and O are causally linked if and only if there is an M connecting them (Glennan 1996; Steel 2004).

In line with Strawson's (1985) comment mentioned earlier, different mechanisms can be proposed to explain the same event although the event was surely the outcome of some specific mechanism(s). Harré (1970: 125) argues that "scientific explanation consists in finding or imagining plausible generative mechanisms for the patterns amongst events." For instance, the interrelationship between the temperature and pressure of a gas is explained in terms of the action of its molecules – the causal mechanism in this case. Typically mechanisms in general and social mechanisms in particular are unobservable (Kiser and Hechter 1991), and their descriptions are therefore bound to consist of constructs that do not appear in empirical data (Bunge 2004).

Consider a typical TCE explanation. As the asset specificity of a transaction increases, redeployability of the asset for alternative uses decreases. This in turn will increase bilateral dependency and contracting hazards between the parties concerned. Owing to bounded rationality, contracts are necessarily incomplete and offer limited protection against opportunistic behavior. The high-powered incentives of the market form of governance impede adaptability among trans-acting parties, resulting in high transaction costs that are required to monitor exchange behavior and guard against opportunism. Thus markets are ill equipped to deal with situations of high bilateral dependency. Transaction-cost-economizing considerations will push transactions with high asset specificity into more inte-grated forms of governance, such as hybrid and hierarchy. How this mechanism actually generates observable events in the empirical domain depends on a number of contingencies, the most prominent of which concerns the institutional environment (political and legal institutions, laws, customs, and norms) (North 1991). Changes in the institutional environment – the context within which a causal mechanism operates – shift the comparative costs of markets, hybrids, and hierarchies (Williamson 1997).

The role of context

Following Falleti and Lynch (2009: 1152), I define context as "the relevant aspects of a setting (analytical, temporal, spatial, or institutional) in which a set of initial conditions leads (probabilistically) to an outcome of a defined scope and meaning via a specified causal mechanism or set of causal mechanisms." Since the phenomena that management researchers study occur in open systems, it is not surprising that context plays a critical role in mechanismic explanation. Pawson and Tilley (1997: 69) argue that "the relationship between causal mechanisms and their effects is not fixed, but contingent," depending on the related context. They sum up their position in what they call the basic realist formula: mechanism + context = outcome. Their claim is not simply that causal relationships vary across contexts; rather it is a more fundamental claim that the context within which a causal mechanism operates is, to a varying extent, intrinsically involved in that mechanism (Maxwell 2004) and cannot be controlled for by adding variables to, say, a regression model.

An important context for management research is related to culture. A good example is Xiao and Tsui's (2007) test of structural holes theory by conducting a questionnaire survey of four high-tech companies in China. The theory main-tains that an individual who holds a brokering position – connecting two or more separate individuals (who form a structural hole between them) – has more social capital than one who does not (Burt 1997, 2000). Brokers enjoy two kinds of benefits: information (having access to more nonredundant information and thus more opportunities) and control (deciding whose interests to serve with those opportunities). Previous empirical studies in this domain were mostly limited to the Western context with a strong individualistic, free-competition orientation (Burt et al. 2000). Xiao and Tsui (2007: 2) phrase the motivation of their study by highlighting the issue of context: "How the mechanisms of social capital operate in other contexts with different cultural norms and market mechanisms remains largely unexplored."

They examined the roles of both national culture and organizational culture and found some significant effects:

> Our empirical results show that, in a collectivistic culture, structural holes in an employee's career network tend to be detrimental to the employee's career development. Further probing at the organizational level revealed that the network consequences of social capital differ across organizations. Although structural holes may bring positive returns to individual actors in a market-like, low-commitment organizational culture, it is network closure that will bring advantages to the actors, by facilitating trust, reciprocity, and reputation, in a clan-like, high-commitment organization with a strong cohesive culture.
>
> (Xiao and Tsui 2007: 23)

In brief, their core finding is that structural holes are detrimental to employees' career performance in Chinese organizations, in sharp contrast to the positive effects of structural holes identified by prior studies that were based on Western samples. In other words, for the same I (employees' network positions), O (their career performance) is different for the former when compared with the latter. Xiao and Tsui attribute the different O to the different M caused by the different contexts within which M operates.

The importance of meaning

Causal mechanisms in the social sciences may include not only impersonal, material factors but also personal intentions and interpretations of the actors involved. The latter often carry more weight than the former. As Sayer (1992: 30) states, "social phenomena are *concept-dependent* . . . What the practices, institutions, rules, roles, or relationships *are* depends on what they mean in society to its members." In this respect, critical realism incorporates insights from the interpretivist approach to explanation that is based on interpretive understanding (*Verstehen*). Weber (1949) regards the motive underlying an action as its cause. A specific feature of this kind of cause is that researchers can understand it by basing it on the assumption that people act rationally.

Weber emphasizes the importance of *Verstehen* as to what actually motivates people to act in individual cases. In line with the hermeneutic tradition (Habermas 1971), this approach takes into account the subjectivity of actors by trying to understand the meanings of their actions and interpretations. Suppose a manager decided to empower his subordinates. To study his decision, a researcher has to first understand the manager's interpretation of the empowerment concept. In other words, the researcher engages in double hermeneutics:

> . . . the subjects of study in the social sciences and the humanities are concept-using beings, whose concepts of their actions enter in a constitutive manner into what those actions are. Social life cannot even be accurately described by a sociological observer, let alone causally elucidated, if that observer does not master the array of concepts employed (discursively or non-discursively) by those involved.
>
> (Giddens 1987: 18–19)

This is in contrast to the single hermeneutics of natural scientists who attempt to understand and theorize the structure and behavior of natural subjects that are not themselves concept-using beings. The only meanings natural scientists have to interpret are those within their own community, whereas social scientists have to mediate between their own frames of meaning and those of their subjects (Sayer 1992).

In spite of its insights, the hermeneutic tradition is not without problems from a critical realist perspective. One such problem is "the tendency of hermeneuticists to assume that society is *only* like a text, requiring *nothing more* than interpretation of its meanings" (Sayer 2000: 143). This tendency leads to a flawed idea of explanation:

> Social *explananda* indeed depend upon (or consist in) intentional human agency, so that reference to beliefs and other conceptual matter will in general be necessary for an adequate social explanation, but it will not – even where the *explanandum* is itself conceptual – in general be sufficient for it. For such action always, or almost always, has a *material* (outer) aspect, so that it cannot be reduced to its *conceptual* component (or inner cause).
>
> (Bhaskar 1998: 136)

More specifically, Bunge (1997) comments that the hermeneutic tradition makes no reference to any social mechanism: it merely hints at a mental source of individual action without any mechanism being conjectured. He suggests that at best hermeneutics may play a supplementary role in the realist process of constructing mechanismic explanations.

A final word of caution is that although the mechanism-based approach is commonly considered superior to the covering law model, it is not a panacea to all the problems associated with empirically establishing a causal relationship.

Gerring (2010) raises a number of thought-provoking challenges to the approach. That said, mechanismic explanation points to a promising direction for future methodological research.

Contrastive explanation

As Hempel (1965) succinctly argues, we do not explain events, but only aspects of events. We structure explanations based on our explanatory interests. The contrastive approach to explanation specifically accommodates this intrinsic characteristic of explanation. A basic tenet is that explanation-seeking questions and explanations have a contrastive form, whether implicit or explicit (Garfinkel 1981; Ruben 1987; van Fraassen 1980). Thus, the contrastive approach takes great pains to analyze and reframe explanation-seeking questions. Two crucial elements of a contrastive question – allomorph as well as fact and foil – are discussed below.

Allomorph

Dretske (1977) argues that a request for an explanation of why a certain event occurred might raise different questions, depending on which word or words in the description of the event are stressed. Consider a fictitious event described by the following statement:

S   Daimler-Benz manufactures its car seats.

The statement may be given different embodiments, which Dretske (1977) calls allomorphs, depending on its contrastive contour. The four different allomorphs of S are:

S_a *Daimler-Benz* manufactures its car seats.
S_b Daimler-Benz *manufactures* its car seats.
S_c Daimler-Benz manufactures *its* car seats.
S_d Daimler-Benz manufactures its *car seats*.

Each allomorph refers to a different aspect of an event and suggests a distinct type of contrastive questions. An allomorph reflects the interest of the questioner. For example, a TCE-related question such as "Why does Daimler-Benz manufacture its car seats instead of purchasing them from the market?" refers to allomorph S_b, whereas another question, "Why does Daimler-Benz, instead of Toyota, manufacture its car seats?" refers to S_a. Needless to say, answers to different contrastive questions normally involve different mechanismic explanations.

As Lewis (1986: 217) argues, "to explain an event is to provide some information about its causal history" usually by someone who possesses the information to someone who does not. However, the entire causal history of an event is often incredibly complex (Marchionni 2006), and providing a complete account of this history is practically impossible (Hitchcock 1999). For every "why" question, there is an almost infinite number of causes that could be cited. Every causal explanation may lead to a further explanation *ad infinitum*. Each of these earlier causes is part of the causal history of the event. If we want to answer the question of why Daimler-Benz manufactures its car seats, we could go as far back as the big bang because without the big bang, Daimler-Benz would not have existed in the first place. In fact, the big bang is part of the causal history of every event but explains only a few (Lipton 1990).

Better questions give rise to better explanations (Mäki 2004). To make the task of explaining an event manageable, we need to indicate which aspect of the event is up for explanation by, for instance, paraphrasing the prior question as, "Why does Daimler-Benz manufacture its car seats instead of purchasing them from the market?" The revision makes clear which aspect of Daimler-Benz's production of car seats needs to be explained. In other words, the contrastive form of questioning eliminates a vast number of elements and aspects of the causal history of an event that are not explanatorily relevant to the explanation-seeking question (Ylikoski 2007) and facilitates the selection of the appropriate explanatory factors from the causal history for which we search an explanation (Marchionni 2006).

Fact and foil

The canonical form of a contrastive question is, "Why P rather than Q?" where P is the fact to be explained and Q is the foil, an alternative to it. Q can be either a single alternative or a set of alternatives. For the aforementioned contrastive question, "Why does Daimler-Benz manufacture its car seats instead of purchasing them from the market?" manufacturing car seats is the fact, and the single alternative – purchasing car seats from the market – is the foil. The idea is that a fact is often not specific enough and we need to add a foil for indicating which aspect of the fact is up for explanation. Thus, a contrastive explanation of a fact is just a partial explanation of that fact. A caveat is that a contrastive question of the form "Why P rather than not-P?" is problematic because the global foil – not-P – is usually too general to narrow down the scope of explanation (Lipton 1993). In fact, this contrastive question adds no content to the plain non-contrastive question "Why P?" (Day and Botterill 2008).

When someone asks, "Why P rather than Q?" there is a presupposition that it was not possible for both P and Q to occur, implying that the fact and the foil are incompatible in this sense. For example, Daimler-Benz's production of car seats is incompatible with its purchasing them from the market, as the two options could not occur at the same time – at least not for a specific lot of car seats. Nevertheless, it is a misconception that contrasts must be incompatible (Barnes 1994). Suppose we revise the contrastive question as, "Why does Daimler-Benz manufacture its car seats rather than seat belts?" Since it was possible for the company to manufacture both, the contrast is compatible.

Because the factors that explain a fact relative to one foil will not generally explain it relative to another foil, a contrastive question imposes a constraint on explanation. It restricts which of the virtually infinite number of causes in the causal history of a fact are explanatorily relevant. If we are lucky or clever enough to work out a contrast where the fact and the foil have very similar causal histories, most potential explanations are immediately "cancelled out," and, as a result, we have a more manageable research program (Lipton 1991).

Uses

Woodward (2003: 146) argues that "all causal claims must be interpretable as having a contrastive structure." The contrastive approach to explanation has been used by social scientists implicitly. A good illustration can be found in Coase's (1937) pioneer work on TCE. Coase asks not just this simple question, "why is there any organisation?" but a contrastive question, "having regard to the fact that if production is regulated by price movements, production could be carried on without any organisation at all, well might we ask, why is there any organisation?" (p. 388). His question can be paraphrased as: why are some production activities organized in firms rather than markets? Before answering the question, he provides information on what "the firm" and "the market" stand for:

> Outside the firm, price movements direct production, which is co-ordinated through a series of exchange transactions on the market. Within a firm, these market transactions are eliminated and in place of the complicated market structure with exchange transactions is substituted the entrepreneur-co-ordinator, who directs production.
>
> (Coase 1937: 388)

This elaboration facilitates Coase's subsequent discussion about the differences between firms and markets in organizing production.

Although Coase's article is entitled "The Nature of the Firm," the question "Why is there any organization?" involves a set of causes that is simply too huge to deal with. Yet Coase's contrastive question helps focus the analysis on the causal histories of organizing production in firms versus markets and is far more manageable. Coase identifies the differences between the situation where production is directed by an entrepreneur and the situation where it is directed by the price mechanism. The main difference is that in the market, contracts have to be negotiated for each exchange transaction. In contrast, an entrepreneur does not have to negotiate a series of contracts with his or her employees, who are supposed to obey the directions of the entrepreneur within certain limits as stated in the employment contract. Hence, the cost of contracting in the market can be avoided by carrying out production activities within the firm.

The functions of contrastive explanation can also be illustrated by the problems that arise due to its absence.[5] A case in point is organizational ecology, also called population ecology, developed by Hannan and Freeman (1977, 1989). In their pioneer article, Hannan and Freeman (1977: 936 and 956) stress twice their core research question: "Why are there so many kinds of organizations?" This question is surely ambiguous. For example, Reydon and Scholz (2009: 417) interpret the question as: "the primary explanandum of organizational ecology should be why we find precisely those organizational forms in the world that we do, rather than different forms or a much larger or much smaller diversity of forms." Their interpretation in fact consists of three distinct contrastive questions:

1   "Why are there these rather than other kinds of organizations?" based on the allomorph "There are so many *kinds* of organizations."
2   "Why is there this number rather than a much larger number of kinds of organizations?" based on the allomorph "There are so *many* kinds of organizations."
3   "Why is there this number rather than a much smaller number of kinds of organizations?" based on the allomorph "There are so *many* kinds of organizations."

Each of the questions requires a different explanation. Hannan and Freeman's (1977) vague question by no means helps advance their research agenda.

Another example is the Uppsala internationalization process model proposed by Johanson and Vahlne (1977). They argue that firms exhibit a pattern of incremental commitment to foreign markets as learning occurs over time. The model seeks to explain two phenomena related to the internationalization process, one of which is that a firm's engagement in a specific foreign market develops according to an establishment chain, reflecting an increasing commitment of resources to the market – "at the start no regular export activities are performed in the market, then export takes place via independent representatives, later through a sales subsidiary, and eventually manufacturing may follow" (Johanson and Vahlne 1990: 13). They constructed the model based on their empirical research on Swedish firms in the 1970s. These firms exhibited a pattern similar to the establishment chain when they expanded abroad.

Unfortunately, in their model building process, Johanson and Vahlne failed to address a very basic contrastive question: "why do firms engage in a foreign market following the establishment chain rather than a leapfrogging pattern?" Leapfrogging refers to the case where a firm does not follow a sequence of steps similar to the one depicted by the establishment chain. For example, a manufacturing facility (the final step in the establishment chain) may be set up in a foreign country at the very beginning without going through the preceding steps. If Johanson and Vahlne had collected further data, say, from leapfrogging firms, to investigate the contrastive question, they might have found that their model would be primarily applicable to overseas expansions motivated by market seeking. If other motives, such as resource or technology seeking, are dominant, the model does not apply (Petersen and Pedersen 1997). For instance, a firm that intends to take advantage of the low labor cost of a developing country (i.e., resource seeking) may not export to that country before it establishes a manufacturing facility there. Hence, the market-seeking motive is an important domain assumption of the model (see chapter 3 for a discussion of the different types of assumptions). Since this assumption was not made explicit (through contrastive reasoning), confusion arose as to how far the model was supported by subsequent empirical tests (Petersen and Pedersen 1997).

The generality of explanations

It is sometimes mistakenly believed that explanations are necessarily general in nature (i.e., with few contextual details). For example, Welch et al. (2011) construct a typology of theorizing from case studies based on the trade-off between causal explanation and contextualization: "we consider how the case study generates causal explanations and how it incorporates context – two features of the case study that are often regarded as being incompatible" (pp. 740–741). A serious problem is that the so-called "trade-off" (a term they use in their paper) simply does not exist; that is, causal explanation and contextualization are not incompatible.

For Welch et al., explaining a phenomenon refers to "showing what makes it what it is" (p. 741). They define causal explanation as one that "makes claims about the capacities of objects and beings to make a difference to their world" (p. 741). According to their own definitions of explanation and causal explanation, there are many explanations that are unequivocally causal and yet highly contextualized. For example, in early 2010, Toyota recalled millions of vehicles in the U.S. because of a problem with the gas pedal. The explanation for Toyota's recall is surely causal – the cause being that there is a problem in the gas pedal of some of its car models. The explanation is also highly contextualized – it is about the recall by a specific automobile manufacturer in a specific country at a specific time because of a specific problem; it is not about product recalls by manufacturers in general. In short, there is simply no relationship between whether a description is a causal explanation and how far the description is contextualized. The extent to which a causal explanation is general depends a great deal on the nature of the explanandum.

In the management literature, there are three main types of explananda. The first type refers to phenomena that have few spatiotemporal constraints. Since such phenomena are often targets of explanation by theories and theories are necessarily general, this may be a reason for the aforementioned belief that explanations are general in nature. Questions such as, "Why is there any organization?" and "Why are there so many kinds of organizations?" discussed earlier are concerned with this type of explananda. The corresponding explanation, such as the one proposed by Coase (1937) or Hannan and Freeman (1977), is necessarily general in the sense that it does not refer to a specific organization or set of organizations, and it does not refer to a specific period of time. The explanation is intended to have a wide domain of applicability such that it can be invoked to explain the other two types of explananda.

The second type refers to phenomena that have clear spatiotemporal boundaries. Researchers often deal with this type of explananda when they attempt to explain the results of quantitative studies. For example, analyzing a sample of U.S. Fortune 500 firms during the period from 1996 to 2003, Su and Tsang (2015) found that secondary stakeholders – as represented by various nonprofit or non-governmental organizations – play a positive moderating role in the relationship between product diversification and financial performance. They propose an explanation that maintaining relationships with secondary stakeholders through donations can help firms pursuing diversification mitigate the costs of external controls in their sociopolitical environments. Strictly speaking their explanation refers to their sample within the specific period only. Whether and how far they can generalize this finding (and the associated explanation) is a different issue (see chapter 5).

The last type of explananda refers to specific events, such as Toyota's massive recall mentioned earlier. More often than not, intensive case studies investigate specific events. For instance, Smets et al. (2012) studied practice-driven institutional change in a global law firm that underwent an Anglo-German merger in the early 2000s. In addition to events investigated by case studies, historical events are also specific. One example is the General Motors–Fisher Body integration in 1926. Another example is the "Honda Effect" – Honda's success in capturing a large share of the U.S. motorcycle market soon after its initial entry in 1959. Using the Honda Effect as an illustrative example, Runde and de Rond (2010: 445) propose three broad criteria for evaluating causal explanations of specific events:

> (1) that the factors cited as causes were present in the run-up to the event in question; (2) that those factors were causally effective in contributing to that event, and (3) that, given an affirmative answer to (1) and (2), the causes actually cited in the explanation explain well, taking into account various contextual and epistemic considerations relating to the intended audience for the explanation, and the interests and theoretical presuppositions of the person providing the explanation.

Since the explanation of specific events is often highly contextualized, the causes evaluated by the criteria are likely to be contextualized as well. Although Runde and de Rond (2010) admit that the criteria are rather general and in some cases may be insufficient for discriminating between competing explanations, it is a commendable step forward in guiding management research.

Atheoretical explanation

A key objective of theory is to explain. However, to explain does not necessarily involve any theory. The explanation for Toyota's massive recall in 2010 is atheoretical because it is not based on any theory in the usual sense of the word used in management research.[6] Unfortunately, atheoretical explanations are coldly received by management journals, especially top journals. For example, the mission of the *Academy of Management Journal* is "to publish empirical research that tests, extends, or builds management theory and contributes to management practice." Hambrick (2007: 1346) laments that the field of management's theory fetish "prevents the reporting of rich detail about interesting phenomena for which no theory yet exists."

A good example of such a phenomenon is the superstitious practices of some Chinese managers who try to seek supernatural sources of information, such as consulting fortune tellers and praying to gods, when they make strategic decisions. Before I changed to my current career, I worked as a corporate banker with HSBC in Hong Kong. Some of my clients frankly told me that they regularly engaged in superstitious activities for the sake of managing their business and personal affairs. This is surely a significant, as well as interesting, phenomenon in Chinese business communities worldwide. More than two decades ago, Kao (1993) maintained that privately owned Chinese firms, most of which were located outside mainland China itself, constituted the world's fourth economic power after Japan, North America, and Europe. With the rapid development of the Chinese economy, the phenomenon is even more important now.

When I embarked on my study of the phenomenon in Hong Kong and Singapore during the late 1990s, I searched the literature, and to my great surprise, I found not even a single piece of academic research on the topic of superstition *and* decision making.[7] My fieldwork consisted of a questionnaire survey in Singapore and dozens of interviews with Chinese businessmen and fortune tellers in both cities. The findings provided some solid and insightful information about the phenomenon. My literature review indicated that the phenomenon lay beyond any existing decision-making theories. While the temptation to create a theory to accommodate my data was great, I suppressed the urge and decided to build the empirical foundation for future theory creation. Although I attempted to explain the phenomenon using two key concepts drawn from the decision-making literature, namely rationality and uncertainty, my explanation is largely atheoretical.

Given top management journals' obsession with theory, I did not even consider submitting my results to journals such as the *Academy of Management Journal* and *Administrative Science Quarterly* because these journals did not (and still do not) have any room for atheoretical discussions of a phenomenon, no matter how important and interesting the phenomenon. I managed to publish my work in *Organization Studies* (Tsang 2004a) and a practitioner version of it in the *Academy of Management Executive* (Tsang 2004b), both of which were the first outlets I tried. One of the three reviewers of *Organization Studies* in fact commented that my study "could become a classic *Organization Studies* piece in the spirit of its founder, David Hickson, who believed that rigor and boredom did not need to go together. It is pieces like that often make a single *Organization Studies* issue more interesting to me than the entire year's crop of AMJs." Later I received e-mails from researchers in Mexico and Brazil, saying that they observed a similar phenomenon in their business communities.

Unexplained empirical regularities

Atheoretical explanations are still explanations. Sometimes researchers may identify an empirical regularity (i.e., a similar phenomenon observed repeatedly) but
are unable to provide any explanation. Needless to say, descriptions of empirical
regularities – not accompanied by any explanation – will face a fate tougher
than that of atheoretical explanations on the desk of management journal editors. This editorial attitude is not in line with the history of scientific research.
There have been incidents in natural science in which the discovery of empirical
regularities alone contributed to the well-being of mankind. An excellent example
is the discovery of penicillin by Alexander Fleming in 1928. The discovery
helped save many lives during the Second World War, although the molecular
structure of penicillin was determined by Dorothy Hodgkin only in 1945 and
the exact generative mechanism that accounted for its healing effect was gradually understood even later (Lax 2004).

Admittedly, the extent of regularities observed in the social world is much
smaller than that in the natural world because social phenomena are historically conditioned and culturally determined (Nagel 1979). Yet social phenomena are not completely chaotic.[8] Observations in the empirical domain indicate
the existence of some invariance in the social world. In addition to law, norms
contribute to the stability of social phenomena (Henderson 2005). Lawson
(1997) describes this situation by creating the term "demi-regularity," which
"is precisely a partial event regularity which *prima facie* indicates the occasional,
but less than universal, actualization of a mechanism or tendency, over a defi-
nite region of time-space" (p. 204). An example is the learning curve, which
indicates the fall in costs per unit as cumulative output increases (see Argote
2013). Where demi-regularities are observed empirically, there is evidence of
relatively enduring structures and mechanisms at play in the real domain.
Danermark et al. (2002: 166) maintain that "social scientific research is about
identifying demi-regularities in the empirical domain and from them trying
to find explanation."

In conclusion, though varying from case to case, scientific research may progress
in three stages: discovery of empirical regularities, construction of explanations,
and creation of theories. Although the first two stages are pre-explanatory and
atheoretical, respectively, they serve unique functions. A serious problem of the
management discipline is its single-minded focus on the last stage at the expense
of the other two.

Notes

1   Ruben (2012: 200–212) discusses some interesting – and intellectually stimulating – examples of non-causal explanations. Since the content of that discussion
verges on what I call "pedantic philosophical issues that have few implications
for management research" in the preface, I exclude it from this chapter. I also
exclude the discussion of functional explanations, such as the Freudian argument
that dreams function to preserve sleep by resolving psychological problems that

might otherwise wake us up. Although Kincaid (1996) shows that functional explanations have a causal structure, they are generally considered non-causal.

2   An analogous distinction between fact (corresponding to causality) and assertion (corresponding to explanation) is made by Russell (1972 [1914]: 61–62):

> Given any fact, there is an assertion which expresses the fact. The fact itself is objective, and independent of our thought or opinion about it; but the assertion is something which involves thought, and may be either true or false.

3   In spite of these problems, the monumental contribution of the covering law model to the development of scientific explanation should be acknowledged. Salmon (1990: 3) comments that Hempel and Oppenheim's (1948) essay "constitutes the fountainhead from which almost everything done subsequently on philosophical problems of scientific explanation flows."

4   In the literature, mechanism has been defined in a variety of ways. Interested readers may refer to Hedström and Ylikoski (2010) and Mahoney (2001) for a collection of examples.

5   It is definitely not my intention to disparage the contributions made by the scholars mentioned below. Rather, I just want to show how failure to address certain contrastive questions could give rise to significant problems in the process of theory building.

6   The term "theory" has been used in a variety of ways:

> Like so many words that are bandied about, the word theory threatens to become meaningless. Because its referents are so diverse – including everything from minor working hypotheses, through comprehensive but vague and unordered speculations, to axiomatic systems of thought – use of the word often obscures rather than creates understanding.
>
> (Merton 1967: 39)

A critical realist definition of theory is: "a description of structures and mechanisms which causally generate the observable phenomena, a description which enables us to explain them" (Keat and Urry 1975: 5). Regardless of how it is defined, a theory should be, to a varying extent, general. As such, the explanation for Toyota's recall cannot be said to be derived from any theory. Sayer (1992: 45–50) discusses the concept of theory and its distinction from fact.

7   Subsequently upon my request, two management scholars, Professors Chi-Nien Chung and Chung-Ming Lau, kindly searched the Chinese academic literature in Taiwan. They also failed to identify any such academic studies. In early 2005, a graduate student of library science at a major university in the Midwestern U.S. searched the English literature for me and found no such studies, other than my two published recently (Tsang 2004a, b).

8   I feel uneasy about including this statement because it is so self-evident. I choose to include it in response to some researchers, such as Lincoln and Guba (2000), who deny the possibility of generalizing from results of case studies (see chapter 5).

References

Achinstein, P. 2000. The symmetry thesis. In J. H. Fetzer (Ed.), *Science, explanation, and rationality: Aspects of the philosophy of Carl G. Hempel*: 167–85. New York: Oxford University Press.

Argote, L. 2013. *Organizational learning: Creating, retaining and transferring knowledge* (2nd ed.). New York: Springer.

Barnes, E. 1994. Why P rather than Q? The curiosities of fact and foil. *Philosophical Studies*, 73: 35–53.

Bhaskar, R. 1998. *The possibility of naturalism: A philosophical critique of the contemporary human sciences* (3rd ed.). New York: Routledge.

Bunge, M. 1997. Mechanism and explanation. *Philosophy of the Social Sciences*, 27: 410–465.

Bunge, M. 2004. How does it work? The search for explanatory mechanisms. *Philosophy of the Social Sciences*, 34: 182–210.

Burt, R. S. 1997. The contingent value of social capital. *Administrative Science Quarterly*, 42: 339–365.

Burt, R. S. 2000. The network structure of social capital. *Research in Organizational Behavior*, 22: 345–423.

Burt, R. S., Hogarth, R. M. and Michaud, C. 2000. The social capital of French and American managers. *Organization Science*, 11: 123–147.

Coase, R. H. 1937. The nature of the firm. *Economica*, 4: 386–405.

Danermark, B., Ekström, M., Jakobsen, L. and Karlsson, J. C. 2002. *Explaining society: Critical realism in the social sciences*. London: Routledge.

Day, M. and Botterill, G. S. 2008. Contrast, inference and scientific realism. *Synthese*, 160: 249–267.

Dretske, F. I. 1977. Referring to events. *Midwest Studies of Philosophy*, 2: 90–99.

Dubin, R. 1978. *Theory building* (revised ed.). New York: Free Press.

Falleti, T. G. and Lynch, J. F. 2009. Context and causal mechanisms in political analysis. *Comparative Political Studies*, 42: 1143–1166.

Friedman, Michael. 1974. Explanation and scientific understanding. *Journal of Philosophy*, 71: 5–19.

Friedman, Milton. 1953. *Essays in positive economics*. Chicago, IL: University of Chicago Press.

Garfinkel, A. 1981. *Forms of explanation: Rethinking the questions in social theory*. New Haven, CT: Yale University Press.

Gasper, P. 1990. Explanation and scientific realism. In D. Knowles (Ed.), *Explanation and its limits*: 285–295. Cambridge, England: Cambridge University Press.

Gerring, J. 2010. Causal mechanisms: Yes, but . . . *Comparative Political Studies*, 43: 1499–1526.

Gidden, A. 1987. *Social theory and modern sociology*. Stanford, CA: Stanford University Press.

Glennan, S. S. 1996. Mechanisms and the nature of causation. *Erkenntnis*, 44: 49–71.

Habermas, J. 1971. *Knowledge and human interests* (translated by J. J. Shapiro). Boston, MA: Bacon Press.

Hambrick, D. C. 2007. The field of management's devotion to theory: Too much of a good thing. *Academy of Management Journal*, 50: 1346–1352.

Hannan, M. T. and Freeman, J. 1977. The population ecology of organizations. *American Journal of Sociology*, 82: 929–964.

Hannan, M. T. and Freeman, J. 1989. *Organizational ecology*. Cambridge, MA: Harvard University Press.

Harré, R. 1970. *The principles of scientific thinking*. Chicago, IL: University of Chicago Press.

Hedström, P. 2005. *Dissecting the social: On the principles of analytical sociology*. Cambridge, England: Cambridge University Press.

Hedström, P. and Ylikoski, P. 2010. Causal mechanisms in the social sciences. *Annual Review of Sociology*, 36: 49–67.

Hempel, C. G. 1942. The function of general laws in history. *Journal of Philosophy*, 39(2): 35–48.

Hempel, C. G. 1965. *Aspects of scientific explanation and other essays in the philosophy of science*. New York: Free Press.

Hempel, C. G. and Oppenheim, P. 1948. Studies in the logic of explanation. *Philosophy of Science*, 15: 135–175.

Henderson, D. 2005. Norms, invariance, and explanatory relevance. *Philosophy of the Social Sciences*, 35: 324–338.

Hitchcock, C. 1999. Contrastive explanation and the demons of determinism. *British Journal for the Philosophy of Science*, 50: 585–612.

Hodgson, G. M. 2004. Opportunism is not the only reason why firms exist: Why an explanatory emphasis on opportunism may mislead management strategy. *Industrial and Corporate Change*, 13: 401–418.

Johanson, J. and Vahlne, J. E. 1977. The internationalization process of the firm – a model of knowledge development and increasing foreign market commitments. *Journal of International Business Studies*, 8: 23–32.

Johanson, J. and Vahlne, J. E. 1990. The mechanism of internationalisation. *International Marketing Review*, 7(4): 11–24.

Kao, J. 1993. The worldwide web of Chinese business. *Harvard Business Review*, 71(2): 24–36.

Keat, R. and Urry, J. 1975. *Social theory as science*. London: Routledge and Kegan Paul.

Kim, J. 1994. Explanatory knowledge and metaphysical dependence. *Philosophical Issues*, 5: 51–69.

Kincaid, H. 1996. *Philosophical foundations of the social sciences*. Cambridge, England: Cambridge University Press.

King, G., Keohane, R. O. and Verba, S. 1994. *Designing social inquiry: Scientific inference in qualitative research*. Princeton, NJ: Princeton University Press.

Kiser, E. and Hechter, M. 1991. The role of general theory in comparative-historical sociology. *American Journal of Sociology*, 97: 1–30.

Kitcher, P. 1981. Explanatory unification. *Philosophy of Science*, 48: 507–531.

Klein, B., Crawford, R. G. and Alchian, A. A. 1978. Vertical integration, appropriable rents, and the competitive contracting process. *Journal of Law and Economics*, 21: 297–326.

Lawson, T. 1997. *Economics and reality*. London: Routledge.

Lax, E. 2004. *The mold in Dr. Florey's coat: The story of the penicillin miracle*. New York: Henry Holt.

Lewis, D. 1986. *Philosophical papers*, Vol. 2. New York: Oxford University Press.

Lincoln, Y. S. and Guba, E. G. 2000. The only generalization is: There is no generalization. In R. Gomm, M. Hammersley and P. Foster (Eds.), *Case study: Key issues, key texts*: 27–44. London: Sage.

Lipton, P. 1990. Contrastive explanation. In D. Knowles (Ed.), *Explanation and its limits*: 247–266. Cambridge, England: Cambridge University Press.

Lipton, P. 1991. *Inference to the best explanation*. London: Routledge.

Lipton, P. 1993. Making a difference. *Philosophica*, 51: 39–54.

Little, D. 1991. *Varieties of social explanation: An introduction to the philosophy of social science*. Boulder, CO: Westview Press.

Mahoney, J. 2001. Beyond correlational analysis: Recent innovations in theory and method. *Sociological Forum*, 16: 575–593.

Mäki, U. 2004. Theoretical isolation and explanatory progress: Transaction cost economics and the dynamics of dispute. *Cambridge Journal of Economics*, 28: 319–346.

Marchionni, C. 2006. Contrastive explanation and unrealistic models: The case of the new economic geography. *Journal of Economic Methodology*, 13: 425–446.

Maxwell, J. A. 2004. Causal explanation, qualitative research, and scientific inquiry in education. *Educational Researcher*, 33(2): 3–11.

Merton, R. K. 1967. *On theoretical sociology: Five essays, old and new.* New York: Free Press.

Mill, J. S. 1843. *A system of logic.* London: John W. Parker.

Nagel, E. 1979. *The structure of science: Problems in the logic of scientific explanation.* Indianapolis, IN: Hackett Publishing.

North, D. C. 1991. Institutions. *Journal of Economic Perspectives*, 5(1): 97–112.

Pawson, R. 1989. *A measure for measures: A manifesto for empirical sociology.* London: Routledge.

Pawson, R. and Tilley, N. 1997. *Realistic evaluation.* London: Sage.

Petersen, B. and Pedersen, T. 1997. Twenty years after – support and critique of the Uppsala internationalization model. In I. Björkman and M. Forsgren (Eds.), *The nature of the international firm*: 117–134. Copenhagen: Copenhagen Business School Press.

Reydon, T. A. C. and Scholz, M. 2009. Why organizational ecology is not a Darwinian research program. *Philosophy of the Social Sciences*, 39: 408–439.

Ruben, D.-H. 1987. Explaining contrastive facts. *Analysis*, 47: 35–37.

Ruben, D.-H. 1990. Singular explanation and the social sciences. In D. Knowles (Ed.), *Explanation and its limits*: 95–117. Cambridge, England: Cambridge University Press.

Ruben, D.-H. 2012. *Explaining explanation* (2nd ed.). Boulder, CO: Paradigm Publishers.

Runde, J. and de Rond, M. 2010. Evaluating causal explanations of specific events. *Organization Studies*, 31: 431–450.

Russell, B. 1972 [1914]. *Our knowledge of the external world.* London: George Allen and Unwin.

Salmon, W. C. 1990. Scientific explanation: Causation and unification. *Critica: Revista Hispanoamericana de Filosofia*, 22(66): 3–23.

Salmon, W. C. 1998. *Causality and explanation.* Oxford, England: Oxford University Press.

Sayer, A. 1992. *Method in social science: A realist approach* (2nd ed.). London: Routledge.

Sayer, A. 2000. *Realism and social science.* London: Sage.

Smets, M., Morris, T. I. M. and Greenwood, R. 2012. From practice to field: A multilevel model of practice-driven institutional change. *Academy of Management Journal*, 55: 877–904.

Steel, D. 2004. Social mechanisms and causal inference. *Philosophy of the Social Sciences*, 34: 55–78.

Strawson, P. F. 1985. Causation and explanation. In B. Vermazen and M. B. Hintikka (Eds.), *Essays on Davidson*: 115–135. Oxford, England: Oxford University Press.

Su, W. and Tsang, E. W. K. 2015. Product diversification and financial performance: The moderating role of secondary stakeholders. *Academy of Management Journal*, 58: 1128–1148.

Suppes, P. 1984. *Probabilistic metaphysics.* Oxford, England: Blackwell.

Sutton, R. I. and Staw, B. M. 1995. What theory is not. *Administrative Science Quarterly*, 40: 371–384.

Tsang, E. W. K. 2004a. Toward a scientific inquiry into superstitious business decision-making. *Organization Studies*, 25: 923–946.

Tsang, E. W. K. 2004b. Superstition and decision-making: Contradiction or complement? *Academy of Management Executive*, 18(4): 92–104.

van Fraassen, B. 1980. *The scientific image*. Oxford, England: Oxford University Press.

Weber, M. 1949. *The methodology of the social sciences* (translated and edited by E. A. Shils and H. A. Finch). New York: Free Press.

Welch, C., Piekkari, R., Plakoyiannaki, E. and Paavilainen-Mäntymäki, E. 2011. Theorising from case studies: Towards a pluralist future for international business research. *Journal of International Business Studies*, 42: 740–762.

Williamson, O. E. 1997. Hierarchies, markets and power in the economy: An economic perspective. In C. Menard (Ed.), *Transaction cost economics: Recent developments*: 1–29. Brookfield, VT: Edward Elgar.

Woodward, J. 2003. *Making things happen: A theory of causal explanation*. New York: Oxford University Press.

Xiao, Z. and Tsui, A. S. 2007. When brokers may not work: The cultural contingency of social capital in Chinese high-tech firms. *Administrative Science Quarterly*, 52: 1–31.

Ylikoski, P. 2007. The idea of contrastive explanandum. In J. Persson and P. Ylikoski (Eds.), *Rethinking explanation*: 27–42. Dordrecht, Netherlands: Springer.

3 Assumptions
Not something to be assumed away

Every theory is based on some assumptions. As stated in chapter 1, the biggest methodological debate in economics was started with Lester's (1946) empirical study that challenged a key assumption of marginal theory – firms maximize profits by producing at a level where marginal revenue equals marginal cost. Friedman (1953) provided a forceful response, arguing that an economic theory should not be criticized for containing unrealistic assumptions. Rather, it should be evaluated by its ability to generate sufficiently accurate predictions. His response sparked off a series of vigorous discussions in the following decades.[1]

In marketing, Shugan (2007) wrote an editorial by restating Friedman's thesis when he was the editor-in-chief of *Marketing Science*, a leading journal with a focus on quantitative research methods. His core argument is that the realism of assumptions does not matter so long as a theory or model generates satisfactory predictions and that unrealistic assumptions in fact breed good theories.[2] The editorial led to a dialogue between Shugan and me concerning whether assumptions have to be realistic (Shugan 2009a, b; Tsang 2009a, b).

With few exceptions (e.g., Ghoshal and Moran 1996; Heiman and Nickerson 2002; Vahlne and Johanson 2014; Wright et al. 2001), management researchers seldom pay close attention to the role played by assumptions in theories. Gartner (2001: 27) laments that "entrepreneurship scholars are not conscious of their assumptions." This chapter aims at achieving two main objectives. First, I discuss the relation between core assumptions and mechanismic explanations covered in chapter 2. I argue that these assumptions often constitute the foundation of such explanations. Second, I distinguish between two ways of theory testing – assumption omitted and assumption based, and recommend that when a new theory is initially tested, the latter should play a more important role than the former. As shown by the following case of transaction cost economics (TCE), which has been dominated by assumption-omitted testing, researchers do not seem to be aware that such bias may slow down theory development and needs to be rectified by incorporating more assumption-based testing.

Types of assumptions

An assumption refers to a fundamental statement, or basic hypothesis, of a theory (Nagel 1963). Simple as it may seem, its meaning is sometimes misunderstood. For example, Shugan (2007: 450) argues that in the case of the prisoner's dilemma, "scholars are seldom prisoners, advising prisoners or advising the police." Therefore, the assumptions of a useful theory need not be realistic. A serious problem of his argument is that the terms "prisoner" and "police" are used metaphorically to construct a plea-bargaining situation. Accordingly, the statements involving these terms are not assumptions. A similar plea-bargaining situation can be represented by a different scenario: a teacher catching two students who collaborate on cheating in a test. In fact, most empirical studies of the prisoner's dilemma do not adopt Tucker's original scenario of suspects caught by the police.[3]

Nagel (1963) distinguishes between three different senses in which assumptions may be said to be realistic or unrealistic. First, if an assumption does not provide an exhaustive description of a certain state of affairs, it is considered unrealistic. This sense is trivial because it is not possible for any finitely long sentence to be realistic. For the second sense, an assumption is considered unrealistic if "it is believed to be either false or highly improbable on the available evidence" (Nagel 1963: 214). Lastly, theories normally posit relations under highly purified conditions between idealized objects or processes, none of which actually exist. As Shugan (2007: 450) comments, "Most published research assumes continuity when virtually no variables are infinitely divisible," whether such variables represent, say, resources or capabilities. Since assumptions are necessarily unrealistic according to the first and the last senses, the following discussion focuses on the second sense – that is, an assumption is said to be unrealistic if it is false or highly improbable based on the available evidence.

Negligibility, domain, and heuristic assumptions

"In order for unrealistic psychological and social assumptions to be acceptable, they must be simplifying idealizations that help the modeling but do not affect the central explanatory relationships in any crucial manner" (Hedström and Ylikoski 2010: 61). In other words, whether an assumption has to be realistic depends on the role that it plays in the theory concerned. In his widely acclaimed critique of Friedman's (1953) thesis, Musgrave (1981) distinguishes among three different kinds of assumptions, namely negligibility, domain, and heuristic. He laments that researchers rarely make a clear distinction among these types of assumptions when they propose their assumptions. As a result, it is often not clear to which type a particular assumption of a theory should belong. This ambiguity is not conducive to theory development.

We make a negligibility assumption whenever we think that we may safely ignore the effect of a factor upon the phenomenon we are investigating. A negligibility assumption enables the researcher to focus on the key determinants postulated by a theory in order to identify its main causes. For instance, when Galileo studied the motion of bodies falling through relatively short distances, he assumed that air resistance had no effect on such motions. For management research, the resource-based view assumes that product market imperfections empirically have little effect on competitive advantage (Foss and Hallberg 2014).

A theory containing a negligibility assumption should be evaluated by testing the consequences of the theory. Galileo's assumption that air resistance was negligible for the phenomena he investigated was justified because his results were in line with the predictions derived from his theory for bodies freely falling in a vacuum. In contrast, the resource-based view's assumption concerning product market imperfections has been criticized by researchers (e.g., Foss and Hallberg 2014; Mathews 2006; Priem and Butler 2001)

A domain assumption specifies the domain of applicability of a theory; it is a statement that theory T works only when factor F is either absent or present (Mäki 2000). In illustrating his argument that realism is a function of personal taste, Shugan (2007: 454) uses the example of "models that assume consumers act in their own best interests." This example can also be an illustration of domain assumptions. In reality, it is very likely that there are consumers who act in their own best interests and those who do not. The relative proportion of each group is an empirical question. If a model assumes that consumers act in their own best interests and this assumption affects how the model explains and predicts, the assumption is a domain assumption in the sense that the model works only when consumers really act in their own best interests.

A negligibility assumption, when refuted, may turn into a domain assumption. Galileo's assumption of negligible air resistance would have been wrong if in the alleged experiment at the Leaning Tower of Pisa, he had dropped a feather and a ball, instead of two balls, from the tower. In that case, the negligibility assumption became a domain assumption in the sense that Galileo's theory would hold only if air resistance was negligible (relative to the density of the falling body). The switch from a negligibility assumption to a domain assumption effectively weakens the applicability of a theory, although it makes the theory more accurate.

Finally, heuristic assumptions facilitate the development of a theory. Heuristic assumptions are first made and then abandoned. They are needed when the theory is so complex that a method of successive approximation has to be employed. Musgrave (1981) illustrates this type of assumption with Newton's inquiry into the solar system where Newton first ignored inter-planetary gravitational forces by assuming that there was only one planet orbiting the sun. The use of heuristic assumptions is also evident in the development of theories in the social sciences. For example, TCE frequently invokes the heuristic assumption of zero transaction costs in order to expose the core issues of a problem. It then gives up the assumption and examines why positive transaction costs arise under certain circumstances (Williamson 1997). Similarly, the supposedly heuristic assumption of two parties in the prisoner's dilemma can be relaxed to form the so-called *n*-person prisoner's dilemma.

Core versus peripheral assumptions

Musgrave's (1981) typology of assumptions is not exhaustive. There are assumptions that do not fall into any of the three types. In this connection, it is also useful to distinguish between core and peripheral assumptions (Mäki 2000). The former are about the major causes posited by a theory while the latter refer to the minor causes. Peripheral assumptions are more likely to be classified into Musgrave's typology than core assumptions. For example, as a core TCE assumption, opportunism does not seem to fall into any of the three types. Opportunism, defined as "self-interest seeking with guile" (Williamson 1975: 6), is a central construct in the TCE logic and is surely not negligible. TCE does not restrict opportunism to certain domains of applicability and has never abandoned the construct as the theory develops. Similarly, the assumption that people act in their own best interests is a core assumption of the prisoner's dilemma. Again, the assumption falls outside Musgrave's typology.

The distinction between core and peripheral assumptions facilitates conceptual discussion. For instance, a common objection against the application of rational choice models outside economics is that they make unrealistic assumptions about individual behavior, such as maximization of self-interest. Lehtinen and Kuorikoski (2007) argue that assumptions have different explanatory roles in different rational choice models. If an assumption of a rational choice model does not play a major causal role, the model may still have satisfactory explanatory power even though the assumption is unrealistic. The gist of their argument is that if the assumption is peripheral, its realism will have little impact on the explanatory power of the model. Making the distinction between core and peripheral assumptions explicit would simplify as well as strengthen the argument.

Assumptions and explanations

Friedman's (1953) emphasis on the connection between assumptions and predictions is derived from his implicit philosophical perspective of instrumentalism (Boland 1979; Caldwell 1980), which is one form of pragmatism. Treating scientific theories as practical instruments, Friedman only cares about the usefulness of a theory in terms of producing sufficiently accurate predictions; he cares much less about how far the theory is true[4] or how far its assumptions are realistic.

If the only goal of science is prediction, Friedman's position is justifiable because all that matters is that a theory or model "works" in the sense of generating sufficiently accurate predictions (Caldwell 1980; Sayer 1992). Yet a major function of a theory is also to explain and not just to predict. As Kaplan (1964: 347) well says, "if we look at the explanations which actually occur in science as well as in everyday life, and not only at what an ideal explanation would be or what all explanations are 'in principle,' it appears that we often have explanations without being able to predict." This is especially the case for social science research due to the open-system nature of social phenomena. Moreover, somewhat contrary to Hempel's (1942) argument for the symmetry between explanation and prediction discussed in chapter 1, a theory that predicts well does not necessarily imply that its explanation is true. For example, before it was overturned by Copernicus, Ptolemaic astronomy was held in high regard because it could not only account for observed planetary movements but also predict future ones to a certain degree of accuracy (see Musgrave 1974).

In a blunt yet insightful critique of Friedman's (1953) thesis, Bunge (1996: 55) proposes the following analogical reasoning: "All humans are vegetables. All vegetables are mortal. Ergo, all humans are mortal." In other words, a ridiculous assumption may lead to a faultless conclusion. His critique concerns the relation between assumptions and the mechanismic explanations offered by a theory, an issue that has been largely neglected by the heated debate aroused by Friedman.

The core of TCE focuses on "transactions and the costs that attend completing transactions by one institutional mode rather than another" (Williamson 1975: 1–2). The transaction, which is a transfer of a good or service between technologically separate units, is the unit of analysis in TCE. The basic structure of TCE consists of four main parts: (1) the assumptions of bounded rationality, opportunism, risk neutrality, and transaction cost minimization; (2) the principal transaction attributes of asset specificity, uncertainty and frequency; (3) a variety of transaction costs; and (4) the various modes of governance. A core assumption of TCE is that managers make contracting decisions in a transaction-cost-economizing manner (Williamson 1975, 1985). This assumption forms the foundation of the theory's mechanismic explanations.

From a critical realist view, need assumptions be realistic? Musgrave (1981) rightly points out that negligibility and domain assumptions have to be realistic. Suppose Galileo had used feathers instead of heavy balls in his experiments. In that case, his assumption that air resistance was negligible would have been false. The contingent condition related to air resistance would be a significant factor affecting the outcome of his experiments and should not be ignored. As an example of a domain assumption, consider an organization theory that applies only if the average salary of senior managers in the organization is lower than that of junior managers. Even if the theory is logically sound, it explains almost nothing empirically. In other words, if a domain assumption is not realistic, the associated theory may be applicable to virtually no actual situation and is not testable. Heuristic assumptions, by their very nature, are often unrealistic. However, this is not a cause for concern because the results based on heuristic assumptions do not reflect the precise predictions of a theory. Rather, they represent the steps toward such predictions (Musgrave 1981). We should expect a heuristic assumption to approximate by steps toward an eventual, complex assumption that *is* realistic (Lakatos 1978).

"I do not wish to deny that false assumptions are useful in economic theory, but only when they are used as auxiliary constructs, not as premises from which empirical theories can be deduced" (Rothbard 1957: 315). This point highlights the different roles played by peripheral and core assumptions. As discussed, Lehtinen and Kuorikoski (2007) argue that the realism of peripheral assumptions has little effect on the explanatory power of a rational choice model. In contrast, a core assumption constitutes the mechanismic explanation of a theory. In marginal theory, the assumption of profit maximization through equating marginal cost with marginal revenue is a vital element of the mechanism concerning how business executives make their production decisions. Similarly, for TCE, opportunism is a key factor affecting the transaction costs of various modes of governance, which in turn determine the choice of a governance arrangement (Wathne and Heide 2000). More often than not, a core assumption is a key element of a mechanismic explanation. Just imagine what TCE would look like without the assumption of opportunism. If the potential for opportunism does not exist, buyers and suppliers will cooperate and promises will be sufficient for protecting market transactions (Williamson 1985).

In parallel with Alchian (1950), Friedman (1953) argues that the assumption of profit maximization is supported by the fact that those who do not manage to maximize profits will probably be eliminated by competition in the course of time. This process of natural selection thus helps validate the assumption. What Friedman fails to realize is that the mechanism associated with natural selection is totally different from that of profit maximization. If natural selection is the actual mechanism operating in the real domain, it implies that marginal theory, including its profit maximization assumption, is false. Koopmans (1957) therefore maintains that if natural selection is the basis for our belief in profit maximization, we should postulate that basis itself and not profit maximization. A similar issue associated with TCE is discussed below.

In summary, an unrealistic core assumption will lead to an unrealistic mechanismic explanation and thus a defective theory. Accordingly, core assumptions have to be realistic. As discussed in the next section, how far an assumption is realistic has to be determined empirically.

Empirical research in transaction cost economics

This section discusses how the empirical research in TCE has handled the core assumptions of the theory. I first distinguish between structural and reduced models. Researchers often employ reduced models in their statistical analyses, although they may derive their hypotheses based on structural models. Such research methods fail to directly put core assumptions to the test. I then examine the transaction-cost-economizing assumption of TCE, the testing of which is crucial for establishing that managerial choice, rather than natural selection, is the key force behind the governance structures observed in the empirical domain.

Structural and reduced models

In econometrics (e.g., Chow 1983; Johnston 1991), there is a distinction
between structural and reduced models. The former contain formulas representing the relation of every dependent variable to its independent variables on
various levels, while the latter exhibit the net or overall relation between the
dependent variable and the ultimate independent variables. Consider a structural
model of the form

$$z = f(x, y) \tag{1a}$$
$$\text{where } x = g(u), \text{ and } y = h(v) \tag{1b}$$

Substituting Equations 1b into Equation 1a results in the corresponding reduced
model:

$$z = \phi(u, v) \tag{2}$$

The variables x, y, z, u, and v presumably represent events in the empirical
domain. There are two crucial methodological differences between the two
models (Bunge 1997). First, Equations 1b "explain" the intermediary variables
x and y whereas Equation 2 does not even contain them. In other words, the
reduced model is simpler and also shallower than the structural model for skipping one level of events represented by x and y. Second, the reduced model
can be derived from the structural model but not the other way around because
the task of working out the structural model from the reduced model is an
inverse problem with an indefinite number of solutions. As illustrated by the
following examples, a core assumption is often eliminated in the process of
converting a structural model into its reduced form. Consequently, the reduced
model is often much less informative with respect to the related mechanism
than the structural model.[5]

The majority of empirical research in TCE is a variation of the discriminating
alignment hypothesis, according to which transactions, which differ in their
attributes, are aligned with governance structures, which differ in their costs
and efficiencies, so as to achieve a transaction-cost-economizing outcome (Williamson 1991). Governance structure is the dependent variable, while transactional properties and control variables serve as independent variables. Among
the three TCE assumptions about human nature – bounded rationality, opportunism, and risk neutrality – opportunism occupies the most important spot in
the theory. Opportunism is the ultimate cause for the failure of markets and
for the existence of hierarchies (Williamson 1993). It is the most frequently
invoked assumption when researchers formulate hypotheses in their empirical
studies. Thus, the discussion here focuses on this assumption.

Consider a pioneer empirical study of TCE. Based on data from the U.S.
automobile industry, Monteverde and Teece (1982a) argue that assemblers will
vertically integrate when the production process of a component generates

specialized, nonpatentable know-how. This is because the existence of transaction-specific know-how and the difficulties of skill transfer imply that it will be costly for the assembler to switch to an alternative supplier. When the assembler is locked into dependence upon a specific supplier, the assembler will be exposed to the possibility of opportunistic recontracting and quasi rent appropriation. They further argue that applications engineering effort reflects the extent of embedded specialized know-how. Thus they formulate their only hypothesis as:

> *Hypothesis 1a: "The greater is the applications engineering effort associated with the development of any given automotive component, the higher are the expected appropriable quasi rents and, therefore, the greater is the likelihood of vertical integration of production for that component"*
> (Monteverde and Teece 1982a: 207).

They obtained from an assembler a list of 133 automotive components, each of which was recorded as either produced internally or sourced externally. They tested the reduced model by operationalizing application engineering effort as the cost of developing a given component and skipping the construct "expected appropriable quasi rents." Hence, they were actually testing the following hypothesis:

> *Hypothesis 1b: The higher is the cost of developing any given automotive component, the greater is the likelihood of vertical integration of production for that component.*

Their finding strongly supports Hypothesis 1b, and so they draw the conclusion: "*Transaction cost considerations* surrounding the development and deepening of human skills appear to have important ramifications for vertical integration in the automobile industry, thereby supporting the transaction cost paradigm advanced by Williamson" (Monteverde and Teece 1982a: 212, emphasis added). This finding "has been widely acclaimed as providing empirical support for the TCE paradigm" (Chiles and McMackin 1996: 74). What has been neglected by this claim is that Hypothesis 1b does not reflect any transaction cost considerations related to opportunism. As argued earlier, there are an indefinite number of solutions when deriving the structural model from the reduced one (Bunge 1997). There is a real possibility that Hypothesis 1b was supported for reasons totally unrelated to the TCE paradigm even if we accept their argument that the cost of developing a component reflects the extent of embedded specialized know-how.

For instance, in developing a knowledge-based view of the firm, Grant (1996) identifies know-how with tacit knowledge. A key characteristic of tacit knowledge is the difficulty of transferring it from one party to another. Thus, in Monteverde and Teece's (1982a) study, if the extent of embedded specialized know-how associated with an automotive component is great, it will be very costly for an assembler to transfer the know-how to the supplier who is supposed to manufacture the component. Unless the supplier can achieve a much lower production cost than the assembler, it is simply not cost-effective for the assembler to outsource the production process, which necessarily incurs a substantial knowledge transfer cost. Moreover, the know-how may be so tacit that transfer is virtually impossible. In fact, for such a component, it is likely that the assembler will be able to manufacture it at a significantly lower cost than the supplier.

Kogut and Zander (1992: 384) argue that "the central competitive dimension of what firms know how to do is to create and transfer knowledge efficiently within an organizational context." Since the know-how associated with the component is firmly embedded within the assembler and becomes its social knowledge (Kogut and Zander 1996), it will be more economical for the assembler than the supplier to coordinate and organize the employees who collectively possess the knowledge to produce the component. Moreover, since the design of the component "must be highly coordinated with other parts of the automobile system" (Monteverde and Teece 1982a: 212), it is arguably more efficient to have such coordination done within the assembler than between the assembler and the supplier. Note that this explanation, which involves a very different mechanism than Monteverde and Teece's, does not invoke any transaction cost considerations related to the opportunistic behavior of suppliers.[6] In fact, Masten et al. (1991) offer a brief alternative explanation of Monteverde and Teece's (1982a) results along a similar line of argument.

Hypothesis 1a, the structural model of Monteverde and Teece, represents a slightly more direct test of TCE. This is because appropriable quasi rents are related to opportunism, which in turn is a core assumption of TCE: the higher are the expected appropriable quasi rents, the greater is the chance that they will be appropriated *if* opportunism exists. In any case, Hypothesis 1a is subject to fewer alternative mechanismic explanations than Hypothesis 1b. In order to provide a much more direct test of TCE in the context of their study, they may test a structural model similar to the following one:[7]

> *Hypothesis 1c: The greater is the applications engineering effort associated with the development of any given automotive component, the higher is the perceived risk of opportunistic recontracting and quasi rents appropriation and, therefore, the greater is the likelihood of vertical integration of production for that component.*

Since Hypothesis 1b required measuring the cost of developing a component, they asked two automotive engineers to provide engineering cost ratings for their sample of components. With further effort and suitable operationalization of the constructs "opportunistic recontracting" and "quasi rent appropriation," it was indeed possible for them to test Hypothesis 1c, which would result in a significantly stronger empirical study of TCE.[8]

In a related study, Monteverde and Teece (1982b) examine the issue of quasi-vertical integration – whereby automotive assemblers own the specialized and dedicated equipment used by suppliers. They argue that when the appropriable quasi rents associated with the tools and dies of an automotive component are high, the supplier of the component is reluctant to own the tooling for fear of being taken advantage of by the assembler. In this case, the assembler will assume owner-ship, resulting in quasi integration. They measured quasi rents originated from asset specificity by the multiplicative composite of tooling cost and degree of specialization and, as expected, found a positive relationship between quasi integration and quasi rents. Their hypothesis, although not explicitly stated in their paper, is of the fol-lowing reduced form:

> *Hypothesis 2a: The higher are the appropriable quasi rents, the greater is the likelihood of quasi-vertical integration.*

They conclude that the "practice of quasi integration . . . appears to be explained, in part, by the desire of suppliers to avoid the possibility of opportunistic recon-structing by downstream customers" (Monteverde and Teece 1982b: 328). (There seems to be a typo here: "reconstructing" should be "recontracting.") Again, their reduced model is silent with respect to their proposed mechanismic explana-tion concerning suppliers' avoidance of opportunistic recontracting and appropria-tion of quasi rents. The existence of appropriable quasi rents does not imply the existence of the *fear* of opportunistic rent appropriation. Whether the latter really exists has to be confirmed empirically by a structural model, such as:

> *Hypothesis 2b: The higher are the appropriable quasi rents, the higher is the perceived risk of opportunistic recontracting and quasi rents appropriation and, therefore, the greater is the likelihood of quasi-vertical integration.*

Monteverde and Teece's two studies are probably the first ever empirical research published in the domain of TCE and have made a significant contribution to filling the empirical void of the theory. Unfortunately, the methods of both studies fail to touch upon the assumption of opportunism, which forms the core of their proposed mechanismic explanations. As such, they have set a flawed precedent for subsequent empirical studies. Although TCE has placed opportun-ism at the center of the agenda of organizational researchers (Beccerra and Gupta 1999), the construct has rarely been studied empirically.

In a systematic assessment of the empirical support for TCE, David and Han (2004) examine 308 statistical tests of TCE constructs and relationships from 63 articles published during 1982–2002. Out of the 308 tests, there are only 7 and 12 tests involving opportunism as independent and dependent variables, respectively, though most of the 308 tests invoke the assumption of opportunism implicitly or explicitly. (Tests on the assumptions of bounded rationality and risk neutrality are completely absent.) For instance, the most frequently tested inde-pendent variable is asset specificity, with a total of 107 counts. Yet, as illustrated by the examples of Monteverde and Teece (1982a, b), the effect of asset specificity on governance choice is based entirely on the assumption of opportunism. Without opportunism, cooperation will be the norm between assemblers and suppliers, and promises will suffice to safeguard market transactions (Williamson 1985). Since the number of tests on asset specificity is far greater than those on opportunism, it is very likely that most of the hypotheses associated with the former are stated in the reduced form similar to Hypotheses 1b and 2a. This conjecture is supported by a key finding of another survey of TCE: "Much of the empirical literature rests on the general presumption of opportunism, but few studies measure opportunism directly" (Macher and Richman 2008: 40).

Managerial choice versus natural selection

As mentioned, TCE assumes that managers utilize a transaction-cost-economizing calculus in making decisions concerning modes of governance (Williamson 1975, 1985). Accordingly, TCE is a theory about the choice of governance structures made by managers in the context of given levels of asset specificity, uncertainty, and frequency of interaction. Similar to the debate about marginal analysis in economics, a pertinent question here is: is this assumption realistic? More specifically, do managers really make use of a transaction-cost-economizing calculus in making contracting decisions? The managerial-choice approach relies on an implicit view that perceived or subjective, rather than objective, transaction costs are what managers take into account when making their decisions (Chiles and McMackin 1996). That is, to answer the aforementioned question, we need to examine how managers actually perceive, weigh, and judge transaction costs (Buckley and Chapman 1997).

This scenario is very similar to that of marginal analysis in economics. While empirical studies assume that governance structures are chosen *as if* the decisions were made based on the transaction-cost-economizing principle (see Friedman 1953 for the as-if formulation), they rarely investigate whether the decisions are *really* made in this manner. There are few exceptions, though. For example, using a questionnaire survey, Lyons (1995) studied the make-or-buy decisions made by British manufacturing firms. His basic methodology was "to ask firms first about the production technology of a specialized input they currently subcontract to another firm to produce, and then also to report the technology of an input currently produced in-house (but which it might be possible to buy-in)" (Lyons 1995: 436). He thus confronted his respondents with a heuristic representation of the make-or-buy decision. In this respect, the study is a significant improvement over a substantial number of TCE studies that are based on secondary data and treat the decision-making calculus as a black box. Nevertheless, we have no means of knowing how far Lyons's questionnaire survey simply forced the results. Using an experimental research method, Pilling et al. (1994) asked purchasing managers to examine the effects of different levels of asset specificity, uncertainty, and frequency on transaction costs and relational closeness. Their study suffers from the same – if not more serious – problem of external validity as Lyons's (see Shadish et al. 2002).

An approach that can better address external validity is illustrated by Buckley and Chapman's (1997, 1998) longitudinal study on a small sample of British and French pharmaceutical companies and British scientific instrument companies. They conducted in-depth, unstructured interviews with managers based on the methodology of social anthropology. This method enabled decisions to be observed in prospect, in concurrent real time, and in retrospect. Their interviews focused on corporate management of the relationships with boundary entities of the company and pertained to the question of internalization versus externalization of activities. When engaging in these activities, managers needed to cope with various transaction cost issues. In common with Lester's (1946) study of production decisions, which sparked off the debate about marginal analysis, Buckley and Chapman (1997: 138) did not find any evidence of transaction cost minimization:

> We have come across no case whatsoever in which managers involved in decisions had access to, or had personally generated for their own purposes, anything like a numerically justified assessment of transaction cost issues . . . They were almost without exception unaware of the existence of the theoretical discourse of transaction cost economics, but they were necessarily engaged in decisions where transaction cost issues were paramount . . . Managers, if offered the idea that there might exist an objective answer to the problems they faced, typically laughed.

Based on two of his previous attempts to collect data from survey respondents, Masten (1996: 48) comments that "respondents had a particularly difficult time distinguishing asset specificity (assets that can produce a product only for a particular customer) from specialized assets (those that can produce only a single product)." Is this an indication that his respondents, similar to Buckley and Chapman's, did not take transaction cost issues into account when making decisions on governance structures?

Buckley and Chapman's (1997) finding suggests that the transaction-cost-economizing assumption is unrealistic, at least as far as his sample firms are concerned. But, does it really matter as long as observed governance structures are consistent with the assumption? It does matter because, as discussed earlier, accurate predictions are by no means substitutes for realistic assumptions. Accurate TCE predictions, if any, can be the outcome of natural selection rather than managerial choice. The natural-selection approach of evolutionary theory "adopts the population of organizations as the level of analysis, the environment as the primary selection mechanism that utilizes some selection criteria (e.g., transaction cost economizing), the long run as the appropriate time frame, and ex post objective view of costs" (Chiles and McMackin 1996: 76). In this framework, firms engage in a random series of configurational changes, some of which are by accident transaction cost reducing while others are not. Firms that happen to arrive at a low transaction cost configuration will succeed relative to those that do not (Buckley and Chapman 1997). In other words, governance structures that are more efficient for economic exchange will supplant less efficient ones, with the result that observed structures are generally consistent with the TCE logic regardless of whether the choice of such structures was based on transaction-cost-economizing decisions (Robins 1987).

The natural-selection approach obviously entails mechanisms very different from those of the managerial-choice approach proposed by TCE (see Hodgson 1993 for a sophisticated treatment of the former). For instance, competitive intensity of an industry is an important factor affecting the outcome of a natural-selection process. Inefficient firms will be eliminated from existence faster in highly competitive than mildly competitive industries. Thus, competitive intensity is a key element of the structure associated with the selection process. However, it is at most a contingent condition affecting the mechanisms of TCE.

The different mechanisms of the two approaches imply different research methods. For example, analysis of secondary archival databases consisting of populations of organizations is a more appropriate method than in-depth case study for the natural-selection approach. Moreover, the two approaches require different methods of measuring transaction costs. Managers choose governance structures according to a subjective interpretation of transaction costs, whereas a selection process is based on objective transaction costs. Unless subjective and objective transaction costs are highly correlated, a study based on, say, the managerial-choice approach measuring transaction costs in an objective way may generate invalid results.

Assumption-omitted versus assumption-based theory testing

From a critical realist perspective, a basic purpose of testing a theory is to investigate how far its proposed mechanisms are consistent with observable events (Sayer 1992). Since the core assumptions of a theory often constitute the foundation of its mechanismic explanations, it is crucial that these assumptions are tested during the early stage of theory development in order to establish a firm foundation for theory development. I call this way of theory testing assumption based. In contrast, assumption-omitted theory testing is to exclude assumptions from empirical tests although assumptions may be invoked in formulating hypotheses. The tests are usually conducted on reduced models that are devoid of core assumptions.

By testing an assumption, I mean investigating whether observed events are consistent with the assumption. For instance, TCE assumes that managers adopt a transaction-cost-economizing calculus when deciding on modes of governance. One way to test this assumption, similar to what Buckley and Chapman (1997) did, is to ask managers whether and how far they really subscribe to the transaction-cost-economizing principle. In the process, it is necessary to explain to the respondents the meaning of not only the principle but also various types of transaction costs that are relevant to their decisions. Consider the assumption of opportunism. In the context of Monteverde and Teece's (1982a, b) studies, a test of the assumption was to examine whether the threat of opportunistic behavior (in the form of opportunistic recontracting and quasi rents appropriation) would lead to vertical or quasi-vertical integration.

Assumption-omitted theory testing

As clearly indicated by the reviews of empirical research in TCE (e.g., David and Han 2004; Macher and Richman 2008; Shelanski and Klein 1995), the history of TCE research since the publication of Williamson's seminal book, *Markets and Hierarchies*, in 1975 has been dominated by assumption-omitted testing. Such dominance has impeded theory development. Simon (1991: 27) cautions that many TCE assumptions are "with no empirical support except an appeal to introspection and common sense." A case in point is the controversy surrounding the assumption of opportunism. An interesting observation is that the debate mainly consists of theoretical exchanges (e.g., Ghoshal and Moran 1996; Granovetter 1985; Williamson 1993, 1996) and that few empirical studies have measured opportunism (David and Han 2004; Macher and Richman 2008; Rindfleisch and Heide 1997). This observation is made against the backdrop that opportunism occupies a central position in TCE and is itself a complex construct (Wathne and Heide 2000). Researchers seem to have missed the simple fact that sciences, whether natural or social, are after all empirically based; no amount of rigorous theorizing can compensate for the lack of empirical testing.

In fact, if opportunism had been tested by some early studies of TCE, certain controversial issues might not have arisen. For example, Conner and Prahalad (1996) argue that knowledge-based considerations can outweigh opportunism-based considerations when governance structures are chosen. Hart (1990) comments that TCE does not specify the mechanisms through which opportunism is reduced in organizations. Similarly, Ghoshal and Moran (1996) lament that TCE errs in the assumption that organizations exist because of their ability to attenuate opportunism through control. The issue of how and how far organizations are able to reduce opportunism has to be tackled by not only theorizing but also empirical research. The latter is the ultimate judge of the validity of the former. Unfortunately, the empirical literature of TCE is virtually silent with respect to this issue. A great deal of intellectual effort is thus wasted on debating issues that can be and should be settled empirically.

Ghoshal and Moran (1996) make the following comment concerning the empirical research in TCE:

> Even though an impressive number of empirical studies have found a positive relationship between asset specificity and internalization . . ., correlation does not demonstrate causation. Relationship-specific assets (e.g., distance, routines) can reduce the costs of internal coordination, *independent of their effects on opportunism.*
>
> (p. 40, emphasis added)

In response, Williamson (1996: 55) claims that TCE "is an empirical success story." Is it? Assumption-omitted theory testing relies heavily on reduced models. As there are an indefinite number of solutions when deriving the structural model from the reduced one (Bunge 1997), a confirmatory test of the reduced model may not offer significant empirical support for the structural model entailed by the theory. Therefore, a theory that has been based predominately on assumption-omitted testing cannot be an empirical success story. Ghoshal and Moran's aforementioned critique pinpoints that the usual reduced-form TCE research on the relationship between asset specificity and internalization does not involve testing opportunism, which constitutes the foundation of TCE mechanismic explanations. Monteverde and Teece's (1982a, b) pioneer TCE studies are typical examples of such reduced-form research.[9]

David and Han's (2004) assessment of the empirical support for TCE delivers mixed results. They found significant empirical support for TCE in some areas (e.g., asset specificity) and weak support in others (e.g., uncertainty and performance). If we take into account the fact that many of the empirical studies are of the reduced form, the overall support will be even weaker. All the previous reviews of the TCE literature seem to have missed this critical point. Nevertheless, I am not dismissing the efforts made by TCE researchers in improving their assumption-omitted methodologies. For example, Masten et al. (1991) contributed some innovative work toward estimating the structure of organization costs in shipbuilding. Monteverde (1995) used a new construct, "unstructured technical dialog," to measure specific human capital investment in his study of the semiconductor industry. The construct is an improvement over similar measures adopted by previous studies, such as Masten (1984) and Monteverde and Teece (1982a). Such efforts surely help develop the theory and should be applauded. What I argue here is simply that if these efforts were complemented by assumption-based testing, the resultant theoretical advancement would be even more remarkable.

Assumption-based theory testing

When we start building a house, we focus on its foundation. After the foundation has been well established, we shift our attention to superstructures. By the same token, theory building starts from the foundation. During the initial empirical research on a new theory, assumption-based testing should play a more important role than assumption-omitted testing. More specifically, assumption-based testing serves three important functions: identifying problematic areas of a theory, opening up new opportunities for strengthening a theory, and clarifying the conceptual domain of an assumption.

First, assumption-based testing helps assess the realism of an assumption and thus facilitates theory development through identifying problematic areas. In the aforementioned Pilling et al.'s (1994) experimental study, they use the TCE reasoning to formulate nine hypotheses about the costs of guarding against opportunism, which are regarded as one type of transaction cost. None of the hypotheses were supported, and in fact, two of them had significant estimates in the opposite direction. Their findings raise questions about the linkage between opportunism and the specific dimensions of governance.

Second, testing an assumption may open up new opportunities for strengthening a theory. For instance, TCE adopts the assumption of risk neutrality, and risk preferences are assumed to have negligible effects on the main mechanisms of TCE. There has been virtually no empirical test of this assumption. Researchers tend to accept it without question. One exception is Chiles and McMackin (1996), who argue that the switch-over level of asset specificity will vary as a function of the risk preference of the firm and therefore that a more realistic assumption of variable risk preferences will improve the predictive efficacy of TCE. If there had been tests on risk neutrality, the effects of risk preferences might have been identified empirically long before Chiles and McMackin's theoretical argument.

Finally, not only the result, but also the process, of assumption-based testing contributes to theory development. To design an empirical test on a core assumption, the researcher often needs to analyze the nature of the assumption carefully. For example, operationalizing a construct involves checking whether it is multi- or unidimensional (see Gerbing and Anderson 1988). Wathne and Heide's (2000) conceptual analysis of opportunism arrives at a distinction between passive and active opportunism. The former is about withholding critical information while the latter concerns committing forbidden acts. Williamson (1996) states that the propensity for opportunism varies between cultures. In particular, Chen et al. (2002) argue that opportunistic propensity is affected by cultural prior conditioning of individualism-collectivism, such that individualists have a higher opportunistic propensity in intra-group transactions and collectivists in inter-group transactions. In other words, individualism-collectivism is a contingent condition affecting how opportunism manifests itself in an exchange relationship. In short, the process of assumption-based testing may clarify the conceptual domain of an assumption.

Testing core assumptions

The history of empirical research in TCE shows that the lack of assumption-based testing was more likely due to neglect rather than the difficulty of conducting the test. For example, Monteverde and Teece (1982a, b) could readily incorporate tests of assumptions in their studies with additional effort. When they (1982a) requested two automotive engineers to rate the engineering cost of each of their sample of components, they could have asked simple questions such as, "What factors does an assembler consider when making make-or-buy decisions?" Similarly, when they (1982b) obtained a small sample of components from a major automotive supplier, they could have asked, "What factors does a supplier consider when deciding whether to own the tools and dies of a component?" If they had asked such simple questions, their studies probably would have made more significant contributions to the TCE literature and prompted more assumption-based testing among subsequent studies.[10]

Following closely after Monteverde and Teece is Stuckey's (1983) in-depth study of vertical integration and joint ventures in the aluminum industry. He uses TCE reasoning throughout his analysis, and yet his 348-page book contains no description of how decisions on governance structures are actually made by managers, let alone any analysis of whether the core assumptions of TCE are realistic. He even states that "[o]pportunism and bounded rationality are presumed always to exist, so bauxite traders are not unusual on these counts" (Stuckey 1983: 74). In other words, he simply presumed that opportunism and bounded rationality existed among bauxite traders without trying to investigate whether and how far this was really the case. Accordingly, his results were based on shaky empirical evidence.

I am arguing neither that assumption-based testing is *always* better than assumption-omitted testing nor that, when a new theory is initially tested, *all* the tests should be assumption based. Sometimes it makes sense to start testing a new theory without examining its core assumptions. For instance, if two variables of a theory are posited to be related via a generating mechanism based on a certain assumption and it is much easier to measure the two variables than the variable(s) associated with the assumption, a cost-effective research strategy may be to first study the relationship between these two variables. If the relationship is as posited, then the assumption is examined and tested; if not, we can stop right there. The problem, as has happened with TCE, is that empirical support accumulates for the relationship between two variables (e.g., asset specificity and hierarchy), but few researchers bother to go deeper and investigate the underlying mechanisms and assumptions.

The main difference between core assumptions and other relationships and constructs embedded in the structure and mechanism of a theory is that the former are often more closely associated with human attitudes, beliefs, and perceptions. To test these assumptions, researchers need to collect data via direct or indirect contact with managers. Quantitative research based on secondary data, such as Brouthers et al. (2003), Dhanaraj and Beamish (2004), Hennart (1988), and Hu and Chen (1993) in the case of TCE, is not likely to yield much meaningful information about these assumptions. Case studies are probably a better option when "how" and "why" questions are being investigated (Yin 2014). As a start, in-depth, unstructured interviews with managers who make transaction cost–related decisions are particularly useful for collecting data about the key factors affecting their decisions.

Buckley and Chapman's (1997, 1998) longitudinal study discussed earlier is a good example. Following the spirit of grounded theory (Strauss 1987), Buckley and Chapman just let respondents describe how they made decisions that involved transaction cost issues, without incorporating any TCE constructs in the probing questions. As far as possible, their interviews were conducted using the terms the manager employed rather than those of the interviewer. That is, they let data tell their own stories. This approach enables researchers to observe how events naturally unfold and understand how managers actually behave. Such data provide a useful preliminary check on the realism of certain TCE assumptions. Depending on the nature of investigation, other research methods that involve managerial contacts, such as questionnaire survey (e.g., Lyons 1995) and experimental research (e.g., Pilling et al. 1994), may also be appropriate. In particular, Lam (2010) suggests two approaches – the experimental-causal-chain and the moderator-of-process designs – that may improve the rigor of testing assumptions under certain circumstances.

Consider an example outside TCE. The classical theory of economic decision making assumes perfect rationality. A standard methodology in economics is to test the theory by its predictions of aggregate phenomena, a typical assumption-omitted approach. In 1934 and 1935, in the course of a field study of the administration of public recreational facilities in Milwaukee, Simon (1979) noticed that the assumption of perfect rationality was not tenable. Subsequently, he and his colleagues conducted several "anthropological" field studies that elicited descriptions of decision-making procedures and observed the course of specific decision-making episodes. These studies led to his path-breaking argument for replacing perfect rationality by bounded rationality as the assumption underlying a decision-making theory.

Other than the aforementioned requirement for collecting data through managerial contacts, testing assumptions does not call for special research designs. While it may not be easy to test a core assumption, it is not likely to be more difficult than testing other relationships posited by a theory, such as the relationship between asset specificity and choice of governance modes in TCE. Operationalizing, for example, opportunism can be a challenging task (see Wathne and Heide 2000); operationalizing asset specificity is not easy either (see Nooteboom 1993). In a similar vein, Blaug (1992: 96) maintains that "direct evidence about assumptions is not necessarily more difficult to obtain than data about market behavior used to test predictions."

Conclusion

> Nothing is more fundamental in setting our research agenda and informing our research methods than our view of the nature of the human beings whose behavior we are studying. It makes a difference, a very large difference, to our research strategy . . .
>
> (Simon 1985: 303)

The core assumptions of a theory often concern the fundamental issue of human nature. More specifically, such assumptions constitute the foundation of the mechanismic explanations of a theory and should play a pivotal role in theory development. An unrealistic core assumption will lead to an unrealistic mechanismic explanation and thus a defective theory. To what extent an assumption is realistic has to be determined empirically.

I have argued for a distinction between assumption-based and assumption-omitted theory testing. In order to establish a solid foundation in the early stage of theory development, researchers should prefer research methods that involve assumption-based testing. This approach, which necessitates collecting data via direct or indirect contact with managers, enables researchers to assess the validity and clarify the conceptual domain of an assumption. It may also open up new opportunities for strengthening a theory. I do not claim that assumption-based testing is a panacea for all the theoretical and methodological problems of TCE. Rather, my modest claim is that assumption-based testing will significantly improve the development of the theory.

The history of empirical research in TCE illustrates how the dominance of assumption-omitted theory testing has slowed down theory development. The overall empirical support for the theory is weakened because reduced models are often subject to alternative mechanismic explanations. It has led to unnecessary debates over the assumption of opportunism. Moreover, although Crook et al.'s (2013: 73) meta-analysis of 143 studies shows that "most of TCE's core predictions are supported by extant evidence," there is still no evidence that managers choose governance structures based on a transaction-cost-economizing rationale, the assumption on which the very foundation of the entire theory relies.

While I have only used TCE to illustrate my arguments, my analysis is applicable to other theories. Consider, for instance, another major organization theory – agency theory. Similar to TCE, empirical research has been biased toward assumption-omitted testing from the very beginning (e.g., Amihud and Lev 1981; Walking and Long 1984). A core assumption of agency theory is that agents exhibit risk-averse behaviors in decision making (Eisenhardt 1989). This assumption has been rarely tested by agency theorists although early research outside the theory shows that individuals may vary significantly in their attitudes toward taking risks (MacCrimmon and Wehrung 1986; March and Shapira 1988). As suggested by the theoretical arguments of Wiseman and Gomez-Mejia (1998) and Wright et al. (2001), empirically investigating how the agent's risk attitude actually affects a principal–agent relationship will tremendously enrich the theory.

As indicated by Wallace's (1971) model of scientific process, theory testing is an integral part of the process. Through empirical research, theories are confirmed or refuted. In view of the critical role of core assumptions in theory development, it is important that these assumptions are put to the test, especially during the early stage of theory testing. Unfortunately, assumption-omitted testing is the norm rather than the exception for management theories. An objective of this chapter is to bring assumption-based testing to the foreground of empirical research. In conclusion, when designing an empirical test on a new theory, researchers should ask, "Have we inadvertently taken the core assumptions of the theory for granted and assumed them away?"

Notes

1 In addition to the number of published discussions, some in top economics journals, the significance of the debate is also reflected by the time span these discussions have covered. For example, Long (2006) is a more recent contribution to the debate, more than half a century after Friedman's (1953) article was published. In fact, the *Journal of Economic Methodology* (Volume 10, Number 4, 2003) published a special issue commemorating the 50th anniversary of the article.

2 For simplicity of discussion, the terms "model" and "theory" are used interchangeably here. Bunge (1998: 125) proposes a useful distinction between theory and model:

> Theoretical models differ from theories in two respects. First, models have a narrower range (or reference class) than theories; to use Merton's expression, models are "theories of the middle range." . . . Second, unlike theories, theoretical models need not contain explicitly any law statements.

3 Goeree and Holt (2001: 1403) have a concise description of the circumstances under which Al W. Tucker invented the prisoner's dilemma story.

4 Here I adopt the correspondence view of truth; that is, truth is a property of a statement referring to a correspondence between that statement and the real world. Hence, a statement "p," such as "The Second World War ended in 1945," is true just in case p is a fact (Moore 1959; Russell 1906).

5 The distinction between structural and reduced models here is different from Masten's (1996). The reduced model of Masten is used by researchers to tackle the methodological issue that transaction costs simply cannot be observed for governance structures not chosen. The model is of a totally different nature than the one shown here. Nevertheless, his reduced model has a similar problem that reduced-form estimates "do not permit identification of the structural relations that underlie those hypotheses" (Masten 1996: 51). Williamson (1991) also uses the term "reduced-form analysis" in the sense that "governance costs are expressed as a function of asset specificity and a set of exogenous variables" (p. 282). He does not mention any problems associated with reduced-form tests but recommends that "[d]eveloping the deeper structures that supports the reduced form – by explicating contractual incompleteness and its consequences in a more microanalytic way and by developing the bureaucratic cost consequences of internal organization more explicitly – is an ambitious but important undertaking" (p. 282). Although he seems to recognize the importance of structural models, his comment is not related to the need for testing core assumptions.

6 This argument is based on a version of the knowledge-based view of the firm, advocated by Conner and Prahalad (1996), Kogut and Zander (1992, 1996), and Madhok (1996, 1997), that explicitly denies the necessity of the assumption of opportunism. Later some scholars, such as Heiman and Nickerson (2002) and Nickerson and Zenger (2004), have tried to further develop the knowledge-based view by incorporating the assumption of opportunism.

7 As Coase (1992: 718) comments, "the interrelationships which govern the mix of market and hierarchy . . . are extremely complex," and it is by no means my intention to claim here that testing Hypothesis 1c will address all the problems associated with TCE empirical research. Rather, I just argue that Hypothesis 1c provides a stronger test of the mechanismic explanation proposed by Monteverde and Teece (1982a) than Hypothesis 1b.

8 One simple, although rather rough, way is to carefully explain the concepts of opportunistic recontracting and quasi rent appropriation in the context of their study to the two automotive engineers and then to ask them to rate the risk of opportunistic recontracting and quasi rent appropriation for each component.

9 In chapter 6, it is noted that some early TCE studies build on Monteverde and Teece's (1982a, b) and form a set of replicated studies in the focal area of vertical integration in manufacturing industries. While this series of replicated studies helps accumulate our knowledge of the focal area, replication will not solve the problem associated with reduced models. No matter how many times

a reduced-form study is repeated, the tests are conducted on somewhat the same reduced model, and the results may be accounted by the same alternative mechanismic explanations. To deal with the problem, assumption-based theory testing is needed.

10 Another possibility is that they did ask questions of a similar nature but did not report them in their articles.

References

Alchian, A. A. 1950. Uncertainty, evolution, and economic theory. *Journal of Political Economy*, 58: 211–221.

Amihud, Y. and Lev, B. 1981. Risk reduction as a managerial motive for conglomerate mergers. *Bell Journal of Economics*, 12: 605–616.

Beccerra, M. and Gupta, A. K. 1999. Trust within the organization: Integrating the trust literature with agency theory and transaction costs economics. *Public Administration Quarterly*, 23: 177–203.

Blaug, M. 1992. *The methodology of economics: Or how economists explain* (2nd ed.). Cambridge, England: Cambridge University Press.

Boland, L. A. 1979. A critique of Friedman's critics. *Journal of Economic Literature*, 17: 503–522.

Brouthers, K. D., Brouthers, L. E. and Werner, S. 2003. Transaction cost-enhanced entry mode choices and firm performance. *Strategic Management Journal*, 24: 1239–1248.

Buckley, P. J. and Chapman, M. 1997. The perception and measurement of transaction costs. *Cambridge Journal of Economics*, 21: 127–145.

Buckley, P. J. and Chapman, M. 1998. The management of cooperative strategies in R&D and innovation programmes. *International Journal of the Economics of Business*, 5: 369–381.

Bunge, M. 1996. *Finding philosophy in social science*. New Haven, CT: Yale University Press.

Bunge, M. 1997. Mechanism and explanation. *Philosophy of the Social Sciences*, 27: 410–465.

Bunge, M. 1998. *Social science under debate*. Toronto: University of Toronto Press.

Caldwell, B. J. 1980. A critique of Friedman's methodological instrumentalism. *Southern Economic Journal*, 47: 366–374.

Chen, C. C., Peng, M. W. and Saparito, P. A. 2002. Individualism, collectivism, and opportunism: A cultural perspective on transaction cost economics. *Journal of Management*, 28: 567–583.

Chiles, T. H. and McMackin, J. F. 1996. Integrating variable risk preferences, trust, and transaction cost economics. *Academy of Management Review*, 21: 73–99.

Chow, G. C. 1983. *Econometrics*. Singapore: McGraw-Hill.

Coase, R. H. 1992. The institutional structure of production. *American Economic Review*, 82: 713–719.

Conner, K. R. and Prahalad, C. K. 1996. A resource-based theory of the firm: Knowledge versus opportunism. *Organization Science*, 7: 477–501.

Crook, T. R., Combs, J. G., Ketchen, D. J. and Aguinis, H. 2013. Organizing around transaction costs: What have we learned and where do we go from here? *Academy of Management Perspectives*, 27: 63–79.

David, R. J. and Han, S.-K. 2004. A systematic assessment of the empirical support for transaction cost economics. *Strategic Management Journal*, 25: 39–58.

Dhanaraj, C. and Beamish, P. W. 2004. Effect of equity ownership on the survival of international joint ventures. *Strategic Management Journal*, 25: 295–305.

Eisenhardt, K. M. 1989. Agency theory: An assessment and review. *Academy of Management Review*, 14: 57–74.

Foss, N. J. and Hallberg, N. L. 2014. How symmetrical assumptions advance strategic management research. *Strategic Management Journal*, 35: 903–913.

Friedman, Milton. 1953. *Essays in positive economics*. Chicago, IL: University of Chicago Press.

Gartner, W. B. 2001. Is there an elephant in entrepreneurship? Blind assumptions in theory development. *Entrepreneurship Theory and Practice*, 25(4): 27–40.

Gerbing, D. W. and Anderson, J. C. 1988. An updated paradigm for scale development incorporating unidimensionality and its assessment. *Journal of Marketing Research*, 25: 186–192.

Ghoshal, S. and Moran, P. 1996. Bad for practice: A critique of the transaction cost theory. *Academy of Management Review*, 21: 13–47.

Goeree, J. K. and Holt, C. A. 2001. Ten little treasures of game theory and ten intuitive contradictions. *American Economic Review*, 91: 1402–1422.

Granovetter, M. 1985. Economic action and social structure: The problem of embeddedness. *American Journal of Sociology*, 91: 481–510.

Grant, R. M. 1996. Toward a knowledge-based theory of the firm. *Strategic Management Journal*, 17(Winter Special Issue): 109–122.

Hart, O. 1990. An economist's perspective on the theory of the firm. In O. E. Williamson (Ed.), *Organization theory: From Chester Barnard to the present and beyond*: 154–171. New York: Oxford University Press.

Hedström, P. and Ylikoski, P. 2010. Causal mechanisms in the social sciences. *Annual Review of Sociology*, 36: 49–67.

Heiman, B. and Nickerson, J. A. 2002. Towards reconciling transaction cost economics and the knowledge-based view of the firm: The context of interfirm collaborations. *International Journal of the Economics of Business*, 9: 97–116.

Hempel, C. G. 1942. The function of general laws in history. *Journal of Philosophy*, 39(2): 35–48.

Hennart, J. F. 1988. Upstream vertical integration in the aluminum and tin industries: A comparative study of the choice between market and intrafirm coordination. *Journal of Economic Behavior and Organization*, 9: 281–299.

Hodgson, G. M. 1993. *Economics and evolution: Bringing life back into economics*. Ann Arbor, MI: University of Michigan Press.

Hu, M. Y. and Chen, H. 1993. Foreign ownership in Chinese joint ventures: A transaction cost analysis. *Journal of Business Research*, 26: 149–160.

Johnston, J. 1991. *Econometric methods* (3rd ed.). Singapore: McGraw-Hill.

Kaplan, A. 1964. *The conduct of inquiry*. San Francisco, CA: Chandler Publishing.

Kogut, B. and Zander, U. 1992. Knowledge of the firm, combinative capabilities, and the replication of technology. *Organization Science*, 3: 383–397.

Kogut, B. and Zander, U. 1996. What firms do? Coordination, identity, and learning. *Organization Science*, 7: 502–518.

Koopmans, T. C. 1957. *Three essays on the state of economic science*. New York: McGraw-Hill.

Lakatos, I. 1978. *Philosophical papers, vol. I: The methodology of scientific research programmes*. Cambridge, England: Cambridge University Press.

Lam, S. Y. 2010. What kind of assumptions need to be realistic and how to test them: A response to Tsang (2006). *Strategic Management Journal*, 31: 679–687.

Lehtinen, A. and Kuorikoski, J. 2007. Unrealistic assumptions in rational choice theory. *Philosophy of the Social Sciences*, 37: 115–138.

Lester, R. A. 1946. Shortcomings of marginal analysis for wage-employment problems. *American Economic Review*, 36: 63–82.

Long, R. T. 2006. Realism and abstraction in economics: Aristotle and Mises versus Friedman. *Quarterly Journal of Austrian Economics*, 9(3): 3–23.

Lyons, B. R. 1995. Specific investment, economies of scale, and the make-or-buy decision: A test of transaction cost theory. *Journal of Economic Behavior and Organization*, 26: 431–443.

MacCrimmon, K. and Wehrung, D. 1986. *Taking risks: The management of uncertainty*. New York: Free Press.

Macher, J. T. and Richman, B. D. 2008. Transaction cost economics: An assessment of empirical research in the social sciences. *Business and Politics*, 10(1): 1–63.

Madhok, A. 1996. The organization of economic activity: Transaction costs, firm capabilities, and the nature of governance. *Organization Science*, 7: 577–590.

Madhok, A. 1997. Cost, value and foreign market entry mode: The transaction and the firm. *Strategic Management Journal*, 18: 39–61.

Mäki, U. 2000. Kinds of assumptions and their truth: Shaking an untwisted F-twist. *Kyklos*, 53: 317–336.

March, J. G. and Shapira, Z. 1988. Managerial perspectives on risk and risk-taking. In J. G. March (Ed.), *Decisions and organizations*: 76–97. Oxford, England: Basil Blackwell.

Masten, S. E. 1984. The organization of production: Evidence from the aerospace industry. *Journal of Law and Economics*, 27: 403–417.

Masten, S. E. 1996. Empirical research in transaction cost economics: Challenges, progress, directions. In J. Groenewegen (Ed.), *Transaction cost economics and beyond*: 43–64. Boston, MA: Kluwer Academic.

Masten, S. E., Meehan, J. W. and Snyder, E. A. 1991. The costs of organization. *Journal of Law, Economics, and Organization*, 7: 1–25.

Mathews, J. A. 2006. *Strategizing, disequilibrium and profits*. Stanford, CA: Stanford Business Press.

Monteverde, K. 1995. Technical dialog as an incentive for vertical integration in the semiconductor industry. *Management Science*, 41: 1624–1638.

Monteverde, K. and Teece, D. J. 1982a. Supplier switching costs and vertical integration in the automobile industry. *Bell Journal of Economics*, 13: 207–213.

Monteverde, K. and Teece, D. J. 1982b. Appropriable rents and quasi-vertical integration. *Journal of Law and Economics*, 25: 321–328.

Moore, G. E. 1959. *Philosophical papers*. London: Allen and Unwin.

Musgrave, A. 1974. Logical versus historical theories of confirmation. *British Journal for the Philosophy of Science*, 25: 1–23.

Musgrave, A. 1981. "Unreal assumptions" in economic theory: The F-twist untwisted. *Kyklos*, 34: 377–387.

Nagel, E. 1963. Assumptions in economic theory. *American Economic Review*, 53: 211–219.

Nickerson, J. A. and Zenger, T. R. 2004. A knowledge-based theory of the firm: The problem-solving perspective. *Organization Science*, 15: 617–632.

Nooteboom, B. 1993. An analysis of specificity in transaction cost economics. *Organization Studies*, 14: 443–451.

Pilling, B. K., Crosby, L. A. and Jackson, D. W. 1994. Relational bonds in industrial exchange: An experimental test of the transaction cost economic framework. *Journal of Business Research*, 30: 237–251.

Priem, R. L. and Butler, J. E. 2001. Is the resource-based "view" a useful perspective for strategic management research? *Academy of Management Review*, 26: 22–40.

Rindfleisch, A. and Heide, J. B. 1997. Transaction cost analysis: Past, present, and future applications. *Journal of Marketing*, 61(4): 30–54.

Robins, J. A. 1987. Organizational economics: Notes on the use of transaction-cost theory in the study of organizations. *Administrative Science Quarterly*, 32: 68–86.

Rothbard, M. N. 1957. In defense of "extreme apriorism". *Southern Economic Journal*, 23: 314–320.

Russell, B. 1906. On the nature of truth. *Proceedings of the Aristotelian Society*, 7: 28–49.

Sayer, A. 1992. *Method in social science: A realist approach* (2nd ed.). London: Routledge.

Shadish, W. R., Cook, T. D. and Campbell, D. T. 2002. *Experimental and quasi-experimental designs for generalized causal inference*. Boston, MA: Houghton Mifflin.

Shelanski, H. A. and Klein, P. G. 1995. Empirical research in transaction cost economics: A review and assessment. *Journal of Law, Economics, and Organization*, 11: 335–361.

Shugan, S. M. 2007. It's the findings, stupid, not the assumptions. *Marketing Science*, 26: 449–459.

Shugan, S. M. 2009a. Commentary – Relevancy is robust prediction, not alleged realism. *Marketing Science*, 28: 991–998.

Shugan, S. M. 2009b. Rejoinder – Think theory testing, not realism. *Marketing Science*, 28: 1001–1001.

Simon, H. A. 1979. Rational decision making in business organizations. *American Economic Review*, 69: 493–513.

Simon, H. A. 1985. Human nature in politics: The dialogue of psychology with political science. *American Political Science Review*, 79: 293–304.

Simon, H. A. 1991. Organizations and markets. *Journal of Economic Perspectives*, 5(2): 25–44.

Strauss, A. L. 1987. *Qualitative analysis for social scientists*. Cambridge, England: Cambridge University Press.

Stuckey, J. A. 1983. *Vertical integration and joint ventures in the aluminum industry*. Cambridge, MA: Harvard University Press.

Tsang, E. W. K. 2009a. Commentary – Assumptions, explanation, and prediction in marketing science: "It's the findings, stupid, not the assumptions". *Marketing Science*, 28: 986–990.

Tsang, E. W. K. 2009b. Rejoinder – Robust prediction and unrealistic assumptions. *Marketing Science*, 28: 999–1000.

Vahlne, J. E. and Johanson, J. 2014. Replacing traditional economics with behavioral assumptions in constructing the Uppsala Model: Toward a theory on the evolution of the multinational business enterprise (MBE). *Research in Global Strategic Management*, 16: 159–176.

Walking, R. and Long, M. 1984. Agency theory, managerial welfare, and takeover bid resistance. *Rand Journal of Economics*, 15: 54–68.

Wallace, W. 1971. *The logic of science in sociology*. Chicago, IL: Aldine Atherton.

Wathne, K. H. and Heide, J. B. 2000. Opportunism in interfirm relationships: Forms, outcomes, and solutions. *Journal of Marketing*, 64(4): 36–51.

Williamson, O. E. 1975. *Markets and hierarchies: Analysis and antitrust implications.* New York: Free Press.

Williamson, O. E. 1985. *The economic institutions of capitalism: Firms, markets, relational contracting.* New York: Free Press.

Williamson, O. E. 1991. Comparative economic organization: The analysis of discrete structural alternatives. *Administrative Science Quarterly*, 36: 269–296.

Williamson, O. E. 1993. Opportunism and its critics. *Managerial and Decision Economics*, 14: 97–107.

Williamson, O. E. 1996. Economic organization: The case for candor. *Academy of Management Review*, 21: 48–57.

Williamson, O. E. 1997. Hierarchies, markets and power in the economy: An economic perspective. In C. Menard (Ed.), *Transaction cost economics: Recent developments*: 1–29. Brookfield, VT: Edward Elgar.

Wiseman, R. M. and Gomez-Mejia, L. R. 1998. A behavioral agency model of managerial risk taking. *Academy of Management Review*, 23: 133–153.

Wright, P., Mukherji, A. and Kroll, M. J. 2001. A reexamination of agency theory assumptions: Extensions and extrapolations. *Journal of Socio-Economics*, 30: 413–429.

Yin, R. K. 2014. *Case study research: Design and methods* (5th ed.). Thousand Oaks, CA: Sage.

4 Theory testing
A seemingly straightforward process

Most students in management doctoral programs are taught the method of null hypothesis statistical testing (NHST) – to test a hypothesis (and its underlying theory) by checking whether its null counterpart can be rejected at a certain level of significance (usually $p < 0.05$).[1] Yet, and more importantly, they are seldom briefed about the complications associated with this seemingly straightforward way of theory testing.[2] In psychology, Nickerson (2000: 241) highlights this problem: "One might think that a method that had been embraced by an entire research community would be well understood and noncontroversial after many decades of constant use. However, NHST is very controversial." In fact, in 2015 *Strategic Management Journal*, as a top journal, took the lead to abolish NHST as a way of presenting empirical findings (Bettis et al. 2016).

NHST is just one – mostly statistics-based – aspect of the much broader and more philosophical domain of theory testing. For example, what Rosenthal (1979) called "the file drawer problem" is closely related to, yet distinct from, the issue of NHST. Even if researchers abolish NHST, they may still hesitate to submit their manuscripts that fail to show significant results (regardless of how "significant results" is defined) for review and publication.[3] This publication bias is in turn related to the predominant verificationist stance among researchers when they test theories. This deficient way of theory testing – accompanied by few falsification attempts – leads to a proliferation of management theories.

The presence of diverse, and even contradictory, theories gives rise to conceptual and managerial confusion. This is an unsatisfactory situation especially if management researchers want to narrow the status gap between their discipline and the natural sciences. Unlike Pfeffer (1993), who advocates for paradigm consensus, I argue here that theories that repeatedly fail empirical tests should be eliminated. This chapter identifies the practical and philosophical difficulties associated with testing management theories and, from a critical realist perspective, proposes methods for improving the rigor of theory testing.

Proliferation of theories

Management researchers have given a great deal of attention and effort to building theories (e.g., Lewis and Grimes 1999; Locke 2007; Pentland 1999; Weick 1989) and much less to falsifying theories. Davis and Marquis (2005: 340) succinctly summarize the situation: "The theories of the 1970s, for instance, continue to hang on independent of empirical confirmation, and efforts at disconfirmation are both rare and relatively ineffective. To our knowledge, no organizational theory has ever been 'rejected' (as opposed to 'falsified')." Failure to falsify is not restricted to the management discipline. For instance, in psychology, Greenwald et al. (1986: 223) lament that "the evidence of history is that the falsification method receives much lip service but little use. Many researchers who would describe their activity as falsification seeking are effectively engaged, instead, in the subtly different activity of theory building." Similarly, Mark Blaug, a noted economic methodologist, describes as a major weakness of economics that much of its theory is not falsifiable and that economists preach falsification but do not practice it (Anonymous 1998).

More than half a century ago, Koontz (1961) used the term "management theory jungle" to describe the various schools of management theory (see also Mintzberg et al. 1998). Without removing any old, rotten trees, and with new trees coming up, the jungle will keep on expanding. Using similarly figurative terms two decades later, Pfeffer (1982: 1) exclaimed that "the domain of organization theory is coming to resemble more of a weed patch than a well-tended garden." Proliferation of theories leads to not only conceptual but also managerial confusion. The persistence of weak, or even false, theories may hinder the development of good theories (Arend 2006) and the field's ability to make scientific progress (Pfeffer 1993). Moreover, misspecified models can produce misguided managerial decisions (Cohen and Axelrod 1984). Managers may be confused by the disparate explanations or conflicting recommendations derived from various theories (Koontz 1980), or they may simply lose interest in what management researchers have to say (Pfeffer and Fong 2002). In short, "modern organization theory offers no consistent advice to practitioners and indeed offers no consistent story about organizations and how they survive and prosper" (Donaldson 1995: 27). In a sarcastic tone, McKinley and Mone (1998: 174) comment that "there is more consensus among organizational employees and other organizational participants about the nature of organizations than there is among organization theorists."

Philosophical discussions of scientific methods point out the important role of falsification in theory development. In his quest for a criterion of demarcation between science and non-science, Popper (1959) argues that a theory is scientific if and only if it is testable. He then equates testability with falsifiability. In other words, what distinguishes scientific from non-scientific theories is that the former are falsifiable whereas the latter are not. Popper cites Freudian psychoanalytic theory as an example that fails to meet his standard of falsifiability and should therefore not be regarded as scientific.

Having reservations about treating falsifiability as the exclusive criterion for distinguishing science from non-science, Grünbaum (1976) argues that instead of focusing on negative evidence only, researchers need to give credit to evidence that supports a theory. That said, falsifiability should be a fundamental feature of scientific research programs. If a management theory is not falsifiable, its scientific status is in jeopardy. Verification and falsification are complementary aspects of science.

Falsification versus verification

Empirical sciences are characterized by their use of inductive inferences: the laws and theories that constitute scientific knowledge are derived by induction from empirical observations (Chalmers 1999). An inference is inductive if the reasoning runs from singular statements, such as descriptions of observed events, to universal statements, such as hypotheses.[4] Suppose in a study of companies that implement total quality management (TQM), researchers find that all the companies in their sample experienced a marked increase in productivity. Based on this evidence, through inductive reasoning the researchers may construct a general theory arguing that TQM always has a positive effect on firm productivity.

Such an inference suffers from the "problem of induction" formulated by the eighteenth-century philosopher David Hume. Hume poses the question of whether we are ever warranted in drawing universal conclusions from particular experiences or observations. According to Hume (2000 [1739]), although we may generalize from individual instances out of habit, we are not logically justified in reasoning from repeated instances that we have experienced to instances that we have not experienced.[5] Consider the hypothetical study of TQM just mentioned. No matter how many observations the researchers may collect that provide confirming evidence for the theory, they can never prove that the theory, which makes a universal statement about the relation between TQM and productivity, is true. The problem of induction is aptly summarized by Hawking's (1988: 10) statement: "no matter how many times the results of an experiment agree with some theory, you can never be sure that the next time the result will not contradict the theory." Based on limited observations relative to the possible cases, a theory can never be verified to be universally true, but it can be shown to be false.

Popper (1959) accepts Hume's conclusion regarding the problem of induction but sought to bypass the problem altogether by putting forward a non-inductive approach to science. He does so by taking a falsificationist approach to scientific inquiry. Although inductive inferences to unobserved cases may not be justified, it is possible to make deductive inferences starting from singular observation statements as premises to arrive at the falsity of universal statements contained in scientific theories. For instance, in the study of TQM, if a company that implements TQM does not show any improvement in productivity or even shows a drop in productivity, the claim that TQM has a universally positive effect on productivity is demonstrated to be false. This asymmetry between falsifiability and verifiability results from the logical form of universal statements, which are not derivable from, but can be contradicted by, singular statements. Popper's reasoning is simple: every theory must contain at least one universal statement (e.g., all swans are white), and as such, it can never be conclusively verified even if it is true, apart from observing all possible cases – past, present, and future.

Nevertheless, universal statements can be refuted easily with just one piece of disconfirming evidence (i.e., the observation of a non-white swan). By establishing falsification, rather than verification, as the method of science, Popper declares Hume's problem of induction simply irrelevant to scientific inquiry.

Falsificationists abandon any claim that theories can be shown to be true in view of observational evidence. Instead, theories are construed as speculative and tentative conjectures created by researchers in an attempt to explain certain phenomena in the world (Popper 1962). Once proposed, theories are to be rigorously and ruthlessly tested through data collection and analyses. According to Popper, such great scientists as Galileo, Kepler, Newton, Einstein, and Bohr made possible a tremendous growth of knowledge by championing bold ideas and subjecting them to severe attempts at refutation, which included severe theoretical analyses and severe empirical tests. A severe test exposes the very foundation of a theory to empirical evidence such that a negative finding may require a wholesale revision of the theory (Losee 2005). Theories that fail to stand up to severe tests should be rejected and replaced by further speculative conjectures. If corroborated through the absence of falsifying evidence, theories may be provisionally accepted. Through such a process of conjectures and refutations, science progresses (Popper 1962). This quest for falsifying evidence never ends. As Agassi (1975: 24) comments, "Popper's theory presents science as an endless series of debates."

Forceful it may seem, Popper's approach is by no means the only possible response to Hume's problem of induction. Thomas Reid (1764), a contemporary of Hume, argues that it is neither logically nor practically possible for people to be universal skeptics. In everyday life, we readily associate our sensory experiences with external realities. By taking for granted our interpretation of sensory data, we draw upon untested assumptions about the nature of reality and speculate about the outcomes of our actions. Instead of being strict falsificationists, people – including researchers – implicitly take a verificationist stance, which presumes the validity of inductive inferences.

Researchers' interest in empirical evidence presupposes that our perceptions of data give some indication of the way things are. A belief is justified presumptively "when there is a *standing presumption* in its favor and no preestablished (rationally justified) reason that stands in the way of its acceptance" (Rescher 1992: 16). Moreover, our use of language to communicate our theories and findings assumes that others will interpret our research in ways that reflect our intended meaning (Campbell 1963). As Polanyi (1962) points out, we cannot possibly doubt all of our beliefs simultaneously; we can only doubt some beliefs on the basis of other beliefs that we hold unquestioningly. Hence, Polanyi (1962) portrays scientists as operating from a "post-critical" or fiduciary perspective, rather than from universal skepticism. Owing to our unexamined assumptions and human fallibility, and our limited access to data, our conclusions are always tentative, and our generalizations are risky. Nevertheless, researchers venture bold claims about the relevance of their findings in settings beyond those studied.

That said, efforts aimed at falsifying theories are important for progress in management research. Stressing verification over falsification has led to a proliferation of theories, including weak and conflicting theories. If falsification were pursued, spread of speculative theories should be less of a concern because theories that fail to pass empirical tests can be eliminated. However, the problem within the management discipline is that proliferation of theories is not accompanied by vigorous attempts at falsification. From a normative and descriptive view of science, verification and falsification are mutually supporting. This chapter chooses to highlight falsification in an effort to encourage a balance that has been neglected by past and current research practices in management research. The next section discusses the major obstacles to testing theories in a rigorous manner, resulting in the dearth of falsification.

Obstacles to rigorous theory testing

Rigorous tests refer to tests that can reduce the chance of biases such as that associated with the file drawer problem. This term should be distinguished from the aforementioned concept of severe tests proposed by Popper (1962) – given a hypothesis H and an observation O in light of background knowledge B, the severity of a test would be greater if O is more probable given H and B and less probable given B alone (see Musgrave 1974). The terms "rigorous test" and "severe test" are related in that reducing biases should contribute to making a test more severe.

Nature of social phenomena

Given the open-system nature of social phenomena, "it is unrealistic to assume that all relevant data will be consistent with a theory even if the theory is correct" (Lieberson 1992: 7). There are several factors that make conclusive theory testing more difficult in the social sciences in general, and management in particular, than in the natural sciences.

First, organizations are inherently complex and changing social phenomena, with multiple levels of analysis, as well as multiple and contingent causal processes (Fabian 2000). Different theories explain different aspects of organizations. From a theory testing view, the availability of competing hypotheses derived from different theories is a fortuitous situation, but it occurs infrequently in management research due to the diverse range of phenomena studied. The boundary conditions surrounding our theories further reduce overlaps that could lead to competing hypotheses. Owing to our inability to identify all the pertinent variables, often we are unable to state precisely the conditions on which different types of behavior depend or even the contingencies that make particular theories relevant to certain empirical contexts. Where boundary conditions are ambiguous, it may not be possible to determine whether hypotheses are direct competitors. Thus, we tend to position our theories as complementary, rather than competing. By contrast, the history of natural science shows that testing competing hypotheses is an effective way to determine the relative merits of different theories (Losee 2005).

A second factor that renders rigorous theory testing difficult concerns the element of personal volition in human behavior. Though constrained by habits, rules, routines, and institutions, humans have freedom to choose their actions (Downward et al. 2002). In management, this belief is reflected in arguments supporting strategic choice as causal, and not merely epiphenomenal (Child 1997). A similar conviction is found in research on creativity in entrepreneurial venturing (e.g., Alvarez and Barney 2010; Sarasvathy 2001). Although contextual factors, such as environment, technology, or scale of operation, have important influences on organizations, Child (1972) maintains that decision makers are not passive. They exercise choice and take actions that enact their organizations' environments. Not only are strategic behaviors nondeterministic, but they can be intentionally unpredictable and deceptive in order to gain competitive advantage. The exercise of free will and creativity curtails the predictive power of theories of human behavior.

Third, researchers' activities may change the beliefs and practices of managers and thereby undermine the continuity of the phenomena investigated (Numagami 1998). Self-fulfilling and self-defeating prophecies are not causes for concern in the natural sciences. A theory of, say, planetary motion will not change how planets actually move. In contrast, managers may alter their behaviors on the basis of the knowledge created by researchers (Ghoshal 2005). Self-fulfilling and self-defeating prophecies are significant issues that researchers need to take into account. The extent to which research influences managerial practice likely varies widely depending on the theory and organization of interest.

Finally, researchers and managers are related to one another such that researchers themselves can, at times, be the direct causal agents in organizational actions (Bradbury and Lichtenstein 2000). For example, making explicit the implicit theory-in-use within organizations can catalyze organizational change (Argyris and Schön 1978), thereby undermining the behavioral relevance of a previously identified theoretical explanation. Conversely, a false theory, if vigorously promoted to managers and given sufficient time, could become a more accurate description of their behavior (Brennan 1994). Ferraro et al. (2005), for example, maintain that economic theories become self-fulfilling as their behavioral assumptions become normative in organizations. A related issue is that unlike the natural sciences, falsification of a theory in the social sciences may not permanently eliminate it because the historical and institutional conditions that originally supported the theory, although subsequently superseded or transformed, may, with further historical change, return again to restore support (Hutchison 1988).

Theorizing

One of the primary obstacles to falsifying management theories is their imprecision. Bacharach (1989: 501) comments that management theories "are often stated in such a vague way that the theorists can rebut any discrediting evidence."

Astley and Zammuto (1992: 446) succinctly note: "while linguistic ambiguity increases the potential number of empirical tests conducted on a theory, it also reduces the chance that those tests can amount to a refutation of the theory." Imprecise wording of hypotheses can make them logically non-falsifiable. For example, Perrow's (1994: 216) contention that "no matter how hard we might try, the characteristics of complexly interactive and tightly coupled systems will cause a major failure, eventually" cannot be falsified due to the open time horizon. Imprecise wording is not unique to management research. Kuhn (1962) and Lakatos (1970) document scientists' tendency to state and interpret theories in ways that make them immune to falsification.

In the natural sciences, a common view is that there can be only one true theory explaining any particular phenomenon. Thus, researchers espousing competing theories are keen to provide not only evidence that supports their theories but also evidence that challenges rival theories (Chalmers 1999).[6] By contrast, among management theorists, it is generally accepted that the same phenomenon can be explained by different theories (Allison 1971; Ghoshal 2005).[7] If explanations are not mutually exclusive, greater space is opened up for researchers to create original theories providing novel explanations.

Taking the view that various theories can co-exist in harmony, some researchers advocate examining organizational phenomena through multiple theoretical lenses (e.g., Lewis and Grimes 1999; Nambisan 2002; Rajagopalan and Spreitzer 1996). For example, in their study of the differential impact of foreign institutional and foreign corporate shareholders on the performance of emerging market firms, Douma et al. (2006) use agency, resource-based, and institutional theories, claiming that a multi-theoretic approach provides a more holistic perspective. In fact, an editorial of the *Academy of Management Review*, a top journal publishing only conceptual papers, makes this claim: "the need to develop multiple-lens explanations in the field of management continues to increase" (Okhuysen and Bonardi 2011: 6).

Viewed positively, this approach is compelling given the complexity of organizations and the lack of a general theory to account for the rich variety of organizational phenomena. Viewed negatively, it could evidence a failure to carefully specify and scrutinize the assumptions, explanations, and implications of different theories to determine whether they are compatible or incompatible. While management researchers are not entirely averse to engaging one another in debates (Fabian 2000), these exchanges tend to remain at a theoretical, and sometimes a philosophical, level (de Cock and Jeanes 2006). For instance, the debate between Ghoshal and Moran (1996) and Williamson (1996) concerning how and how far organizations are able to reduce opportunism has remained at the theoretical level, stimulating few follow-up empirical studies. A similar situation is found in the debate between Barney (2001) and Priem and Butler (2001a, b) concerning whether Barney's (1991) core resource-based view arguments are tautological. By avoiding clearly stating competing hypotheses and digging into the evidence, empirical claims within our theories are never at risk in such debates.

Empirical research

Since management theories often do not provide guidance that is precise enough to know if our models are properly and fully specified, we cannot assess the nature and extent of misspecification. For example, our theories specify causes and effects, but rarely tell us the precise lag structure (Mitchell and James 2001). A theory may alert us to causality running in one direction, but neglect direct or indirect causal relations running the other way. Rarely are our models derived from mathematical identities, which provide some assurance against specification errors. Instead, researchers are left to their own discretion as they choose which variables to include and the functional forms of their models. Because our theories are incomplete, we augment our models with control variables to reflect alternative explanations. Exercising discretion in model specification does not present an inherent bias against falsification, but it can be an occasion for opportunistic behavior by researchers intent on verification. Researchers seeking validation for their theories can search for specifications that produce favorable results (Leamer 1978).

Closely related to the nature of social phenomena is the fact that most tests of management theories are not conducted under the conditions of a closed system. Regularity of events occurs when a phenomenon is buffered from outside influences, but conditions of closure are rarely achievable in the nonexperimental social sciences. Macro-organizational phenomena are not amenable to laboratory research, although it may be possible to extrapolate, *mutatis mutandis*, from laboratory research on individuals and groups to the organizational level. Efforts to isolate social phenomena in laboratory experiments can introduce artificiality, which alters behavioral responses (Harré and Second 1972). It is impossible to specify all the necessary initial conditions in a test situation, even in controlled experiments (Caldwell 1984). The openness of the social world entails that a mechanism that is under study will not *alone* determine the course of events observed by researchers (Peacock 2000).

Testing management theories under the conditions of an open, rather than closed, system further aggravates the problems associated with isolating the relations of interest from other confounding effects. Specifying the boundary conditions of a theory is critical to advancing theory testing (Bacharach 1989). For instance, as discussed in chapter 2, the Uppsala internationalization process model proposed by Johanson and Vahlne (1977) maintains that firms exhibit a pattern of incremental commitment to foreign markets as learning occurs over time. Early statements of the model were vague about its boundary condition that the model applies primarily to overseas expansions motivated by the objective of market seeking. If other motives – such as resource seeking – are dominant, the model does not apply. For years, lack of clarity about this boundary condition caused confusion about how far empirical data supported the model (Petersen and Pedersen 1997).

We can learn more from disconfirming cases than from confirming cases, yet our reasoning and sampling tend to have a confirmatory bias (Wason and Johnson-Laird

1972). The originators of a theory may hold it with such affection that they uncon-sciously pay attention only to supporting results. Observing this more than a century ago, Chamberlin (1965 [1890]) advocated the method of multiple working hypoth-eses: instead of basing empirical tests on one theory, researchers should try to develop tenable hypotheses for the phenomenon of interest from as many conceiv-able perspectives as possible. By so doing, they are less likely to be biased by theory when collecting observations and conducting analyses.

Researchers tend to adopt what Klayman and Ha (1987) called a "positive test strategy" – examining instances in which a theory is expected to hold. "A theory-confirming researcher perseveres by modifying procedures until prediction-supporting results are obtained" (Greenwald et al. 1986: 220). Another common research practice along the lines of positive test strategy is to develop hypotheses after the results are known. Kerr (1998) coins the term "HARKing" (Hypothesizing After the Results are Known) to label this practice of post hoc hypothesis development. With the exception of studies based on either the grounded theory approach or case studies, most quantitative studies are presented in a format suggesting that hypotheses are first deduced from related theories and then data are collected and analyzed for hypothesis testing using the method of NHST. Yet this positivist hypothetico-deductive approach advocated by Hempel (1965) may not represent the actual practice. Bettis (2012) reports the reply of a second-year Ph.D. student to his question "So what are you studying?" as follows:

> His reply of "I look for asterisks" momentarily confused me. He proceeded to tell me how as a research assistant under the direction of two senior faculty members he searched a couple of large databases for potentially interesting regression models within a general topical area with 'asterisks' (10 percent or better significance levels) on some variables. When such models were found, he helped his mentors propose theories and hypotheses on the basis of which the 'asterisks' could be explained.
>
> (pp. 108–113)

The student's reply indicates the practice of HARKing, which is the opposite of the hypothetico-deductive approach that is supposed to follow; hypotheses are formulated based on post hoc reasoning but presented as if they were a priori. In addition to being an ethically questionable practice (Leung 2011), HARKing has a number of harmful consequences such as reporting greatly exaggerated levels of statistical significance, preventing the identification of plausible alternative hypotheses, and developing flawed theories (Bettis 2012; Kerr 1998).

Journal review processes reinforce this confirmatory orientation by favoring theory-supporting results (Pfeffer 2007), leading to the file drawer problem (Rosenthal 1979). Aldrich (1992: 36) laments that management research "sys-tematically disdains the two processes central to scientific endeavor: attempted replication of previous findings, and publication of negative findings." Positive test strategy obviously contradicts the principle of falsification and leads to inflated confidence in a theory's corroborating evidence and generalizability. It also blinds us to possible unexplored alternative explanations.

Another problem of positive test strategy concerns the methodological issue of accommodation. Miller (1987: 308) argues that "when a hypothesis is developed to explain certain data, this can be grounds for a charge that its explanatory fit is due to the ingenuity of the developer in tailoring hypotheses to data, as against the basic truth of the hypothesis." Similarly, Starbuck (2004: 1248) notes that "human minds have the ability to generate seemingly credible explanations for virtually any data, including data that were nonsense." These researchers refer to what Lipton (1991) calls the "fudging" of a theory. When data need to be accommodated, there is a motive for the researcher to fudge a theory to make the accommodation. Likewise, researchers intending to find the effects that a theory anticipates may do whatever it takes to arrive at supporting results from empirical data by "massaging" the data. For example, opportunistic researchers may engage in model specification searches, delete observations to improve model fit, and achieve statistically significant coefficients with the expected signs.

The Duhem-Quine thesis

Popper's falsificationism has been challenged by the Duhem-Quine thesis, named after Pierre Duhem (1954) who first raised it and William Quine (1961) who revived it. According to this thesis, which threatens to undermine the prospects for theory testing, theories are never tested alone. Rather, they are tested in conjunction with other untested auxiliary hypotheses, which include background assumptions and rules of inference.

For the TQM research example mentioned earlier, when the relation between TQM and productivity is tested, it involves not only the theory that argues for a positive relation but also a set of auxiliary hypotheses, such as the practices associated with TQM, how to measure productivity, data collection methods, statistical analysis, and so on. A theory and its associated auxiliary hypotheses together form a *test system*. Let H be the principal hypothesis derived from a substantive theory of interest, A the set of auxiliary hypotheses, and O the observational consequence entailed by the conjunction of H and A so that $H \wedge A \Rightarrow O$.[8] An observation "not O" implies "not $(H \wedge A)$" rather than "not H" alone. In other words, the whole test system, instead of the principal hypothesis, is falsified by the contradictory outcome (Grünbaum 1960), and the existence of auxiliary hypotheses confounds tests of the principal hypothesis. When a finding does not support a theory, one can argue that the problem resides in the failure to control for certain conditions of the theory, rather than in the theory itself (Nooteboom 1986).

A critical problem posed by the Duhem-Quine thesis is that when an instance of falsification occurs, logic alone cannot isolate which elements of a test system are responsible for the falsification. Suppose a researcher found that contrary to the theory, TQM had a negative effect on productivity. The researcher cannot simply conclude that the theory has been falsified. Adjusting the auxiliary hypotheses may allow the theory to stand without alterations. This problem of under-determination is particularly serious in the social sciences where there is little agreement among researchers as to how certain auxiliary hypotheses should be independently tested (Meehl 1978). For instance, researchers may not agree on a reliable and valid way of measuring productivity or whether various TQM practices constitute a single construct or multiple constructs.

Incommensurability of theories

Donaldson (1995) portrays management theories as oriented toward different levels of analysis and different value assessments of organizations and managers, as well as having distinct languages and methodologies. For each theory, there is a dedicated group of scholars working on research to test hypotheses derived from their theory. To establish their distinct niches within a research field, such groups of researchers emphasize how their theories differ from one another (Mone and McKinley 1993). Over time, boundaries between groups of theorists become insurmountable (Aldrich 1992). As researchers perceive their theories to be incommensurable and discontinue conversations with advocates of alternative theories (Mahoney 1993), integration becomes very difficult, if not impossible (Jackson and Carter 1991).[9]

Incommensurability of theories also complicates the issue of theory testing. The notion of incommensurability has been used by management researchers in a "loose and imprecise fashion" (Weaver and Gioia 1994: 584). Hintikka (1988: 25) defines the commensurability of two theories "(relative to a given set of questions) as the ratio of the total information of their shared answers to the total information of the answers yielded by the two theories combined." That is, if there is little overlap in terms of the explanations given by two theories for a certain phenomenon, the theories are highly incommensurable with respect to explaining that phenomenon. More generally, incommensurability refers to the unintelligibility of theories to outsiders due to alien assumptions (e.g., ontologies and epistemologies) and vocabularies (i.e., the absence of a neutral observation language). A frequently perceived consequence of incommensurability is that without common ground, meaningful communication between theorists operating within distinct frameworks is virtually impossible.

For instance, in an interesting exchange between Amihud and Lev (1999), Denis et al. (1999), and Lane et al. (1999) concerning the relation between equity ownership structure and corporate diversification strategies, there appears to be a problem of incommensurability between agency theory, as understood by finance researchers, and the strategic management theorists' approach. Researchers in the two fields measure key constructs differently and use disparate reasoning to qualify and interpret empirical evidence (Lane et al. 1999). These differing auxiliary assumptions lead to the perception that the two research streams are not mutually informing and obstruct reaching a shared conclusion based on the evidence from past research. Lane et al. (1999) claim that agency theory and strategic management present two different worldviews. Such claims of incommensurability imply difficulty in comparing – logically and empirically – the merits of distinct theories and preclude theory testing by those who are outsiders. In short, incommensurability protects theories from competition (Jackson and Carter 1991).

Professional incentives

The problem of confirmatory bias may be motivated by the professional incentives that researchers face: "Given that professional advancement may be based more on the success of one's own theories than one's success in falsifying others', few researchers may be prompted to invest themselves in falsification efforts" (Greenwald and Ronis 1981: 136). Stinchcombe (1986) goes further by charging that those who call themselves theorists often embrace empirical emptiness (by putting forward theories having no empirically investigable implications) and fail to take seriously the stream of research findings generated by rival theories that contradict their own theories. In short, a rule of the game is to myopically focus on establishing the credibility of one's own theory, with little penalty associated with neglecting rival explanations and their empirical evidence. Researchers who are closely associated with a theory have a vested interest in seeing the theory supported and may tend to publish only confirming results. This attitude is surely unscientific. As Richard Feynman (1985), a noted Nobel laureate in physics, commented in his 1974 Caltech commencement address, "If you make a theory, for example, and advertise it, or put it out, then you must also put down all the facts that disagree with it, as well as those that agree with it" (p. 341).

Publishing in leading journals is an important indicator of a scholar's performance. Assuaging the preferences of reviewers and editors is a key factor in publishing success. As explicitly specified in the editorial policies of many journals, journal review processes strongly favor novel contributions to theory. Researchers respond accordingly, leading to a proliferation of sparsely tested theories or theoretical arguments. To the extent that theories are tested, authors generally want to show that empirical data corroborate their hypotheses derived from these theories, as reflected by the file drawer problem. Likewise, reviewers and editors generally favor hypothesis-supporting empirical results. Reviewers selected by editors (because they are subject experts) are vested in their own theories. Unless authors can provide some sound theoretical explanations for refuted hypotheses, reviewers and editors often frown on negative findings.[10]

In summary, the current situation is like what Arend (2006) candidly describes as academia's version of a pyramid scheme:

> Those researchers who enter earlier have the payoff of increased citations and legitimacy from further empirical support. Those adding to the pyramid have three potential benefits from towing the line: simpler exposition of

context and hypothesis generation; a greater possibility of reviewer acceptance due to reviewer knowledge and support of the theory; and a greater
possibility of future citations given the popularity of invoking the theory.

(p. 419)

A consequence of this incentive system is that management researchers' duty of
providing theories that inform practice is compromised: "the benefits of supporting and invoking a popular theory are substantial, while the costs of supporting
a theory that turns out to be benign or even damaging to practitioners are mini-
mal" (Arend 2006: 417). This cost-benefit asymmetry motivates verification at
the expense of falsification. From a critical realist perspective, the next section
discusses theory testing methods that address some of these obstacles.

Methods of theory testing

Most researchers work from an implicit *empiricist ontology*, which conflates the
empirical and the real domains, rather than a *realist ontology* informed by Bhaskar's (1978) distinction between the real, the actual, and the empirical domains.
Using variance designs (Mohr 1982), researchers often study empirical regularities expressed as correlations, rather than examining causal explanations directly.
Although research methods training sensitizes us to the distinction between
closed and open systems, our theories and empirical tests reflect to only a limited
extent the critical realist emphasis on outcomes as resulting from contingent
conjunctions of mechanisms.

Some critical realists acknowledge the gap between critical realism's contribution to philosophy of science and the dearth of methodological guidance in this
literature (e.g., Wuisman 2005; Yeung 1997). The situation has been improving,
but those who have begun to address this gap have done so primarily for the
purposes of theory *generation* and *verification*, rather than theory *falsification*.[11]
There is a need to augment critical realist writings by specifying methods for
testing theories. To the extent possible, proposed methods should address the
obstacles to theory testing identified earlier.

This section advances practical guidance for evaluating theories – particularly
management theories – that would facilitate theory testing. First a four-step
approach to theory testing is proposed, and then research programs that combine
both extensive and intensive designs are introduced.

Testing mechanisms

Within critical realism, to theorize is to propose mechanisms that explain events.
To identify mechanisms, researchers rely upon *retroduction*, which lies beyond
the two forms of inference traditionally emphasized in philosophy of science –
deduction and induction (Wuisman 2005). As briefly mentioned in chapter 1,
retroduction is the mode of inferential reasoning that reconstructs the conditions
for the occurrence of an empirical phenomenon (Danermark et al. 2002).

Retroduction seeks to identify the generative mechanisms that transcend the immediate instance of the phenomenon and are critical to its occurrence. To abstract from specific empirical instances to mechanisms, we attempt to distinguish general and essential conditions that underpin the phenomenon from incidental and non-essential conditions (i.e., spurious effects).

Less emphasized in the coverage of critical realist methods is the needed complementary process of *testing* postulated mechanisms. Sayer (1992) advocates testing mechanisms directly instead of testing their observable implications. This view reflects an analytical shift from empirical correlations to real mechanisms. While correlation analyses can evaluate the predicted implications of a theory, they fail to substantiate or refute a theory's causal explanation directly or to rule out alternative explanations. If mechanisms are to be truly explanatory, they must be amenable to testing directly (Bromiley and Johnson 2005). How-ever, critical realist discussions identify two characteristics that present formidable obstacles to testing explanations: (1) mechanisms may not be directly observable and (2) their effects are contingent. If critical realists are to engage in both theory generating and theory testing research, they must overcome these two obstacles by providing methods to (1) identify and measure the relevant mecha-nisms in play in a situation and (2) test for conjunctions of mechanisms as explanations for empirical outcomes.

The concern about unobservable mechanisms has been addressed elsewhere in management research. Godfrey and Hill (1995) distinguish between constructs that are *measurement unobservable* (i.e., there is no instrument appropriately calibrated) and *state unobservable* (i.e., observation perturbs the state). In the former case, the key emphasis needs to be on advances in measurement; for the latter case, effort should be directed toward techniques for unobtrusive data collection (Webb et al. 2000). The two forms of unobservability are not unique to critical realist research, and the methods for addressing both challenges are well established, although success in overcoming them is by no means guaran-teed. Mechanisms that are unobservable from the researcher's perspective may be apparent, nevertheless, to participants within the research setting. Questioning participants (using interviews or questionnaires) can elicit evidence regarding mechanisms, although self-report measures are susceptible to various kinds of biases and must be treated with caution (Schwarz et al. 1998).

Management research tends to move from theoretical arguments motivating sets of hypotheses directly to theory testing using multivariate models that incor-porate proxies for multiple theoretical and control variables. Such research seeks to test full theoretical systems using variance (i.e., correlation) methods. Bolstering this approach is the concern that regression models that are less than fully speci-fied produce biased coefficients. The use of multivariate correlational methods should be commendable, but they do not, by themselves, fulfill the exigencies of critical realism. In particular, they neglect the requirement of testing causal mechanisms as part of the process of verifying or falsifying a theory. Examining mechanisms directly calls for added research steps that specify the hypothesized mechanisms, test for the presence of these mechanisms, and determine whether they function as hypothesized. These three steps, together with testing the full theoretical system, make up the four-step approach to theory testing.

Step 1

The initial step involves identifying the causal mechanisms believed to account for the hypothesized relations in a study. This step requires interpretive work at the interface of theory and the empirical context of interest. Researchers must resolve ambiguities in their theories and derive their implications for particular settings. The goal is a contextualized specification of the explanatory properties and processes that underlie hypothesized causal relations. Since a theory may propose different mechanisms to explain different phenomena, researchers need to select those mechanisms that they believe operate in their particular research setting. More than one mechanism may be relevant to a given causal relation; furthermore, mechanisms may have complementary or conflicting implications for a hypothesized relation. To illustrate the importance of identifying all relevant mechanisms, Bromiley and Johnson (2005) point out the varied and conflicting ways that top management team diversity affects firm performance.

Consider a simple theory contending that variables x_1 and x_2 jointly determine y. The top portion of Figure 4.1 shows the path diagram representing this theoretical system. The hypothesized mechanisms, m_1 and m_2, link x_1 and x_2, respectively, to y. It is important to distinguish between the parameters relating x_1 and x_2 to y (designated β_1 and β_2 in step 4) and the mechanisms themselves, m_1 and m_2. The circle encompassing the path diagram reflects the explicit or implicit *ceteris paribus* condition, which treats the theoretical system as closed. Specifying a model according to step 1 of Figure 4.1 challenges theorists to clarify theoretical mechanisms (Anderson et al. 2006) and boundary conditions (Bacharach 1989).

Step 2

The next step in testing this theory is to consider whether the proposed mechanisms are indeed present in the empirical setting. Step 2 of Figure 4.1 conveys the emphasis on substantiating the existence of the causal mechanisms. Failure to validate the presence or the nature of postulated mechanisms provides compelling evidence to reject a theory's arguments. Prioritizing testing for mechanisms, rather than jumping directly to testing their hypothesized relations to dependent variables, runs contrary to the pattern in management research (Bromiley and Johnson 2005).

Tests for the presence of a mechanism can involve looking for collateral implications of the mechanism beyond those predicted by the theory of interest (Goldthorpe 2001). Even if a particular mechanism is not directly observable, the more observable effects that logically are attributable to the mechanism, the more compelling is the case for its presence. For example, consider an argument claiming that experience with an alliance partner leads to greater willingness

Step 1: Identify the hypothesized mechanisms.

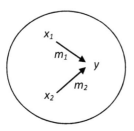

Step 2: Test for the presence of the mechanisms (m_1 and m_2) in the empirical setting.

Step 3: Test isolated causal relations.

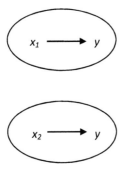

Step 4: Test the theoretical system.

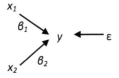

Figure 4.1 Steps in a critical realist approach to testing theories

to make asset-specific investments, with growth in trust as the explanation. Trust between alliance partners may not be directly observable, but it should produce a variety of manifest effects on negotiations, contracts, and coordination processes. In this case, multiple observable indicators provide indirect support for the presence of an unobserved mechanism. The reasoning here parallels the use of multiple indicators for latent constructs in structural equation modeling but, in this case, the construct of interest is a causal mechanism.

Bhaskar (1998) maintains that people's reasons can operate as causes, which in turn are responsible for producing or inhibiting change. Such intentional human behavior provides an opportunity for testing the mechanism of a theory. Retroducing intentions relies upon either truthful disclosure by the individuals involved, generalizations about similarly situated others, or projections of the researcher's own intentions onto the studied subjects. In order to infer reasons and evaluate the subjects' espoused reasons, we draw heuristically upon our own self-understanding for insights into others' unobservable intentions. Our common humanity and experiences, rather than a posture of objectivity, inform the hermeneutical act of inferring intentions from others' actions (Gadamer 2002; Ricoeur 1981).

Step 3

If the available evidence affirms the presence of the theorized mechanisms, we move to testing their causal effects. Before attempting to verify or falsify an entire theoretical system in an open context, a precautionary step is to test binary or more complex subsets of relations under controlled circumstances. For the hypothetical example shown in Figure 4.1, we seek tests of the component x_1-y and x_2-y relations in contexts that isolate each relation from other effects. Step 3 of Figure 4.1 depicts such tests. To do so, we must move from the open system of the empirical context of ultimate interest to experimental or quasi-experimental settings.

In spite of the threats to external validity (Guala and Mittone 2005), *laboratory experiments* allow for testing the effects of mechanisms under conditions similar to those of a closed system and, due to random assignment of treatments, generally provide stronger evidence that supports or rejects hypotheses than do nonexperimental designs. Many theories invoke mechanisms that consist of chains of causal links in which one event leads to another; experiments help isolate and test these links. Moreover, experiments enable researchers to assess the merits of competing theories by, for example, testing competing mediating relations proposed by those theories (Shadish et al. 2002). Although experiments have been a popular research method in psychology and organizational behavior, they are seldom used in the macro areas of management research, such as strategy, to facilitate tests of mechanisms (Croson et al. 2007). A notable exception is the experiment conducted by Sutcliffe and Zaheer (1998) to study the effects of different kinds of uncertainty on the likelihood of vertical integration.

Another is Schweiger et al.'s (1989) experiment involving managers in dialectical inquiry, devil's advocacy, and consensus approaches to group strategic decision making.

A *behavioral simulation* involves individuals in a setting constructed to mimic key aspects of a naturally occurring organizational situation. The realism of the constructed setting is the key feature distinguishing behavioral simulations from laboratory experiments. In an interactive behavioral simulation, researchers control the simulated context and observe the behaviors and decisions coming from participants' interactions with one another. The method is particularly suited for strategy process research (Dutton and Stumpf 1991). For example, Hough and White (2003) used an interactive behavioral simulation to study the moderating effect of environmental dynamism on the relation of decision-making comprehensiveness to decision quality. Gist et al. (1998) report that interactive behavioral simulations remain quite rare in management research – even among studies published in organizational behavior journals.

Quasi-experiments share some characteristics of laboratory experiments, but they occur in field settings, and researchers have less than full control over the assignment and scheduling of effects (Shadish et al. 2002). Thus, quasi-experiments have some merit by offering conditions that approximate randomly assigned treatments. In contrast with laboratory experiments, quasi-experiments trade off some control for external validity (Grant and Wall 2008). Again, with few exceptions, management researchers outside the domain of organizational behavior rarely use quasi-experimental designs. An example of such exceptions is Szulanski and Jensen's (2004) investigation of the role of templates in the replication of organizational routines, which was based on an eight-year longitudinal case study that took the form of a naturally occurring, repeated-treatment quasi-experiment.

Management researchers in the macro streams are recommended to further explore the potential of laboratory experiments, behavioral simulations, and quasi-experiments for rigorously testing the relations invoked in their theories. Because such methods fall outside the training typically acquired in strategy or international business doctoral programs, there are opportunities for collaborating with scholars in fields such as organizational behavior and psychology where such methods are in the mainstream.

Step 4

If empirical data corroborate a theory's mechanisms and their effects, then the next step is to examine the implications of its mechanisms jointly. This step moves the analysis from isolated mechanisms to the entire theoretical system, thereby adding complexity to the evaluative procedure. At this stage, we are interested in whether all of the theory's mechanisms are necessary and whether they are jointly sufficient to explain the outcome. For a complicated management theory, it may not be feasible to test all of its mechanisms in a single study. In such cases, a second-best alternative is to design tests of subsets of mechanisms that are unbiased by omitted theoretical variables through choosing research settings where the unmeasured variables can be assumed to be either invariant or irrelevant.

The openness of social systems complicates jointly testing a theory's hypotheses. Although the theoretical system is closed (see step 1), the empirical contexts of organizations and industries are not. Step 4 of Figure 4.1 depicts the open theoretical system in which outside influences give rise to unexplained variance that is relegated to the error term, ε. Here, the error term results from omitting variables relevant to the empirical context but outside the scope of the theory itself. Failure to account for some of the relevant mechanisms diminishes the proportion of variance explained by a model and potentially biases the estimated effects of the theoretical variables. Step 4, in contrast with the original theoretical model (step 1), focuses on estimable partial correlations (β_1 and β_2) and omits the generative mechanisms (m_1 and m_2). This switch from mechanisms to correlations accommodates established multivariate methods. Fitting empirical data to a multivariate model treats the process generating the dependent variable as a black box, and, as such, correlational analysis can only complement other research that directly tests mechanisms, not substitute for such tests.

Acknowledging potentially relevant outside contingencies, researchers conducting large-sample studies attempt to include control variables that account for effects beyond those in their theory and interactions. However, the situation may lead to an "interactionist regress" (Sayer 1992: 189) in which explaining outcomes as contingent conjunctions of mechanisms results in complex interactions that are difficult to understand conceptually and test empirically. Large-sample analytical methods require simplifying assumptions regarding the contingencies affecting observations, whereas case research can identify and take into account idiosyncratic contingencies (Nash 1999). The next section discusses how different research designs contribute to theory testing.

Research designs

Critical realism is highly pluralist in terms of empirical research methods. Since different methods focus on different aspects of reality, combining several methods together in a research program yields a rich understanding of the phenomenon of interest (Mingers 2001). Critical realists distinguish between *extensive* and *intensive designs* and maintain that both approaches are needed and complementary (Danermark et al. 2002; Sayer 1992, 2000). Extensive research tests empirical generalities across cases and typically employs quantitative methods. Intensive research tries to uncover the explanatory mechanisms relevant in particular cases and is often associated with qualitative modes of analysis. *Mixed designs* combine both extensive and intensive designs, thereby utilizing their complementary strengths and weaknesses. Critical realism encourages mixed designs in an effort to cope with the complexity of studied phenomena, aspects of which may go undetected by any single research approach (Mingers 2006).

Extensive designs

Critical realist concerns about extensive designs revolve around (1) their focus on empirical correlations rather than specifying explanatory mechanisms, (2) assumptions of model stability and closure, and (3) reliance upon statistical tests of significance (Mingers 2004). Conveying similar concerns, Sayer (1992: 194) observes:

> Given the disjunction between mechanisms and events, a strong correlation (or some other quantitative association) need not imply causation, or a weak one absence of a causal or structural relation. If a theory is to help solve this type of problem it must postulate causal mechanisms and not merely specify how total variation in the dependent variable might relate quantitatively to variation in the independent variables.

Even Starbuck's (2006) prioritization of effect size over statistical significance omits the goal of explanation through identifying mechanisms and their surrounding contingencies. Estimated effect sizes capture causal importance only if models are specified in terms of contingent relations reflecting complex conjunctures of mechanisms.

However, Ron (2002) offers some counterarguments to address such concerns. He points out that open systems do not *necessarily* undermine empirical regularities and that the occurrence of such regularities can provide insights into the operative mechanisms. Working from a critical realist perspective, a researcher uses regression analysis to demonstrate the effects of theorized causal mechanisms after controlling for other mechanisms that also could affect the outcome. Ron submits that researchers' repeated respecification of regression models exhibits an exploratory search for mechanisms affecting an empirical outcome. Such exploratory use of regression analysis seeks to explain empirical patterns retrospectively, and, for open systems, the result should not be interpreted as a predictive model, and conventional criteria for evaluating the statistical significance of coefficients for theory-determined models do not apply. If our intent is to falsify theories, researchers ought to pursue model respecifications that *undermine* hypothesized relations, not just post hoc respecifications that favor the theory (Caudill and Holcombe 1987, 1999; Kennedy 2005) or adjustments in theoretical arguments to fit findings (Lipton 1991), as practitioners of HARKing do.

Manicas (1987, 2006) raises the concern that the causes postulated in critical realist research are not linearly additive and, thus, violate a key assumption of regression modeling. Such a critique misses some possibilities for using multivariate modeling in critical realist research. For example, researchers can use regression models with interaction terms to test contingent effects. If a hypothesized effect varies over the range of values for a regressor, then a spline function can be used. Using regression analysis, relations for which empirical tests are feasible consist primarily of direct effects and lower-level (two-way or three-way) curvilinear effects, rather than more complex contingent relations. Hierarchical linear modeling allows coefficients to vary contingent upon moderating and mediating effects at other levels of analysis (Hofmann et al. 2000; Zhang et al. 2009) and, as such, is another tool suitable to critical realists' interest in testing the effects of intervening mechanisms on theoretical relations.

For models with complex and dynamic conjunctions, computer simulation modeling offers a means to transition from theoretical arguments to empirical testing. Experimentation with a simulation model generates data for a *response surface* reflecting the effects of multiple variables on a particular outcome of interest. Such data permit estimation of an algebraic function, often called a *meta-model,* that captures the effects of a set of independent variables on the dependent variable. *Response surface methods* estimate a multivariate equation that approximates the functional relation of explanatory variables to an outcome variable as generated by a complex simulation model (Law and Kelton 2000). Provided relevant empirical data are available, an estimated meta-model can be tested. This combination of simulation modeling of complex systems resulting in an empirically testable regression model provides a way to move from complex (nonlinear) dynamic systems to empirical tests using established methods. Such methods can advance empirical testing in research areas such as organizational structure and learning, where simulation research has enhanced our understanding of the relevant mechanisms (e.g., Lin and Hui 1999; Rahmandad 2008).

Intensive designs

Intensive designs complement extensive designs by addressing the differences across cases that one would expect if empirical outcomes result from conjunctions of multiple mechanisms in open systems. The purpose behind intensive designs is to identify and describe the generative mechanisms operating in particular cases, which is often not feasible for extensive designs. An intensive design emphasizes the collection of detailed data within one or more cases. The data are often qualitative, as are the analytic methods. Established methods for case study, ethnography, historiography (discussed in chapter 7), and action research guide intensive designs.

A distinctive feature of critical realist deployment of these methods is the emphasis on retroduction. Intensive investigation of a case affords a unique opportunity to evaluate whether the mechanisms proposed by a theory jointly affect empirical outcomes as expected, while taking into consideration intervening and countervailing contextual mechanisms. Easton (2000: 212) concludes:

> Case research which would wish to lay claim to a realist philosophy should be carried out in a different way: to be inquisitive, to look for the roots of things, to disentangle complexities and to conceptualize and re-conceptualize, test and retest, to be both rigorous and creative and above all to seek for the underlying reality through the thick veil which hides it.

For instance, Porter's (1993) ethnographic study of how racism affected the occupational relationships between nurses and doctors in a hospital adopted a critical realist perspective for identifying mechanisms that generated the racist events and found that the universalist-achievement ethos of professionalism was a mechanism countering the ascriptive nature of racist tendencies.

Intentional sampling is an important step if intensive designs are to yield evidence verifying or falsifying theoretical claims. Contrasting cases can provide evidence from natural experiments regarding how mechanisms operate under different conditions. Intertemporal comparisons through repeated studies of the same case can reveal how continuities and discontinuities in mechanisms and contexts affect outcomes (Harrison and Easton 2004). Pathological or extreme cases can reveal conditions where mechanisms are undermined or unimpeded (Danermark et al. 2002). As Collier (1994: 165) explains, "by seeing how something goes wrong we find out more about the conditions of its working properly than we ever would by observing it working properly."

Auxiliary hypotheses

The aforementioned Duhem-Quine thesis informs how we test mechanisms and theoretical systems. Since the presence of auxiliary hypotheses (A) confounds the testing of any theoretical hypothesis (H), it is possible to accept a given theoretical hypothesis under one set of auxiliary hypotheses and reject the hypothesis under another set of auxiliary hypotheses. Although the confounding effects implied by the Duhem-Quine thesis cannot be eliminated, Sawyer et al. (1997) suggest two ways of assessing the effects of auxiliary hypotheses.

One method is to conduct sensitivity analyses, where the auxiliary hypotheses are altered. For example, researchers can draw different samples, use alternative measures, vary model specifications, or employ dissimilar statistical methods for fitting and evaluating models. Consistent falsifying or supporting evidence using alternative auxiliary hypotheses is more conclusive than if alternative auxiliary hypotheses produce conflicting findings. Typical robustness checks found in quantitative papers belong to this method.

A second method is to test the auxiliary hypotheses directly. As discussed in chapter 3, Mäki (2000) distinguishes between the core and peripheral assumptions of a theory: core assumptions indicate the major causes postulated by a theory while peripheral assumptions refer to the minor causes. Although tests of theories center on core assumptions, direct tests of peripheral assumptions can provide further evidence qualifying theories and throw light on auxiliary hypotheses.

Replications that extend prior studies can also help researchers examine the implications of alternative auxiliary hypotheses by focusing their attention on one part of the test system at a time. Suppose the findings of a study did not support the test system, $H \wedge A$. Suspecting that a certain auxiliary hypothesis caused the result, a researcher replicates the study with an alternative auxiliary hypothesis (A') while keeping the rest of the test system intact. Finding support for the new test system, $H \wedge A'$, confirms the researcher's conjecture.[12] If the system is still not supported, the researcher needs to consider whether H should be rejected. In a similar vein, Søberg (2005) submits that a series of experiments can be used to locate the source of disconfirming evidence.

Critical tests

Critical tests involve data that allow researchers to judge the relative merits of competing theories (Stinchcombe 1968). This approach involves finding theories within a particular research area that make arguments leading to conflicting empirical predictions. Researchers should look for opportunities to conduct critical tests of two sorts: (1) tests of differing explanatory mechanisms and (2) tests of conflicting implications of alternative theories.

As an example of the first type of study, Gimeno et al. (2005) empirically examine the competitive and noncompetitive rationales for strategic mimicry put forward by different theories. As an example of the second type – testing the conflicting empirical implications of different theories – Singh (1986) argues for a negative relation between organizational performance and risk taking but notes that theoretical arguments based on hubris or boredom would motivate a relation with the opposite sign. This framing makes his empirical evidence a critical test between these alternative predictions. Setting up direct empirical tests of conflict-ing theoretical predictions provides more complete evidence regarding their relative merits than does testing the implications of a single theory and then invoking the alternative as a post hoc explanation for unanticipated findings. Although these two examples are based on extensive designs, critical tests also can be con-ducted under intensive designs. Sagan's (1993) case study of the Cuban missile crisis discussed in chapter 5 is an exemplar of testing competing mechanisms and implications proposed by the two major theories that explain accidents in hazard-ous high-technology organizations – normal accident theory (Perrow 1999) and high reliability theory (La Porte and Consolini 1991; Roberts 1989).

Conclusion

Proliferation of competing theories contributes positively to scientific progress (Kuhn 1962; Lakatos 1970). Within the management field, March (2004) highlights the adaptive value of diverse beliefs. The interdisciplinary nature of management research and the multifaceted nature of organizations make plural-ism a strength. The problem is not that we have too many theories; the problem is that we rarely, if ever, winnow out any.

The approach advocated here is neither falsificationist nor verificationist. Science must include both stances, as they logically and practically complement one another. Yet the proliferation of management theories indicates that the current practices within the field favor verification at the expense of falsification. To remedy the situation, this chapter proposes to enhance falsification efforts through testing theories more rigorously.

To successfully test theories, management researchers must overcome a for-midable set of practical and philosophical obstacles, such as the complexity and contingency of social phenomena, the openness of social systems, imprecisely specified theories, and the limitations of research designs. Career and profes-sional considerations, such as protecting the credibility of one's own theory, sometimes also stand in the way of rigorous theory testing.

This chapter discusses a series of four complementary steps for testing manage-ment theories: (1) identify the hypothesized mechanisms, (2) test for the presence of the mechanisms in the empirical setting, (3) test isolated causal relations using experimental or quasi-experimental designs, and (4) test the theoretical system using correlational methods. Although there have been scattered discussions of these steps and the methods they entail in the literature, there is no other attempt to organize them into an integrative research process.

Most empirical studies in management, especially those based on extensive research designs, seek to identify empirical regularities expressed as correlations and thus are located at step 4 of the recommended four-step approach. Although many research studies also touch upon step 1 during the development of hypoth-eses, steps 2 and 3 have been neglected for the most part. Without examining causal mechanisms directly, it is difficult to adjudicate conflicting explanations for empirical findings. Even in the face of cumulative, mostly confirming empiri-cal findings, omitting tests for the presence and causal effects of mechanisms leaves theoretical explanations in doubt. Both intensive and extensive designs can provide such tests.

Identifying and testing causal mechanisms calls for increased use of designs and methods found most frequently elsewhere in the social sciences – such as generating data through laboratory experiments, behavioral simulations, quasi-experiments, historiography, ethnography, or grounded theory building in field settings. Cross-disciplinary collaborations and drawing guidance from the meth-ods literature in other academic fields can facilitate such research designs. Since each of the four steps requires specific research techniques and no researcher is well versed in all these techniques, there is a need for specialization, with different researchers focusing on different steps, and the potential for collabora-tion as researchers coordinate sequential steps or work together on more than one step.

Last but not least, researchers should heed Locke's (2007: 887) advice, "Never tie your self-esteem (ego) to the correctness of your theory," and should be prepared to adjust or even abandon their theories when the evidence calls for new directions in their thinking. The shift expressed by Raymond Vernon in his product life cycle theory is a commendable example. In the initial formulation, Vernon (1966) postulated sequential involvement of firms beginning with the home-country market as the source of innovative products, followed by participation in foreign markets through exports and eventually foreign direct investment. In his later article, Vernon (1979) acknowledged that many multinational firms had moved away from the home-country orientation postulated in his initial theory and were introducing products simultaneously in multiple country markets. He pointed out that the evidence falsified sequential market rollout as a general theory of multinational behavior and stipulated some contingencies where it could still apply. As members of the scientific community, we need not make consistent arguments over the duration of our careers. Acknowledging changes in our thinking indicates that we are learning and that our field is progressing.

Notes

1 Nickerson (2000: 242) distinguishes between two meanings of null hypothesis: "the hypothesis whose nullification, by statistical means, would be taken as evidence in support of a specified alternative hypothesis" and "the hypothesis of 'no difference' between two sets of data with respect to some parameter." In the former meaning, a null hypothesis may or may not state "no difference." Note that management researchers normally adopt the former meaning, which is also the meaning used in this chapter.

2 At least this was the case for my own doctoral training received at the Judge Institute of Management Studies (now Cambridge Judge Business School) during the 1990s in the U.K. Myself and (as far as I know) my classmates took NHST for granted in our research activities. In fact, NHST has been institutionalized in the sense that it is readily available in most software packages for doing statistical analyses: "most researchers mindlessly test only nulls of no difference or of no relationship because most statistical packages only test such hypotheses" (Thompson 1998: 799).

3 Along with abolishing NHST, *Strategic Management Journal* welcomes submissions that report studies with non-results (Bettis et al. 2016).

4 This is just one form of inductive inference. Chapter 5 offers a formal definition of induction and discusses other forms of inductive inference.

5 It is beyond the scope of this book to explain the nature of Hume's problem of induction. Interested readers may refer to Tsang and Williams (2012) for a non-technical treatment.

6 Chalmers (1999: 92–101) relates how supporters of the Aristotelian worldview put forward various pieces of evidence to discredit the Copernican theory.

7 This contrast is partly related to the nature of natural versus social phenomena. For instance, if one theory proposes that the earth revolves around the sun and another theory proposes the opposite, it is logically impossible that both theories are accurate descriptions. In contrast, a firm's decision to manufacture a certain component in-house instead of purchasing it from the market can be based partly on transaction cost considerations (transaction-cost-economics explanation) and partly on legitimacy considerations (institutional explanation). Such explanations are not mutually exclusive; managers' motivations can encompass both. Ghoshal

(2005: 86) points out that in the social sciences, "many different and mutually inconsistent theories explain the same phenomenon, often to very similar extents."

8 The logical operators ∧ and ⇒ signify "and" as well as "imply," respectively.

9 Unlike the other obstacles discussed here, this one is more apparent than real. Even Kuhn, who originated the idea of incommensurable paradigms in his 1962 landmark work on the history of the natural sciences, admitted subsequently that incommensurability does not necessarily rule out meaningful communication and mutual understanding between researchers working within distinct paradigms (Kuhn 1990). Likewise, Laudan (1996: 9) argues that the problem of incommensurability is not as severe as some assert: "From the beginning of its vogue in the early 1960s, incommensurability has been a philosophical conundrum in search of instantiation." In a stronger tone, Hunt (1991) maintains that paradigm incommensurability has been thoroughly discredited in philosophy. Similarly, Hintikka (1988: 38) concludes that "the frequent arguments that strive to use the absolute or relative incommensurability of scientific theories as a reason for thinking that they are inaccessible to be purely scientific (rational) comparisons are simply fallacious." In other words, theories are commensurable and can be fairly compared and appraised based on common standards (Losee 2005). In light of these critiques of incommensurability, it is unfortunate that incommensurability has been used by some management researchers as "an excuse for not trying to understand or reconcile different theories" (Donaldson 1998: 269). Chapter 6 discusses the relation between incommensurability and theory-ladenness of observation.

10 I would like to be able to provide some large-sample data to support this claim, but for now I can only draw upon my own and colleagues' anecdotal experiences with journal review processes. For example, an associate editor of a top management journal once told me that he was in charge of a manuscript whose hypotheses were mostly not supported. A reviewer strongly recommended rejection citing that fact as the main justification.

11 A recent edited book, Edwards et al. (2014), includes a number of papers discussing various research methods and techniques from a critical realist perspective. Such papers nicely illustrate the claim here that there is a bias toward theory generation and verification.

12 An assumption here is that the study has to be repeated in order to examine the auxiliary hypothesis in question; that is, a simple reanalysis of the prior data will not do. This is the case when, for example, the auxiliary hypothesis is about the measurement of a certain variable in a questionnaire survey. In such a case, a new survey with a different set of measurement items for that variable is needed.

References

Agassi, J. 1975. *Science in flux*. Dordrecht, the Netherlands: D. Reidel Publishing.

Aldrich, H. E. 1992. Incommensurable paradigms? Vital signs from three perspectives. In M. Reed and M. Hughes (Eds.), *Rethinking organization: New directions in organization theory and analysis*: 17–45. London: Sage.

Allison, G. T. 1971. *Essence of decision: Explaining the Cuban missile crisis*. Boston, MA: Little, Brown and Company.

Alvarez, S. A. and Barney, J. B. 2010. Entrepreneurship and epistemology: The philosophical underpinnings of the study of entrepreneurial opportunities. *Academy of Management Annals*, 4: 557–583.

Amihud, Y. and Lev, B. 1999. Does corporate ownership structure affect its strategy towards diversification? *Strategic Management Journal*, 20: 1063–1069.

Anderson, P. J. J., Blatt, R., Christianson, M. K., Grant, A. M., Marquis, C., Neuman, E. J., Sonenshein, S. and Sutcliffe, K. M. 2006. Understanding mechanisms in organizational research: Reflections from a collective journey. *Journal of Management Inquiry*, 15: 102–113.

Anonymous. 1998. The problems with formalism: Interview with Mark Blaug. *Challenge*, 41(3): 35–45.

Arend, R. J. 2006. Tests of the resource-based view: Do the empirics have any clothes? *Strategic Organization*, 4: 409–422.

Argyris, C. and Schön, D. A. 1978. *Organizational learning: A theory of action perspective*. Reading, MA: Addison-Wesley.

Astley, W. G. and Zammuto, R. F. 1992. Organization science, managers, and language games. *Organization Science*, 3: 443–460.

Bacharach, S. B. 1989. Organizational theories: Some criteria for evaluation. *Academy of Management Review*, 14: 496–513.

Barney, J. 1991. Firm resources and sustained competitive advantage. *Journal of Management*, 17: 99–120.

Barney, J. B. 2001. Is the resource-based "view" a useful perspective for strategic management research? Yes. *Academy of Management Review*, 26: 41–56.

Bettis, R. A. 2012. The search for asterisks: Compromised statistical tests and flawed theories. *Strategic Management Journal*, 33: 108–113.

Bettis, R. A., Ethiraj, S., Gambardella, A., Helfat, C. and Mitchell, W. 2016. Creating repeatable cumulative knowledge in strategic management: A call for a broad and deep conversation among authors, referees, and editors. *Strategic Management Journal*, 37: 257–261.

Bhaskar, R. 1978. *A realist theory of science* (2nd ed.). Hassocks, England: Harvester Press.

Bhaskar, R. 1998. *The possibility of naturalism: A philosophical critique of the contemporary human sciences* (3rd ed.). New York: Routledge.

Bradbury, H. and Lichtenstein, B. M. B. 2000. Relationality in organizational research: Exploring *the space between*. *Organization Science*, 11: 551–564.

Brennan, M. J. 1994. Incentives, rationality, and society. *Journal of Applied Corporate Finance*, 7(2): 31–39.

Bromiley, P. and Johnson, S. 2005. Mechanisms and empirical research. In D. J. Ketchen Jr. and D. D. Bergh (Eds.), *Research methodology in strategy and management*, Vol. 2: 15–29. Amsterdam, NL: Elsevier.

Caldwell, B. J. 1984. Some problems with falsificationism in economics. *Philosophy of the Social Sciences*, 14: 489–495.

Campbell, K. 1963. One form of scepticism about induction. *Analysis*, 23(4): 80–83.

Caudill, S. B. and Holcombe, R. G. 1987. Coefficient bias due to specification search in econometric models. *Atlantic Economic Journal*, 15: 30–34.

Caudill, S. B. and Holcombe, R. G. 1999. Specification search and levels of significance in econometric models. *Eastern Economic Journal*, 25: 289–300.

Chalmers, A. F. 1999. *What is this thing called science?* (3rd ed.). Maidenhead, England: Open University Press.

Chamberlin, T. C. 1965 [1890]. The method of multiple working hypotheses. *Science*, 148(3671): 754–759.

Child, J. 1972. Organizational structure, environment and performance: The role of strategic choice. *Sociology*, 6: 1–22.

Child, J. 1997. Strategic choice in the analysis of action, structure, organizations and environment: Retrospect and prospect. *Organization Studies*, 18: 43–76.

Cohen, M. D. and Axelrod, R. 1984. Coping with complexity: The adaptive value of changing utility. *American Economic Review*, 74: 30–42.

Collier, A. 1994. *Critical realism: An introduction to Roy Bhaskar's philosophy*. London: Verso.

Croson, R., Anand, J. and Agarwal, R. 2007. Using experiments in corporate strategy research. *European Management Review*, 4(3): 173–181.

Danermark, B., Ekström, M., Jakobsen, L. and Karlsson, J. C. 2002. *Explaining society: Critical realism in the social sciences*. London: Routledge.

Davis, G. F. and Marquis, C. 2005. Prospects for organization theory in the early twenty-first century: Institutional fields and mechanisms. *Organization Science*, 16: 332–343.

de Cock, C. and Jeanes, E. L. 2006. Questioning consensus, cultivating conflict. *Journal of Management Inquiry*, 15: 18–30.

Denis, D. J., Denis, D. K. and Sarin, A. 1999. Agency theory and the influence of equity ownership structure on corporate diversification strategies. *Strategic Management Journal*, 20: 1071–1076.

Donaldson, L. 1995. *American anti-management theories of organization: A critique of paradigm proliferation*. Cambridge, England: Cambridge University Press.

Donaldson, L. 1998. The myth of paradigm incommensurability in management studies: Comments by an integrationist. *Organization*, 5: 267–272.

Douma, S., George, R. and Kabir, R. 2006. Foreign and domestic ownership, business groups, and firm performance: Evidence from a large emerging market. *Strategic Management Journal*, 27: 637–657.

Downward, P., Finch, J. H. and Ramsay, J. 2002. Critical realism, empirical methods and inference: A critical discussion. *Cambridge Journal of Economics*, 26: 481–500.

Duhem, P. 1954. *The aim and structure of physical theory*. Princeton, NJ: Princeton University Press.

Dutton, J. E. and Stumpf, S. A. 1991. Using behavioral simulations to study strategic processes. *Simulation and Gaming*, 22: 149–173.

Easton, G. 2000. Case research as a method for industrial networks: A realist apologia. In S. Ackroyd and S. Fleetwood (Eds.), *Realist perspectives on management and organisations*: 205–219. London: Routledge.

Edwards, P. K., O'Mahoney, J. and Vincent, S. (Eds.) 2014. *Studying organizations using critical realism: A practical guide*. Oxford, England: Oxford University Press.

Fabian, F. H. 2000. Keeping the tension: Pressures to keep the controversy in the management discipline. *Academy of Management Review*, 25: 350–371.

Ferraro, F., Pfeffer, J. and Sutton, R. I. 2005. Economics language and assumptions: How theories can become self-fulfilling. *Academy of Management Review*, 30: 8–24.

Feynman, R. P. 1985. *"Surely you're joking, Mr. Feynman!": Adventures of a curious character*. New York: W. W. Norton and Company.

Gadamer, H. 2002. *Truth and method* (2nd revised ed.). New York: Continuum.

Ghoshal, S. 2005. Bad management theories are destroying good management practices. *Academy of Management Learning and Education*, 4: 75–91.

Ghoshal, S. and Moran, P. 1996. Bad for practice: A critique of the transaction cost theory. *Academy of Management Review*, 21: 13–47.

Gimeno, J., Hoskisson, R. E., Beal, B. D. and Wan, W. P. 2005. Explaining the clustering of international expansion moves: A critical test in the U.S. telecommunications industry. *Academy of Management Journal*, 48: 297–319.

Gist, M. E., Hopper, H. and Daniels, D. 1998. Behavioral simulation: Application and potential in management research. *Organizational Research Methods*, 1: 251–295.

Godfrey, P. C. and Hill, C. W. L. 1995. The problem of unobservables in strategic management research. *Strategic Management Journal*, 16: 519–533.

Goldthorpe, J. H. 2001. Causation, statistics, and sociology. *European Sociological Review*, 17: 1–20.

Grant, A. M. and Wall, T. D. 2008. The neglected science and art of quasi-experimentation: Why-to, when-to, and how-to advice for organizational researchers. *Organizational Research Methods*, 12: 653–686.

Greenwald, A. G. and Ronis, D. L. 1981. On the conceptual disconfirmation of theories. *Personality and Social Psychology Bulletin*, 7: 131–137.

Greenwald, A. G., Pratkanis, A. R., Leippe, M. R. and Baumgardner, M. H. 1986. Under what conditions does theory obstruct research progress? *Psychological Review*, 93: 216–229.

Grünbaum, A. 1960. The Duhemian argument. *Philosophy of Science*, 27: 75–87.

Grünbaum, A. 1976. Is falsifiability the touchstone of scientific rationality? Karl Popper versus inductivism. In R. S. Cohen, P. K. Feyerabend and M. W. Wartofsky (Eds.), *Essays in memory of Imre Lakatos*: 213–252. Dordrecht, the Netherlands: D. Reidel Publishing.

Guala, F. and Mittone, L. 2005. Experiments in economics: External validity and the robustness of phenomena. *Journal of Economic Methodology*, 12: 495–515.

Harré, R. and Second, P. F. 1972. *The explanation of social behavior*. Oxford, England: Basil Blackwell.

Harrison, D. and Easton, G. 2004. Temporally embedded case comparison in industrial marketing research. In S. Fleetwood and S. Ackroyd (Eds.), *Critical realist applications in organisation and management studies*: 194–210. London: Routledge.

Hawking, S. 1988. *A brief history of time: From the big bang to black holes*. New York: Bantam Books.

Hempel, C. G. 1965. *Aspects of scientific explanation*. New York: Free Press.

Hintikka, J. 1988. On the incommensurability of theories. *Philosophy of Science*, 55: 25–38.

Hofmann, D. A., Griffin, M. A. and Gavin, M. B. 2000. The application of hierarchical linear modeling to organizational research. In K. J. Klein and S. W. J. Kozlowski (Eds.), *Multilevel theory, research, and methods in organizations: Foundations, extensions, and new directions*: 467–511. San Francisco, CA: Jossey-Bass.

Hough, J. R. and White, M. A. 2003. Environmental dynamism and strategic decision-making rationality: An examination at the decision level. *Strategic Management Journal*, 24: 481–489.

Hume, D. 2000 [1739]. *A treatise of human nature*. Oxford, England: Oxford University Press.

Hunt, S. D. 1991. Positivism and paradigm dominance in consumer research: Toward critical pluralism and rapprochement. *Journal of Consumer Research*, 18: 32–44.

Hutchison, T. W. 1988. The case for falsification. In N. de Marchi (Ed.), *The Popperian legacy in economics*: 169–181. Cambridge, England: Cambridge University Press.

Jackson, N. and Carter, P. 1991. In defense of paradigm incommensurability. *Organization Studies*, 12: 109–127.

92 *Theory testing*

Johanson, J. and Vahlne, J.-E. 1977. The internationalization process of the firm – a model of knowledge development and increasing foreign market commitments. *Journal of International Business Studies*, 8(1): 23–32.

Kennedy, P. E. 2005. Oh no! I got the wrong sign! What should I do? *Journal of Economic Education*, 36: 77–92.

Kerr, N. L. 1998. HARKing: Hypothesizing after the results are known. *Personality and Social Psychology Review*, 2: 196–217.

Klayman, J. and Ha, Y. W. 1987. Confirmation, disconfirmation, and information in hypothesis testing. *Psychological Review*, 94: 211–228.

Koontz, H. 1961. The management theory jungle. *Academy of Management Journal*, 4(3): 174–188.

Koontz, H. 1980. The management theory jungle revisited. *Academy of Management Review*, 5: 175–187.

Kuhn, T. S. 1962. *The structure of scientific revolutions*. Chicago, IL: University of Chicago Press.

Kuhn, T. S. 1990. Dubbing and redubbing: The vulnerability of rigid designation. In C. W. Savage (Ed.), *Minnesota studies in the philosophy of science, vol. XIV: Scientific theories*: 298–318. Minneapolis, MN: University of Minnesota Press.

Lakatos, I. 1970. Falsification and the methodology of scientific research programmes. In I. Lakatos and A. Musgrave (Eds.), *Criticism and the growth of knowledge*: 91–196. Cambridge, England: Cambridge University Press.

Lane, P. J., Cannella, A. A. and Lubatkin, M. H. 1999. Ownership structure and corporate strategy: One question viewed from two different worlds. *Strategic Management Journal*, 20: 1077–1086.

La Porte, T. R. and Consolini, P. M. 1991. Working in practice but not in theory: Theoretical challenges of "high reliability organizations". *Journal of Public Administration Research and Theory*, 1: 19–47.

Laudan, L. 1996. *Beyond positivism and relativism: Theory, method, and evidence*. Boulder, CO: Westview Press.

Law, A. M. and Kelton, W. D. 2000. *Simulation modeling and analysis* (3rd ed.). Boston, MA: McGraw-Hill.

Leamer, E. E. 1978. *Specification searches: Ad hoc inference with non-experimental data*. New York: Wiley.

Leung, K. 2011. Presenting post hoc hypotheses as a priori: Ethical and theoretical issues. *Management and Organization Review*, 7: 471–479.

Lewis, M. W. and Grimes, A. J. 1999. Metatriangulation: Building theory from multiple paradigms. *Academy of Management Review*, 24: 672–690.

Lieberson, S. 1992. Einstein, Renoir, and Greeley: Some thoughts about evidence in sociology. *American Sociological Review*, 57: 1–15.

Lin, Z. and Hui, C. 1999. Should lean replace mass organization systems? A comparative examination from a management coordination perspective. *Journal of International Business Studies*, 30: 45–79.

Lipton, P. 1991. *Inference to the best explanation*. London: Routledge.

Locke, E. A. 2007. The case for inductive theory building. *Journal of Management*, 33: 867–890.

Losee, J. 2005. *Theories on the scrap heap: Scientists and philosophers on the falsification, rejection, and replacement of theories*. Pittsburgh, PA: University of Pittsburgh Press.

Mahoney, J. T. 1993. Strategic management and determinism: Sustaining the conversation. *Journal of Management Studies*, 30: 173–191.

Mäki, U. 2000. Kinds of assumptions and their truth: Shaking an untwisted F-twist. *Kyklos*, 53: 317–336.

Manicas, P. T. 1987. *A history and philosophy of the social sciences*. Oxford, England: Basil Blackwell.

Manicas, P. T. 2006. *A realist philosophy of social science: Explanation and understanding*. Cambridge, England: Cambridge University Press.

March, J. G. 2004. Parochialism in the evolution of a research community: The case of organization studies. *Management and Organization Review*, 1: 5–22.

McKinley, W. and Mone, M. A. 1998. The re-construction of organization studies: Wrestling with incommensurability. *Organization*, 5: 169–189.

Meehl, P. E. 1978. Theoretical risks and tabular asterisks: Sir Karl, Sir Ronald, and the slow progress of soft psychology. *Journal of Consulting and Clinical Psychology*, 46: 806–834.

Miller, R. W. 1987. *Fact and method: Explanation, confirmation and reality in the natural and social sciences*. Princeton, NJ: Princeton University Press.

Mingers, J. 2001. Combining is research methods: Towards a pluralist methodology. *Information Systems Research*, 12: 240–259.

Mingers, J. 2004. Future directions in management science modeling. In S. Fleetwood and S. Ackroyd (Eds.), *Critical realist applications in organisation and management studies*: 164–193. London: Routledge.

Mingers, J. 2006. A critique of statistical modelling in management science from a critical realist perspective: Its role within multimethodology. *Journal of the Operational Research Society*, 57: 202–219.

Mintzberg, H., Ahlstrand, B. and Lampel, J. 1998. *Strategy safari: A guided tour through the wilds of strategic management*. New York: Free Press.

Mitchell, T. R. and James, L. R. 2001. Building better theory: Time and the specification of when things happen. *Academy of Management Review*, 26: 530–547.

Mohr, L. B. 1982. *Explaining organizational behavior*. San Francisco, CA: Jossey-Bass.

Mone, M. A. and McKinley, W. 1993. The uniqueness value and its consequences for organization studies. *Journal of Management Inquiry*, 2: 284–296.

Musgrave, A. 1974. Logical versus historical theories of confirmation. *British Journal for the Philosophy of Science*, 25: 1–23.

Nambisan, S. 2002. Designing virtual customer environments for new product development: Toward a theory. *Academy of Management Review*, 27: 392–413.

Nash, R. 1999. What is real and what is realism in sociology? *Journal for the Theory of Social Behaviour*, 29: 445–466.

Nickerson, R. S. 2000. Null hypothesis significance testing: A review of an old and continuing controversy. *Psychological Methods*, 5: 241–301.

Nooteboom, B. 1986. Plausibility in economics. *Economics and Philosophy*, 2: 197–224.

Numagami, T. 1998. The infeasibility of invariant laws in management studies: A reflective dialogue in defense of case studies. *Organization Science*, 9: 2–15.

Okhuysen, G. and Bonardi, J. P. 2011. The challenges of building theory by combining lenses. *Academy of Management Review*, 36: 6–11.

Peacock, M. S. 2000. Explaining theory choice: An assessment of the critical realist contribution to explanation in science. *Journal for the Theory of Social Behaviour*, 30: 319–339.

Pentland, B. T. 1999. Building process theory with narrative: From description to explanation. *Academy of Management Review*, 24: 711–724.

Perrow, C. 1994. The limits of safety: The enhancement of a theory of accidents. *Journal of Contingencies and Crisis Management*, 2: 212–220.

Perrow, C. 1999. *Normal accidents: Living with high-risk technologies* (2nd ed.). Princeton, NJ: Princeton University Press.

Petersen, B. and Pedersen, T. 1997. Twenty years after – support and critique of the Uppsala internationalization model. In I. Björkman and M. Forsgren (Eds.), *The nature of the international firm*: 117–134. Copenhagen, Denmark: Copenhagen Business School Press.

Pfeffer, J. 1982. *Organizations and organization theory*. Marshfield, MA: Pitman.

Pfeffer, J. 1993. Barriers to the advance of organizational science: Paradigm development as a dependent variable. *Academy of Management Review*, 18: 599–620.

Pfeffer, J. 2007. A modest proposal: How we might change the process and product of managerial research. *Academy of Management Journal*, 50: 1334–1345.

Pfeffer, J. and Fong, C. T. 2002. The end of business schools? Less success than meets the eye. *Academy of Management Learning and Education*, 1: 78–95.

Polanyi, M. 1962. *Personal knowledge: Toward a post-critical philosophy*. Chicago, IL: University of Chicago Press.

Popper, K. 1959. *The logic of scientific discovery*. London: Hutchinson.

Popper, K. 1962. *Conjectures and refutations*. New York: Basic Books.

Porter, S. 1993. Critical realist ethnography: The case of racism and professionalism in a medical setting. *Sociology*, 27: 591–609.

Priem, R. L. and Butler, J. E. 2001a. Is the resource-based "view" a useful perspective for strategic management research? *Academy of Management Review*, 26: 22–40.

Priem, R. L. and Butler, J. E. 2001b. Tautology in the resource-based view and the implications of externally determined resource value: Further comments. *Academy of Management Review*, 26: 57–66.

Quine, W. V. O. 1961. *From a logical point of view*. New York: Harper and Row.

Rahmandad, H. 2008. Effect of delays on complexity of organizational learning. *Management Science*, 54: 1297–1312.

Rajagopalan, N. and Spreitzer, G. M. 1996. Toward a theory of strategic change: A multi-lens perspective and integrative framework. *Academy of Management Review*, 22: 48–79.

Reid, T. 1764. *An inquiry into the human mind, on the principles of common sense*. Edinburgh, Scotland: A. Millar and A. Kincaid and J. Bell.

Rescher, N. 1992. *A system of pragmatic idealism, vol. I: Human knowledge in idealistic perspective*. Princeton, NJ: Princeton University Press.

Ricoeur, P. 1981. *Hermeneutics and the human sciences: Essays on language, action and interpretation*. Cambridge, England: Cambridge University Press.

Roberts, K. H. 1989. New challenges in organization research: High reliability organizations. *Organization and Environment*, 3: 111–125.

Ron, A. 2002. Regression analysis and the philosophy of social science: A critical realist view. *Journal of Critical Realism*, 1: 119–142.

Rosenthal, R. 1979. The file drawer problem and tolerance for null results. *Psychological Bulletin*, 86: 638–641.

Sagan, S. D. 1993. *The limits of safety: Organizations, accidents, and nuclear weapons*. Princeton, NJ: Princeton University Press.

Sarasvathy, S. D. 2001. Causation and effectuation: Toward a theoretical shift from economic inevitability to entrepreneurial contingency. *Academy of Management Review*, 26: 243–263.

Sawyer, K. R., Beed, C. and Sankey, H. 1997. Underdetermination in economics. The Duhem-Quine thesis. *Economics and Philosophy*, 13: 1–23.

Sayer, A. 1992. *Method in social science: A realist approach* (2nd ed.). London: Routledge.

Sayer, A. 2000. *Realism and social science*. London: Sage.

Schwarz, N., Groves, R. M. and Schuman, H. 1998. Survey methods. In D. T. Gilbert, S. T. Fiske and G. Lindzey (Eds.), *The handbook of social psychology* (4th ed.), Vol. 1: 143–179. Boston, MA: McGraw-Hill.

Schweiger, D. M., Sandberg, W. R. and Rechner, P. L. 1989. Experiential effects of dialectical inquiry, devil's advocacy and consensus approaches to strategic decision making. *Academy of Management Journal*, 32: 745–772.

Shadish, W. R., Cook, T. D. and Campbell, D. T. 2002. *Experimental and quasi-experimental designs for generalized causal inference*. Boston, MA: Houghton Mifflin.

Singh, J. V. 1986. Performance, slack, and risk taking in organizational decision making. *Academy of Management Journal*, 29: 562–585.

Søberg, M. 2005. The Duhem-Quine thesis and experimental economics: A reinterpretation. *Journal of Economic Methodology*, 12: 581–597.

Starbuck, W. H. 2004. Why I stopped trying to understand the *real* world. *Organization Studies*, 25: 1233–1254.

Starbuck, W. H. 2006. *The production of knowledge: The challenge of social science research*. New York: Oxford University Press.

Stinchcombe, A. L. 1968. *Constructing social theories*. New York: Harcourt, Brace and World.

Stinchcombe, A. L. 1986. *Stratification and organization: Selected papers*. Cambridge, England: Cambridge University Press.

Sutcliffe, K. M. and Zaheer, A. 1998. Uncertainty in the transaction environment: An empirical test. *Strategic Management Journal*, 19: 1–23.

Szulanski, G. and Jensen, R. J. 2004. Overcoming stickiness: An empirical investigation of the role of the template in the replication of organizational routines. *Managerial and Decision Economics*, 25: 347–363.

Thompson, B. 1998. In praise of brilliance: Where that praise really belongs. *American Psychologist*, 53: 799–800.

Tsang, E. W. K. and Williams, J. N. 2012. Generalization and induction: Misconceptions, clarifications, and a classification of induction. *MIS Quarterly*, 36: 729–748.

Vernon, R. 1966. International investment and international trade in the product cycle. *Quarterly Journal of Economics*, 80: 190–207.

Vernon, R. 1979. The product cycle hypothesis in a new international environment. *Oxford Bulletin of Economics and Statistics*, 41: 255–267.

Wason, P. C. and Johnson-Laird, P. N. 1972. *Psychology of reasoning: Structure and content*. Cambridge, MA: Harvard University Press.

Weaver, G. R. and Gioia, D. A. 1994. Paradigms lost: Incommensurability vs structurationist inquiry. *Organization Studies*, 15: 565–590.

Webb, E. J., Campbell, D. T., Schwartz, R. D. and Sechrest, L. 2000. *Unobtrusive measures* (revised ed.). Thousand Oaks, CA: Sage.

Weick, K. E. 1989. Theory construction as disciplined imagination. *Academy of Management Review*, 14: 516–531.

Williamson, O. E. 1996. Economic organization: The case for candor. *Academy of Management Review*, 21: 48–57.

Wuisman, J. J. J. M. 2005. The logic of scientific discovery in critical realist social scientific research. *Journal of Critical Realism*, 4: 366–394.

Yeung, H. W.-C. 1997. Critical realism and realist research in human geography: A method or a philosophy in search of a method? *Progress in Human Geography*, 21: 51–74.

Zhang, Z., Zyphur, M. J. and Preacher, K. J. 2009. Testing multilevel mediation using hierarchical linear models problems and solutions. *Organizational Research Methods*, 12: 695–719.

5 Generalization

A controversial endeavor

A key objective of the social sciences is to elucidate and articulate the generalities of social life (Danermark et al. 2002; Hägg and Hedlund 1979). In management research, in particular, Mintzberg (2005: 361) astutely comments, "If there is no generalizing beyond the data, no theory. No theory, no insight. And if no insight, why do research?" In fact, according to the U.S. Office of Human Subjects Research, scientific research refers to "a systematic investigation, including research development, testing and evaluation, designed to develop or contribute to generalizable knowledge" (Title 45, Part 46, Code of Federal Regulations, revised January 15, 2009).

Simple as it may appear, the concept of generalization is in fact complex and causes frequent confusions. A piece of supporting evidence is the recent debate that my colleague and I engaged in with two prominent information systems researchers concerning the concepts of generalization and induction and their differences (Lee and Baskerville 2003, 2012; Tsang and Williams 2012; Williams and Tsang 2015). A simple illustration is Lee and Baskerville's use of the term "generalization" to refer to inference from sample points (such as the heights of individuals in a group) to a sample statistic (such as the average height of the group). An obvious problem is that a sample statistic is *deduced* and not *induced* from sample points. Deduction is not induction, and generalization is one form of induction.[1]

The issue of generalization is particularly salient for qualitative research. For example, case studies are often criticized on the grounds that their findings are not generalizable to other settings because of the small-N problem (Gerring 2007; Hillebrand et al. 2001; Sharp 1998; Steinmetz 2004; Stoecker 1991). Gibbert et al. (2008) reviewed all case studies published during the period 1995–2000 in 10 leading management journals and examined how case study researchers discussed the procedures associated with the four usual criteria for assessing the rigor of field research: internal validity, construct validity, generalizability (or external validity), and reliability. They found that case studies were more likely to provide reports on generalizability than on the other three criteria. This finding indicates the serious concern of authors, editors, and reviewers over the generalizability of case study results and supports Mjøset's (2009: 51) observation: "How can the study of cases contribute to general knowledge? The question is a classical one in debates on qualitative methodology."

Case study researchers themselves hold different views regarding the generalizability of their results. The prevailing view is that case studies are weak in generalizability. For example, Ferner et al.'s (2005) study of cross-national transfer of employment diversity policies was based on six U.S. multinational corporations in the U.K. They "would acknowledge the limitation of a small-N study that does not allow broad generalisations to be drawn about the patterns of occurrence of the dependent variable" (p. 311). In another example, de Rond and Bouchikhi (2004) investigated the dialectics of strategic alliances based on a longitudinal case study of an alliance in biotechnology. They arrive at this conclusion: "Case studies do not lend themselves easily to generalization" (p. 68).

On the other hand, some case study researchers hold very different opinions about the generalizability of their results. Kochan and Rubinstein (2000) in their study of the Saturn Corporation argue that "while the role of the union may appear to be one of the idiosyncratic features of Saturn, in fact, the functions served by the union may have implications that are generalizable well beyond this particular type of stakeholder organization" (p. 383). In fact, Gerring (2004) defines a case study as "an intensive study of a single unit with an aim to *generalize* across a larger set of units" (p. 341, emphasis added).

A more extreme view is to deny generalizability as a legitimate criterion for evaluating case studies (Lincoln and Guba 1985). A basic premise is that "generalization is neither possible nor desirable" (Halkier 2011: 787). Chreim et al. (2007), for example, investigated the reconstruction of professional role identity in a Canadian health clinic. They challenge the usual caution against single-case designs in this way:

> Our study is based on one case. Although some may view this as a limitation impeding generalizability, it should be noted that naturalistic case studies should be judged not on the basis of generalizability, but on the basis of transferability and comparability.
>
> (p. 1535)

These prior examples illustrate three major views: (1) the results of case studies do not generalize well; (2) the results generalize well; and (3) generalizability is not relevant to case studies. Such conflicting opinions concerning the generalizability of case findings suggest that this important methodological issue is contentious and has generated a growing volume of muddled debates.

This chapter aims to achieve three objectives: (1) to clearly define generalization and induction and propose a classification of induction, (2) to dispel some major misconceptions of generalization, and (3) to rebut the prevailing view that case studies are weak in generalizability. The first two objectives are motivated by the fact that a major factor causing the divergent views about the generalizability of case study results is that the concept of generalization itself is often misconceived. Another factor is the philosophical perspective held by the researcher. As such, I compare the positivist, interpretivist, and critical realist views of generalizing from case findings. For the last objective, I argue that case studies have an advantage over quantitative methods in terms of theoretical generalization, identifying disconfirming cases, and providing useful information for evaluating the empirical generalizability of results. However, my position is not that case studies are definitely superior to quantitative methods, but just that the former have some merits over the latter with respect to certain aspects of generalizing from research findings. Some of these merits have not been sufficiently recognized by case study researchers.

Before proceeding, it is necessary to define the term "case study" as different researchers may have different things in mind when they talk about case study as a research method. I follow Yin (2014) and define a case study as "an empirical inquiry that investigates a contemporary phenomenon (the 'case') in depth and within its real-world context, especially when the boundaries between phenomenon and context may not be clearly evident" (p. 16). As a case study usually involves intensively investigating a single case or a small number of cases in their naturalistic contexts (Piekkari et al. 2009), it is likely that there will be more variables of interest than data points. As such, researchers often rely on "multiple sources of evidence, with data needing to converge in a triangulating fashion" (Yin 2014: 17). Taking naturalistic contexts into account may give rise to the difficulty of identifying the exact boundary of a case. On the other hand, the contexts provide rich information that helps researchers develop a theoretical explanation of the phenomenon in question, as discussed in the following sections. There is a variety of case studies. Some focus on identifying relationships among variables whereas others focus on examining process dynamics over time.

Although case studies occasionally involve the collection and analysis of quantitative data (e.g., Eisenhardt and Bourgeois 1988), methodologically case studies are often considered one form of qualitative research, which comprises an array of non-statistical research practices with an intention of capturing the actual meanings and interpretations that actors ascribe to the phenomenon under study (Johnson et al. 2006). This chapter focuses on case studies rather than the broad domain of qualitative research partly because some of the qualitative methods, such as ethnography, are rather rare in management research and partly because case studies are the most popular qualitative method used by management researchers (Welch et al. 2013) and are also increasingly popular among social scientists (Gerring 2007).[2]

A classification of induction

Following Schwandt (1997: 57), generalization is defined as a "general statement or proposition made by drawing an inference from observation of the particular."[3] This characterization of generalization is consistent with that proposed by logicians, such as Cohen and Nagel (1934), Copi and Cohen (1990), and Hurley (2003). In empirical research, generalization is an act of inferring from specific, observed instances, such as those in a case setting, to general statements.

As discussed below, generalization is sometimes confounded with its closely related concept, induction, which refers to inference from matters of fact that we have observed to those we have not (*Cambridge Dictionary of Philosophy* 1999: 745). Induction has a broader meaning than generalization because generalization denotes a directional inference from something particular to something more general whereas induction does not. There are at least two forms of induction that are not generalization. One of these is what logicians call "statistical syllogism" (Gensler 2001), for example:

> P1 Nearly all senior accounting managers in the U.K. have college degrees.
> P2 Tom is a senior accounting manager in the U.K.
> C Tom has a college degree.

This inference is inductive because it goes from observed matters of fact (P1 and P2) to unobserved matters of fact (C). Yet the inference goes from a *general* premise and a particular premise to a *particular* conclusion. So it is not a generalization.

Another form of inductive inference is what logicians call "inductive analogy" (Copi and Cohen 1990; Hurley 2003), for example:

> P1 Dan is male, mature, speaks Japanese, has received training in cross-cultural communication, and is culturally sensitive.
> P2 Tim is male, mature, speaks Japanese, has received training in cross-cultural communication, and is culturally sensitive.
> P3 Dan experiences little culture shock when working in Japan as an expatriate manager.
> C Tim experiences little culture shock when working in Japan as an expatriate manager.

This inference is also inductive because it also goes from observed matters of fact (P1, P2, and P3) to unobserved matters of fact (C). But the inference goes from *particular* premises to a *particular* conclusion. So this is not generalization either.

To classify induction, it is necessary to first distinguish two levels of research activities, namely empirical and theoretical. On the empirical level, researchers collect data through observation, and on the theoretical level, researchers develop theories based on data collected on the empirical level, pure conjectures, or a combination of both. The classification is pictorially presented in Figure 5.1, where the arrows represent inferences. There are five basic types of generalization: (1) theoretical, (2) within population, (3) cross population, (4) contextual, and (5) temporal, with theoretical generalization being across the empirical and theoretical levels and the rest within the empirical level. The whole classification also includes the two aforementioned kinds of inductive reasoning that do not belong to the domain of generalization – statistical syllogism and inductive

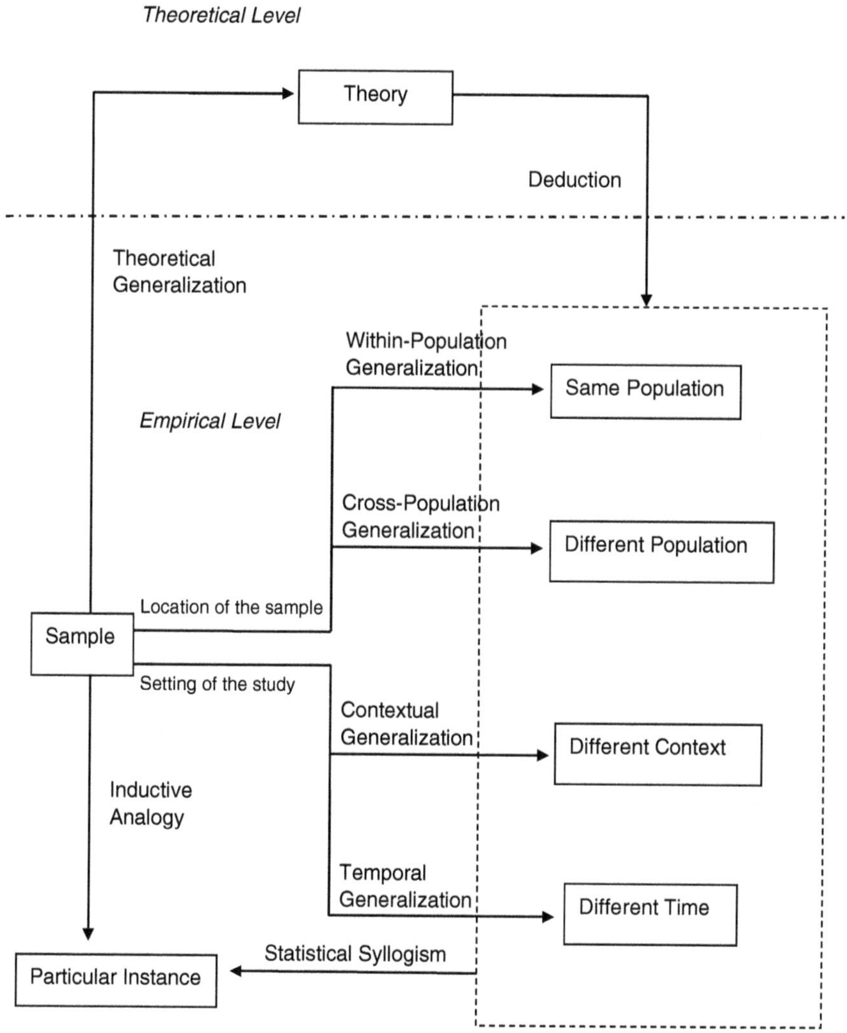

Theoretical Level

Figure 5.1 Types of induction

analogy. Both are within the empirical level. For easy reference, Table 5.1 lists the definition of each type of induction.

The five types of generalization have their roots in the literature. To begin with, Gomm et al. (2000) and Sharp (1998) classify generalization into two main types: theoretical and empirical. The current typology further classifies empirical generalization into four types. Within-population generalization and cross-population generalization are concerned with where a sample is

Table 5.1 Definition of types of induction

Type of Induction	Definition
Theoretical generalization	Generalizing from research findings to theories
Within-population generalization	Generalizing from the characteristics of a sample to those of the corresponding population
Cross-population generalization	Generalizing from a sample in one population to members of another population, with both populations existing in a similar context and a similar period of time
Contextual generalization	Generalizing from a sample in one population to members of another population, with both populations existing in significantly different contexts but within a similar period of time
Temporal generalization	Generalizing from a sample in one population at one point in time to members of the same or a different population at another point in time, assuming that the context remains more or less the same
Statistical syllogism	An inference of the form P1 N% of Fs are Gs. P2 X is an F. C X is a G. where N denotes a precise statistic or a vague range of statistics as in "Most" or "Nearly all"
Inductive analogy	An inference of the form P1 X has properties $a, b, c \ldots$ and z. P2 Y has properties $a, b, c \ldots$ C Y has property z.

located – inside or outside – relative to the population at which generalization is targeted. A similar distinction between these two kinds of generalization can be found in the literature. For example, Maxwell (1992) distinguishes between internal and external generalizability in qualitative research, corresponding to within- and cross-population generalization, respectively. Similarly, Schofield (1990: 201) states, "the aspect of external validity that has typically received the lion's share of attention in textbook and other treatments of the concept is generalizing to and across populations."[4] Contextual generalization and temporal generalization are derived from the insightful comment of Nagel (1979) concerning the space-time constraint of social phenomena. There are scattered discussions of these two types of generalization in the literature. Lucas (2003), for example, discusses generalizing across settings, corresponding to contextual generalization. Cronbach's (1975) argument that generalizations in the social sciences decay rather fast over time is related to temporal generalization.

In the following discussion, Gefen and Straub's (1997) study is used to illustrate the classification. The study extends the work on information technology implementation and diffusion by investigating gender effects in the context of the technology acceptance model (Davis 1989) and a subsequent addendum to the model (Straub 1994). Data were collected from the e-mail system in one U.S., one Swiss, and one Japanese airline through a questionnaire survey measuring self-reported e-mail use, perceived ease of use, usefulness, and social presence.

Five types of generalization

Theoretical generalization consists in generalizing from research findings to theories. Deriving theories from data collected in the empirical world is a traditional view of scientific research (Chalmers 1999). Gefen and Straub's study is a good example. Their findings suggest that the same mode of communication may be perceived differently by men versus women, and so they propose to extend the technology acceptance model by including the effects of gender. In other words, they generalize their results to a revised theoretical model.

Within-population generalization, which is equivalent to the more commonly used term "statistical generalization," consists in generalizing from the characteristics of a sample to those of the corresponding population. "Within-population generalization" instead of "statistical generalization" is used here in order to contrast this type of generalization with cross-population generalization. To perform within-population generalization, researchers need to first clearly specify the intended population in which their study is conducted and then follow a sampling procedure that allows statistical inference from sample characteristics to population characteristics. Unfortunately, difficulties of research access often prevent researchers from discussing how far their findings are statistically generalizable. That said, researchers should at least clearly describe their sampling procedure. Gefen and Straub's study is deficient in this respect. They distributed questionnaires to users of the e-mail system in one U.S., one Swiss, and one Japanese airline, without mentioning the number of employees in each airline. The only piece of information about the sampling frame is this sentence: "The sample included workers across managerial, professional, and technical ranks" (Gefen and Straub 1997: 395). That is, employees across these three ranks in each airline constituted a population. Although they report the response rate in each airline, they do not report the sample size drawn from each airline. A larger sample size will usually increase the within-population generalizability of the results of a study.

Cross-population generalization consists in generalizing from a sample in one population to members of another population, with both populations existing in a similar context and a similar period of time. Assume that Gefen and Straub had broken up their data into three parts, each of which contained data collected from one airline. In this case, cross-population generalization might consist in generalizing the results of the American airline (in which Gefen and

Straub collected data) to another American airline that existed at the time of data collection. The contexts in which the two firms operate are similar in the sense that they are in the same industry and the same country. Note that a different way of defining a population will give rise to a different kind of cross-population generalization. Suppose that Gefen and Straub had conducted their study in only one of the three airlines and had drawn a sample from the male employees of the airline only. The population would be the collection of male employees, and one kind of cross-population generalization would consist in generalizing the findings to the population of female employees within that airline. As the actual findings of Gefen and Straub's study indicate that women and men differ in their perceived social presence and perceived usefulness of e-mail, the cross-population generalizability from male to female employees would be weak.

In comparing the social sciences with the natural sciences, Nagel (1979: 459) observes that "unlike the laws of physics and chemistry, generalizations in the social sciences therefore have at best only a severely restricted scope, limited to social phenomena occurring during a relatively brief historical epoch within special institutional settings." This observation implies that social scientists have to investigate whether their research findings collected in one space-time setting are generalizable to other significantly different space-time settings, in other words, whether these findings are contextually and temporally generalizable.

In contextual generalization, researchers generalize from a sample in one population to members of another population, with both populations existing in significantly different contexts but within a similar period of time. Some scholars call for contextualization as "a way of approaching research where knowledge of the settings to be studied is brought to bear in design and implementation decisions" (Rousseau and Fried 2001: 6). By paying greater attention to the context in which a study is conducted, researchers are in a better position to assess the contextual generalizability of their findings. For example, Gefen and Straub specifically included the effect of cultural differences in their structural equations and found that the effect was significant. This suggests that the generalizability of their findings to other cultural contexts would be limited. There are other types of context in addition to cultural or national context. Gefen and Straub conducted their study in the airline industry. The generalizability of their findings to another industry depends on whether the new industrial context significantly affects people's perception and usage of e-mail.

Temporal generalization consists in generalizing from a sample in one population at one point in time to members of the same or a different population at another point in time, assuming that the context remains more or less the same. Temporal generalization is the least discussed in the literature. Yet it is implicitly present in any form of generalization in the sense that the act of generalizing and the findings to be generalized necessarily occur at different times. Temporal generalization is a more important issue in the social than the natural sciences. Nature is unaffected by scientific research. The fact that the earth revolves around the sun will not be changed by a theory proposing otherwise. However, activities of management researchers may change the beliefs and practices of managers and thus undermine the stability of the phenomena investigated (Numagami 1998). Temporal generalization is a very important concern when one tries to generalize the findings of a study conducted in a distant past to a current situation. Gefen and Straub's study was done about 20 years ago. Can their findings be generalized to today's airlines in the U.S.? Note that the airline industry in the U.S. has undergone significant changes since the September 11 terrorist attack. The much tighter security control in the industry may affect how e-mail systems are structured and how e-mails are used and monitored.

Generalization within the empirical level often involves a combination of some of the four basic types discussed here. For example, if researchers try to generalize Gefen and Straub's findings to today's airlines in Germany, this involves across-population, contextual, and temporal generalization. A major problem of this kind of generalization is that if the generalization is subsequently found to be wrong, it may be difficult to identify whether the failure is due to differences in population or contextual or temporal factors.

As indicated by Figure 5.1, theory, or the collection of theoretical knowledge, may be able to provide some useful information about the four types of generalization within the empirical level through deductive inference. Gefen and Straub, for instance, draw heavily on Hofstede's (1980) cultural dimension of masculinity-femininity in their study. The three countries in which they conducted their fieldwork, namely Japan, Switzerland, and the U.S., are high in masculinity. In these countries, gender roles are clearly defined and nurtured. So the gender effects that Gefen and Straub found in their study will probably be less generalizable to countries that are low in masculinity, such as the Scandinavian countries. In short, knowledge of the cultural dimension of masculinity-femininity throws light on the contextual generalizability of their findings.

Statistical syllogism and inductive analogy

Figure 5.1 shows that in statistical syllogism, researchers draw a conclusion about a particular instance from a generalization. Gefen and Straub's findings support the proposition that women perceive a higher social presence and usefulness of e-mail than men. Suppose we are interested in the differences in the perception of e-mail between a particular pair of male and female employees in the American airline in which Gefen and Straub collected data. We may use statistical syllogism and conclude that the female employee is likely to perceive a higher social presence and usefulness of e-mail than her male counterpart.

In inductive analogy, researchers proceed from particular premises to a conclusion about a particular instance. Assume that Gefen and Straub had run their analysis separately on the data collected from the American airline, and suppose we are interested in the gender differences in the perception of e-mail among a group of employees drawn from another American airline. If there are substantial relevant similarities between this airline and Gefen and Straub's as well as between this group of employees and Gefen and Straub's sample, we may conclude that their results probably also reflect the characteristics of the group. Should Gefen and Straub provide more information about the airline and its employees that they studied, this would facilitate inductive analogy.

Implication for empirical research

The current classification helps management researchers articulate the limitations of their studies. Since there are distinct types of generalization, when researchers discuss the generalizability of their findings, it is important that they specify the kind of generalization they have in mind. However, this is often not the case. A typical example is: "As a single case study, it has inevitably limited generalizability" (Maguire et al. 2004: 675). A pertinent question is: generalize to what? The classification highlights the need for researchers to think about the kind of generalization they refer to when they discuss the generalizability of their findings. This would help researchers delineate the limitations of their studies and point to concrete future research directions that may address these limitations.

Gefen and Straub's discussion is an excellent illustration:

> From the standpoint of external validity, the study gathered data from three firms in one industry across three countries, which, *per force*, limits the generality of the results. It may well be, for instance, that there is a systematic bias in the airline industry that restricts our ability to generalize to other industries. Moreover, knowledge workers in managerial, professional, or technical positions in Japan tend to be overwhelmingly male, which very likely explains a relatively smaller number of Japanese women in our sample.
>
> (p. 397)

Their reference to the airline industry is about generalizing across industrial contexts. Their highlighting of the idiosyncrasy of Japan seems to indicate their concern about the contextual generalizability of their Japanese case to companies in other countries. Further studies may be designed to test the generalizability of their findings along these directions.

Among the five types of generalization, temporal generalization is the most neglected. Researchers are usually aware of it when there is some significant structural change in the context of the original study. For example, researchers would hesitate to generalize the results of a study that investigated labor relations during the Soviet Union era (e.g., Filtzer 2002) to present-day Russia. However, temporal generalization can also be an issue when progressive change is gradual. A study of people's attitudes toward online shopping conducted 20 years ago is probably outdated as online shopping has become more popular and secure during the last 20 years. In brief, management researchers should pay more attention to temporal generalization when citing previous studies.

How philosophy informs views of generalization

As mentioned, researchers hold diverse opinions concerning how far the results of a case study can be generalized. These opinions are based on different philosophical perspectives. This section discusses the critical realist view concerning how case findings are generalized empirically and theoretically and compares it to the positivist and interpretivist views (Table 5.2). The latter two views are chosen for comparison because they are the more common ones explicitly stated in the literature.

Positivism has been briefly covered in chapter 1, and interpretivism is one stream of postmodernism also covered in that chapter. Interpretivists aim to "interpret the meanings and actions of actors according to their own subjective frame of reference" (Williams 2000: 210) and adopt a relativist stance "such that diverse meanings are assumed to exist and to influence how people understand and respond to the objective world" (Gephart 2004: 457). Intentional

Table 5.2 Comparison of positivism, interpretivism, and critical realism with respect to generalizing from case findings

	Positivism	*Interpretivism*	*Critical Realism*
Empirical Generalization	Empirical generalization is downplayed because it is often equated with statistical generalization, and case findings cannot be generalized statistically.	Empirical generalization is inconsistent with interpretivists' idea that interpretations of reality are dynamic and may shift over time. Naturalistic generalization is actually inductive analogy, not generalization.	A representative case can help identify the characteristics of demi-regularities in the population to which the case belongs. This knowledge serves as the raw material for subsequent theory building.
Theoretical Generalization	Theoretical generalization is stressed as a reaction to the usual challenge that case studies are weak in generalizability. Attempts are made to justify theoretical generalization by arguing that cases should be treated as natural science experiments.	Some interpretivists (e.g., Klein and Myers 1999) deem that case findings can be generalized to theory, but others (e.g., Denzin 1983) do not.	Case studies provide useful information concerning how the postulated mechanisms operate under a set of contingent conditions. Researchers work out the related mechanismic explanations.

phenomena are therefore meaningful in the sense that they are what they are according to the interpretation of those who are involved.

Empirical generalization

Empirical generalization concerns whether the findings of a case study are typical of the population from which the cases are drawn or of another population. Thus, it is confined to the empirical domain and excludes the domain of deep reality structures (Danermark et al. 2002). Empirical generalization sometimes serves as the first stage of the process that aims at generating theoretical generalization. However, this implies neither that theoretical generalization is necessarily preceded by empirical generalization nor that empirical generalization is necessarily followed by theoretical generalization. Either kind of generalization can exist on its own. Within-population generalization is a common type of empirical generalization. A key objective of empirical generalization is to establish whether or not there is some kind of empirical regularity in the population the researcher is interested in rather than providing an explanation of the regularity.

From a positivist perspective, a case study is based on a very small sample, and its contribution to establishing law-like relationships is therefore marginal. Accordingly, positivist discussions of case study research have focused on theoretical generalization at the expense of empirical generalization (Eisenhardt and Graebner 2007; Yin 2009). For instance, Yin's (2009) work is based on the premise that "the investigator is striving to generalize a particular set of results to some broader theory" (p. 43). This may be a knee-jerk reaction to the popular view that case studies are weak in generalizability, which is usually taken to mean within-population generalization.

The idea of empirical regularity does not fit well with interpretivists' emphasis on interpreting meanings and actions according to the actor's own and probably unique frame of reference because "interpretations of reality may shift over time as circumstances, objectives, and constituencies change" (Orlikowski and Baroudi 1991: 14). Thus, empirical generalization is not generally recognized by interpretivists. Stake and Trumbull's (1982) "naturalistic generalization" is somewhat related to empirical generalization in the sense that it concerns comparing one empirical setting with another. Nevertheless, as elaborated in the next section, naturalistic generalization is actually inductive analogy rather than generalization. In sum, Orlikowski and Baroudi (1991) comment that, for interpretivist studies, "generalization from the setting (usually only one or a handful of field sites) to a population is not sought" (p. 5).

Although the ultimate goal of scientific research is to develop theories that can explain the empirical phenomenon in question (i.e., theoretical generalization), critical realism does recognize the function of empirical generalization. Owing to the existence of demi-regularities in the social world (see chapter 2), it is meaningful for management researchers to make claims based on empirical generalization. Researchers may consider identifying demi-regularities as the first step of an inquiry into possible mechanisms that reside in the real domain

(Manicas 2006), and this step can inform subsequent data-gathering and analysis of qualitative data collected from case studies (Zachariadis et al. 2013).

Critical realists deem that although it is not possible to statistically generalize case findings to the population from which the cases were drawn (Cavaye 1996), case studies do have something to contribute if we consider the broader domain of empirical generalization. A representative case can provide useful information regarding certain characteristics of the population to which the case belongs.

Theoretical generalization

Theoretical generalization refers to generalizing from the findings of a case study to theory, which under critical realism consists of postulated structures and mechanisms that operate in the real domain. In contrast to empirical generalization, researchers make theoretical generalizations by developing explanations for the relationships between variables observed in their case studies (Sharp 1998). Hopefully such explanations are applicable to either the population from which the cases were drawn or to other populations (Firestone 1993). The belief is that the mechanism or mechanisms that caused the observable events in a case setting will also cause similar outcomes in other settings (Zachariadis et al. 2013).

As mentioned, positivists underscore theoretical generalization. Their aim is to discover law-like relations embedded in a theory, which is supposed to explain certain general empirical phenomena. Yin (2014) strengthens the methodological legitimacy of case studies by arguing that a "fatal flaw in doing case studies is to consider statistical generalization to be the way of generalizing the findings from your case study" (p. 40) because cases are not sampling units and should be treated as experiments. His intention seems to associate case study research with the experimental method adopted by the prestigious natural sciences.

Denzin (1983: 133) claims that "the interpretivist rejects generalization as a goal and never aims to draw randomly selected samples of human experience." Other than this more extreme view, interpretivists are more receptive of theoretical than empirical generalization: "interpretivists often maintain that rather than making empirical generalizations, they are making *theoretical inferences*, that is they draw conclusions from their data about the necessary relationships that exist amongst categories of phenomena" (Williams 2000: 218). Similarly, among the principles that Klein and Myers (1999) propose for conducting and evaluating interpretive field studies, the principle of abstraction and generalization requires relating the idiographic details revealed by data interpretation to "theoretical, general concepts that describe the nature of human understanding and social action" (p. 72). However, interpretivists' emphasis on theoretical generalization while downplaying or even ignoring empirical generalization is problematic because a major function of theory is to explain empirical phenomena that usually display a certain degree of regularity across time and space. Without empirical generalization, it is not sensible to talk about theoretical generalization.

From a critical realist perspective, scientific theories offer mechanismic explanations of empirical phenomena that unveil the phenomena's actual or possible mechanisms (Bunge 1997). Case study researchers not only observe events in the empirical domain, but also aim to understand the mechanisms in the real domain leading to the events. Unlike studies based on quantitative methods, case studies seek to investigate phenomena within their contexts rather than independent of context (Gibbert et al. 2008). The case study method is an excellent way to explore the interaction of structures, events, human actions, and contexts for identifying and explicating mechanisms (Wynn and Williams 2012). When compared with quantitative methods, such as questionnaire survey and analysis of archival data, case study research is more likely to discover relations that are "causal, structural, and substantial, i.e., relations of connections" (Sayer 1992: 246). Such discoveries often have generalization implications as detailed in the following discussion.

Misconceptions of generalization

Despite frequent discussions of the concept by case study researchers, misconceptions of generalization abound in the literature.[5] This section focuses on some common misconceptions that are related to case studies and is not meant to provide a comprehensive coverage. These misconceptions are not due to the philosophical perspectives on which they are based. Rather, their problems are related to contradicting the meaning of generalization, violating basic philosophical principles, or logical inconsistencies.

Analytic generalization

Yin's *Case Study Research: Design and Methods*, which is in the fifth edition and is widely considered a landmark work on case study, makes a distinction between statistical generalization – inferring from a sample to the population – and what he calls "analytic generalization" – inferring from case findings to theory, as pictorially presented in Figure 2.2 of Yin (2014). Statistical generalization corresponds to within-population generalization in this chapter's classification of induction. As mentioned, Yin (2014) argues against considering statistical generalization to be the way of generalizing case findings, a point underscored by Lee and Baskerville (2003). Instead, the mode of generalization should be analytic generalization, treating cases as experiments. His argument has been used by other researchers to strengthen the methodological legitimacy of case studies (e.g., Danis and Parkhe 2002; Eisenhardt 1989; Eisenhardt and Graebner 2007).

A major problem is that Yin does not clearly and consistently define analytic generalization, which is probably the most common kind of generalization claimed to be used by management researchers when they conduct case studies. In his book, analytic generalization refers to "the logic whereby case study findings can extend to situations outside of the original case study, based on the relevance of similar theoretical concepts or principles" (Yin 2014: 237).[6] The definition is more similar to that of inductive analogy than generalization; that is, the findings of a case study are applied to another situation.

In an entry of the *Encyclopedia of Case Study Research*, Yin (2010: 21) provides a significantly different definition:

> Analytic generalization may be defined as a two-step process. The first involves a conceptual claim whereby investigators show how their case study findings bear upon a particular theory, theoretical construct, or theoretical (not just actual) sequence of events. The second involves applying the same theory to implicate other, similar situations where analogous events also might occur.

The first step is vague as the meaning of "bear upon" is not clear (although it seems to imply theoretical generalization), and the second step is about theory testing, not generalization. Bengtsson and Hertting (2014: 726) rightly point out that "Yin is not particularly clear about the logic" of analytic generalization and that "the rationale behind his approach remains largely undefined."

Case studies as natural science experiments

Yin's analogy between case studies and experiments is echoed in the literature to the extent that researchers sometimes refer to natural science experiments as a way of justifying case studies as a scientific method. For example, Flyvbjerg (2006) maintains that Galileo's famous experiment of falling bodies that overturned Aristotle's law of gravity "was a matter of a single experiment, that is, a case study" and "did not involve a large random sample of trials of objects falling from a wide range of randomly selected heights under varying wind conditions and so on" (p. 225). His argument intends to show that case studies are as credible as quantitative studies that are based on large samples.

Similarly, Lee (1989) argues that case studies should be treated as a form of natural experiment. While his argument sounds reasonable, a serious problem arises when he tries to boost the generalizability of case study results by referring to laboratory experiments in the natural sciences: "a single organizational case study, conducted as a natural experiment, can assure no more, but no less generalizability than any single laboratory experiment conducted in the natural sciences" (p. 135). Assuming that both a case study in the social sciences and a laboratory experiment in the natural sciences are rigorously conducted, the result of the latter is surely more generalizable than that of the former because of the uniformity of nature.[7] Our daily lives actually rely on our belief in the uniformity of nature – we jump into a swimming pool, believing that our bodies will float rather than sink to the bottom of the pool. Suppose in a laboratory experiment, copper expands when heated; this finding is generalizable to all copper on earth. In contrast, if a case study discovers that a Japanese trading company provides lifetime employment to all of its employees, the finding is not likely to be generalizable to all Japanese trading companies, not to mention all Japanese companies. In the social sciences, "it is unrealistic to assume that all relevant data will be consistent with a theory even if the theory is correct" (Lieberson 1992: 7).

The uniformity of nature is not applicable to most, if not all, social phenomena, which are historically conditioned and culturally determined (Nagel 1979). This simple fact jeopardizes the generalizability of the results of social studies, whether quantitative or qualitative (see Hamilton 1981; MacIntyre 2007). Thus, it makes little sense to equate case studies with natural science experiments as far as generalizability is concerned.

Naturalistic generalization

Adopting a strategy similar to that of Yin, Stake and Trumbull (1982) distinguish between two kinds of generalization, namely formal and naturalistic. Formal generalization is rational, propositional, and law-like – the attributes associated with positivism. Naturalistic generalization, in contrast, is more intuitive, empirical, and based on personal direct and vicarious experience – the attributes associated with interpretivism. Stake (1995: 85) puts forward a definition: "Naturalistic generalizations are conclusions arrived at through personal engagement in life's affairs or by vicarious experience so well constructed that the person feels as if it happened to themselves." This definition is not only vague but also inconsistent with the usual meaning of generalization that it is about inference from something specific to something general. This is because the conclusions that people draw from their experiences are not necessarily general in nature.

From an interpretivist point of view, case studies may not contribute much in terms of formal generalization, but cases are a powerful means for building naturalistic generalization: "case studies will often be the preferred method of research because they may be epistemologically in harmony with the reader's experience and thus to that person a natural base for generalization" (Stake 1978: 5). The reader of a case, which provides a thick description and a vicarious experiential account, should be able to determine if and how far the case can be used to understand a new setting (Stake 1994). In this sense, naturalistic generalization is a kind of tacit recognition of the similarities and differences between a case and a new setting, based on personal experience and knowledge of the reader. Or, in the words of Stake (1978: 7), its nature is about "generalization to a similar case rather than generalization to a population of cases."

In brief, a key problem of naturalistic generalization is its misuse of the term "generalization." The core idea of naturalistic generalization – making inference from one case to a new setting – resembles inductive analogy, which does not involve generalization.[8]

The impossibility of generalization

Instead of naturalistic generalization, other researchers in fact use terms like "transferability" (Lincoln and Guba 2000) as well as "comparability" and "translatability" (Goetz and LeCompte 1984) to describe the extent to which findings from one qualitative study are applicable to another situation. Chreim et al.

(2007), for example, use such terms to describe the results of their case study mentioned earlier. In particular, Lincoln and Guba (2000) use the term "transferability" instead of any variant of "generalizability" because they argue that generalization is impossible in qualitative research: "The aim of inquiry is to develop an idiographic body of knowledge. This knowledge is best encapsulated in a series of 'working hypotheses' that describe the individual case. Generalizations are impossible since phenomena are neither time- nor context-free" (Guba and Lincoln 1982: 238).

Unfortunately their argument – generalization being impossible because phenomena are neither time- nor context-free – is flawed. In the social sciences, although quantitative research collects less temporal or contextual information than qualitative research, the former is not inherently more time- or context-free than the latter. More importantly, all empirical studies – whether natural science or social science – are neither time- nor context-free. However, generalization is still possible. The whole discipline of the natural sciences is in fact based on the possibility of generalization.[9] Admittedly, owing to the non-applicability of the uniformity of nature to social phenomena and the open-system nature of social science research (Bhaskar 1978), results of social science research are less generalizable than those of natural science research. As Cronbach (1975: 125) aptly comments, "When we give proper weight to local conditions, any generalization is a working hypothesis, not a conclusion." Yet weak generalization is not equivalent to no generalization.

Generalization of theory

Another misconception is that generalizability is sometimes used to describe a theory, such as Lee and Baskerville's (2003: 221) discussion of "the generalizability of an IS theory to different settings." Similarly, Eisenhardt and Graebner (2007: 26) mention the term "generalizable theory" and ask, "How can the theory generalize if the cases aren't representative?" Winer (1999: 352) also mentions something along the same line: "it is not only the theory that can be replicated and generalized but the empirical results as well." The fact is, generalizability is a property of research findings, not a property of the theory itself (Gibbert 2006). Theories consist of general statements, not specific instances, whereas generalization is an act of reasoning based on the observation of specific instances. Thus theories are not generalizable; only research findings are.

When researchers discuss the generalizability of a theory, what they in fact refer to is whether the theory covers certain empirical phenomena. For instance, drawing on the resource-based view (RBV), Wilson and Amine's (2009) longitudinal case study investigated resource asymmetry between global and local advertising agencies operating in Hungary. They claim that their results "increase confidence in the generalizability of RBV theory by demonstrating its usefulness and flexibility when applied to an unusual context in terms of time and space" (p. 62). The term "applicability" should be used instead because the issue here concerns whether the RBV can be applied to the phenomenon in Hungary. A theory is more general when its domain of applicability is wider. As discussed in chapter 3, the switch from a negligibility assumption to a domain assumption reduces the applicability of a theory.

The impossibility of theory testing

Generalization is sometimes inappropriately linked with theory testing: "while the opponents of case studies accept exploratory case research, they feel that the results of case studies cannot be used for theory-testing, because the findings cannot be generalized" (Hillebrand et al. 2001: 652). There are two problems. First, as elaborated in the next section, if a quantitative study does not employ a probability sampling method, its results are also not generalizable statistically. However, few would challenge that quantitative studies cannot be used for theory testing. Second, those who deny theory testing by case studies often hold a traditional view that theory must be tested by statistical analysis based on large samples. This view is flawed epistemologically. To test a theory is to judge whether the hypotheses derived from it are consistent with the empirical data collected, regardless of whether the data are based on one case or one thousand cases (see Bitektine 2008 for a discussion of theory testing using the prospective case study design). In short, whether a piece of finding can be generalized and whether it can be used to test a theory are two totally unrelated issues. The issue of falsification is discussed further in the next section.

This misconception has created the impression of a second-class status of case studies that they are necessarily exploratory in nature and have to be followed by more "rigorous," large-sample kind of studies for the purpose of theory testing. It seems that some case study researchers readily accept this inferior status. For instance, in their review of 135 case studies published in four leading international business journals from 1995 to 2005 and 22 published in the *Journal of International Business Studies* from 1975 to 1994, Piekkari et al. (2009) found that over half of these studies explicitly stated that they had an exploratory purpose. A typical example is the conclusion of Levy's (1995) case study of the international supply chain of a single company in the personal computer industry: "The exploratory nature of this study does not permit the results to be generalized to other firms or industries, but it does suggest directions for future research" (p. 356). This viewpoint is succinctly reflected in this statement: "critics and advocates alike suggest that using the case study for anything more than exploratory purposes is risky" (Stoecker 1991: 91). The viewpoint itself is a serious misconception.

To summarize, the prior discussion indicates that debates about the ability of case studies to inform generalization results remain contentious partly because of the various misconceptions, some of which are held by prominent scholars, in the literature. Generalizing from case study results is either mixed up with theory testing (e.g., Yin 2010), exaggerated (e.g., Flyvbjerg 2006; Lee 1989), improperly conceived (e.g., Stake 1995), or wrongfully denied (e.g., Guba and

Lincoln 1982). Moreover, the concept of generalization is inappropriately linked with theory application (e.g., Eisenhardt and Graebner, 2007; Winer 1999) and theory testing (e.g., Hillebrand et al. 2001). Based on a critical realist perspective, the next section presents a better conceived view of how case studies contribute to generalizable results and thus theory development.

Comparative advantages of case studies

Contrary to the prevailing view that case studies are weak in generalizability, results of case studies can be more generalizable than those of quantitative studies in several important respects. As elaborated below, case studies may be better than quantitative studies in terms of theoretical generalization and falsification, which are associated with theory building and theory testing, respectively. In addition, case studies are not totally inferior to quantitative studies in terms of empirical generalization that establishes whether there is some kind of empirical regularity in the population under investigation.

Since different case study designs may affect the strength of generalization claims, the following discussion covers two major dimensions that classify these designs: single- versus multiple-case study and cross-sectional versus longitudinal case study. These two dimensions are often referred to in the case study literature, and in fact Leonard-Barton (1990) uses them to construct her dual methodology for case studies.

Theory building

A traditional view of scientific research is to build theories from data collected in the empirical world through observation (Chalmers 1999). Although it is not likely that a new theory can be developed from a single study, whether qualitative or quantitative, theoretical frameworks or implications can still be generated. Theory building from case studies, or theoretical generalization, is "an increasingly popular and relevant research strategy that forms the basis of a disproportionately large number of influential studies" (Eisenhardt and Graebner 2007: 30). Walton (1992: 129) goes further to argue that "case studies are likely to produce the best theory." Why? The reason lies in the ability of case studies to offer a better channel than quantitative methods through which researchers generalize theoretically.

As mentioned, scientific theories offer mechanismic explanations of empirical phenomena (Bunge 1997). Case studies allow researchers to tease out ever-deepening layers of reality in the search for mechanisms and influential contingencies and to peer into the box of causality to locate the factors lying between some critical cause and its purported effect (Brady et al. 2006). This process creates the depth and detail necessary for capturing the "hows" and "whys" rather than only the "whats" (Harrison and Easton 2004). A key difference between case studies and quantitative methods is that case studies seek to investigate phenomena in their contexts, rather than independent of context (Gibbert et al. 2008). By trying to understand empirical events in their rich context, case studies also throw light on the specific contingent conditions under which the postulated mechanisms operate (Tsoukas 1989).

Consider, for instance, Ferner et al.'s (2005) study of the transfer of diversity employment policies by U.S. multinational corporations to their U.K. subsidiaries mentioned earlier. The authors carefully describe the labor-market context for their study, tracing the historical origin of the U.S. diversity policy and the different emphases of the U.K. counterpart. Five of their six cases attempted to transfer their diversity policies from the headquarters to the U.K. subsidiaries. Although managers of the subsidiaries were generally favorable to the idea of diversity, they perceived that the transfer was driven by parochial U.S. problems, which were alien to a non-U.S. environment, and thus that some policy measures were not suitable for the U.K. This gave rise to tensions during the implementation of the transfer. Subsidiary managers used available power resources to shape the content and impact of the transferred policies, resulting in a pattern of uneasy subsidiary accommodation to these policies. In brief, the study clearly describes the mechanisms that generate the observed pattern. Moreover, it also indicates the operation of influential contingencies, such as the extent of integration in global operation, degree of diversity of product markets, and management philosophy of the founding family.

Another example is Greenwood and Suddaby's (2006) study of institutional entrepreneurship in the accounting industry of Canada. The study investigates "the paradox of embedded agency – that is, the paradox of how actors enact changes to the context by which they, as actors, are shaped" (p. 27). The core research question concerns a particular incident of institutional entrepreneurship: why did the Big Five accounting firms introduce a new organizational form of multidisciplinary practice in the 1980s and 1990s? The authors interviewed senior partners of three of the Big Five and regulatory personnel. They also reviewed a variety of archival data. Their results are generalized to a model of institutional entrepreneurship that unpacks the mechanisms by which embeddedness is weakened and the scope for action is enlarged. Boundary bridging and boundary misalignment, as neglected features of network location, are two key structural elements of the model. Boundary bridging leads to institutional contradictions and affects awareness, while boundary misalignment leads to resource asymmetries and affects openness. When boundary misalignment and boundary bridging are under the contingent condition of poor performance, elite organizations, such as the Big Five, attain the motivation, awareness, and openness necessary for institutional entrepreneurship. In short, their study clearly delineates the structure, mechanisms, and contingent conditions that underlie the phenomenon of institutional entrepreneurship.

Although theoretical generalization does not necessarily call for a multiple-case design (Mitchell 1983), the "evidence from multiple cases is often considered more compelling" (Yin 2014: 57) for a major reason that it can be difficult to separate theoretical relationships found in a case, which are generalizable, from idiosyncrasies associated with the case. Thus, keeping other things constant, a multiple-case design provides a stronger basis for theoretical generalization than a single-case design.

A multiple-case design relies on theoretical, instead of random, sampling for case selection (Eisenhardt 1989). A case is chosen because it is expected to predict either (1) similar results or (2) contrasting or opposite results based on known theoretical reasons (Yin 2014). In the former case, when a finding is observed in more than one case, its generalizability is enhanced. The latter case helps establish the boundary conditions of the theory concerned so that the theory would not be applied to inappropriate situations. Take, for example, Ferner et al.'s (2005) study of cross-national transfer of workforce diversity policy. It is well-known that in European countries, unions and collective bargaining constitute an essential element underpinning the legal framework of equality, which in turn affects companies' workforce diversity policies. Thus they included both unionized and non-unionized companies in their sample to enhance theoretical generalizability. In other words, researchers can manipulate the contexts in which their cases are embedded to achieve the desired extent of generalization. On the other hand, since quantitative methods are less context dependent, this tool is not as readily available.

Other things being equal, a longitudinal case study provides stronger evidence for theoretical generalization than a cross-sectional case study because the former enables researchers to track cause and effect more effectively. For example, Leonard-Barton (1990) reports her study of the transfer of new technologies from their developers into the hands of their users. The study consisted of nine cross-sectional cases (where data were collected within a short period of time from each case based on respondents' retrospective accounts) and one three-year, real-time longitudinal case (where data were collected as the process of transfer unfolded). A direct causal link between the innovation's level of transferability and transfer success or failure was observed in one of the cross-sectional cases. However, the longitudinal case suggested that the degree of mutual technical and organizational adaptation undertaken by the transferring and the recipient organizations was a mediating factor in the causal link. She concludes that the mediating factor was missing in the cross-sectional case because respondents might confuse the direction of causality based on their somewhat biased memories of the events that happened during the transfer. On the other hand, for the longitudinal case, the possibility of confusion was eliminated when similar events were observed in real time as the process of transfer unfolded. This again shows the advantage of investigating cases in their naturalistic contexts, which in this example helped Leonard-Barton explain the different findings of her cross-sectional and longitudinal cases.

High-quality mechanismic explanations are not likely to be achieved by quantitative studies that rely on, for instance, archival data. Although quantitative studies usually discuss the mechanisms underlying their hypotheses, "the distance between conceptual constructs and measurable variables is often rather large" (Siggelkow 2007: 22). More importantly, quantitative studies often use correlational methods that do not directly examine mechanisms (Bromiley and Johnson 2005). As discussed in chapter 3, the history of empirical research on transaction cost economics has been dominated by quantitative studies that fail to rule out alternative mechanismic explanations of the phenomenon under investigation. In brief, although mechanisms are not logically precluded from quantitative research, they are more likely to be investigated directly in qualitative research such as case studies.

Theory testing

While theoretical generalization concerns theory building, falsification is about theory testing. Chapter 4 discusses the obstacles to testing, in particular falsifying, management theories. Case studies can contribute to management research through facilitating falsification. As theory evolves through cycles of verification and falsification, the important role of case studies in falsification has been neglected by existing literature, which only focuses on theory building based on case study research.

To illustrate the principle of falsification, consider the statement "All swans are white." While the statement cannot be proven to be true no matter how many white swans are observed, just one observation of a black swan will falsify the statement regardless of whether the observation can be generalized to other swans. Thus, disconfirming research findings play an important epistemological role in theory development. Owing to its in-depth investigation approach to revealing explanatory mechanisms, the case study is well suited to identifying "black swans" (Flyvbjerg 2006). Such disconfirming results may lead to the setting of the boundary conditions of the theory concerned. If the results are widespread, the validity of the theory itself is doubtful.[10] It goes without saying that a multiple-case design is in a better position than a single-case design to show how far a disconfirming finding is a widespread phenomenon. For a good example of "black swans," consider Buckley and Chapman's (1997, 1998) longitudinal case study discussed in chapter 3. One of their findings challenges a core assumption of transaction cost economics that managers make contracting decisions in a transaction-cost-economizing manner (Williamson 1975, 1985). This finding is by no means a conclusive falsification of the assumption as there could be other factors affecting it. For example, managers might have engaged in some sort of transaction cost consideration but failed to communicate the practice to the researchers. That said, their finding indicates the need for further testing the assumption. It is not surprising that Buckley and Chapman's study is the first to identify this "black swan" given that most of the empirical studies of transaction cost economics have used quantitative methods (David and Han 2004).

Moreover, case studies can be used to test mechanisms proposed by competing theories, thereby distinguishing between "white swans" and "black swans." Sagan's (1993) study of the Cuban missile crisis is an exemplar. There are two major competing theories explaining accidents in hazardous high-technology organizations. Perrow's normal accident theory is one. Perrow (1999) created the theory mostly based on his study of the nuclear power accidents at Three Mile Island, supplemented by an examination of other high-risk systems such as petrochemical plants and air-traffic control systems. The other theory is high reliability theory, represented by a multidisciplinary group of scholars based at the University of California at Berkeley. Their studies focused on aircraft carriers, air-traffic control systems, and electric power systems (see La Porte and Consolini 1991; Roberts 1989). While normal accident theory predicts that certain kinds of system accidents are inevitable, high reliability theory predicts smooth sailing if the entire organization, including the leadership, is committed to safety.

Sagan (1993) nicely summarized and contrasted the key mechanisms of both theories. He then evaluated these mechanisms based on his study of near misses in the U.S. nuclear weapons command-and-control system during the Cuban missile crisis, which represented a new context for both theories, and found support for normal accident theory. For instance, high reliability theory argues that extreme discipline and intense socialization will reduce the chance of accidents. However, in line with the argument of normal accident theory, Sagan's study discovered a set of severe side effects that could significantly increase the risk of serious accidents. The support of Sagan's results for normal accident theory was even more significant if we take into account the fact that his study was what he called a "tough test" for normal accident theory: "the apparent excellent safety record, the importance with which political leaders viewed nuclear weapon safety, and the strict discipline and socialization present in professional military organizations, all led to a logical expectation that U.S. nuclear weapons operations would be exceptionally safe" (p. 252). To summarize, Sagan's deep probe into the key mechanisms of both theories has provided rich materials for the theories, especially high reliability theory, to be further developed. These two examples also indicate that other things being equal, a longitudinal case design, which enables researchers to tease out causal relationships, provides stronger evidence than a cross-sectional design.

Identification of empirical regularities

One of the objectives of empirical generalization is to establish whether there is some sort of empirical regularity in the population concerned. Again take the example of Ferner et al.'s (2005) study. Their findings "show a pattern of uneasy subsidiary accommodation to transferred diversity policies" (p. 316). Rather than being idiosyncratic to their six cases, this pattern could be an empirical regularity in the population of U.S. multinational corporations in the U.K. Empirical regularities may not fall neatly within the domain of any existing theory and thus do not provide immediate contributions to theory building. However, they could form the empirical basis for future theory building (Hambrick 2007; Helfat 2007).

Contrary to a usual saying that it is not necessary to select cases that are representative of the population to which they belong (Mitchell 1983), it makes more sense to choose representative cases if the aim of a study is to generate empirical generalization.[11] In other words, the logic of theoretical sampling discussed earlier is less applicable here. Moreover, a multiple-case design provides a stronger basis for empirical generalization than a single-case design because the former is in a better position to show that what is to be generalized is not an idiosyncratic trait of one case. Depending on whether a causal or a correlational relation is in question, a longitudinal case design may not necessarily be stronger than a cross-sectional one.

Following the prior argument that a multiple-case design offers a stronger basis for empirical generalization, the findings of a quantitative study, such as a large-scale survey, are more generalizable than those of a case study within the population concerned. Yet a caveat is that the generalizability of survey results depends a great deal upon whether a probability sampling method is used to construct a representative sample. Owing to various practical constraints, such as the ability to include every member of a population in the sampling process, probability sampling is often not feasible in surveys. Hence, within-population generalizability of many survey results is more doubtful than certain, an issue that has been neglected by those who challenge case studies on the grounds of generalizability (Gobo 2004).

For cross-population generalization, there is simply no reason to believe that survey results are inherently more generalizable than case study results. It all depends on how far the two populations in question are similar with respect to the characteristic or relationship that is generalized. For example, the results of an extensive employment policy survey of U.S. multinational corporations in the U.K. will not be more generalizable to U.S. multinational corporations in other countries than the results of Ferner et al.'s (2005) study unless the country concerned has similar labor legislation, ethnic diversity policy, and so on as the U.K. Hence, the view that survey results are always more generalizable empirically than case study results is unwarranted.

An often neglected merit of case studies is that they provide useful information for assessing the empirical generalizability of their results. In order to judge whether and how far a piece of research finding is generalizable to, say, members of other populations, it is often necessary to clearly understand the context in which the study was conducted because the context can have a direct or indirect effect on the relationship under consideration. Since case studies generally provide more such contextual information than quantitative methods, the former are superior to the latter in this respect.

Ferner et al.'s (2005) report of their findings, for instance, indicates the effects of certain factors specific to the U.K. Race-based discrimination, for instance, has been a major policy issue of U.S. firms whereas ethnic minorities account for only 9 percent of the total population in the U.K., compared with almost 30 percent in the U.S. Hence, the implementation of ethnic diversity policies created tensions in some of the U.K. subsidiaries as local managers thought that ethnic diversity should not be a major priority. This finding is not likely to be generalizable to countries, such as Singapore and Malaysia, where ethnic minorities constitute a substantial portion of the population. Promoting more women to management positions, as an element of diversity policy, also encountered problems because it was inconsistent with U.K. and even E.U. legislation outlawing positive discrimination. The result may not be generalizable to countries that do not have such legislation. In short, the detailed description of the context helps determine the empirical generalizability of the results.

Summary

Figure 5.2 summarizes the role played by case studies in theory development. A major objective of empirical generalization is to establish if there is any empirical regularity associated with the events under study. The existence of such a regularity is a prerequisite for theory creation because a theory is supposed to explain a rather general phenomenon rather than some isolated, idiosyncratic events (see Runde and de Rond 2010). The information provided by case studies can throw light on existing theories or form an empirical foundation for creating new theories. Although ideally speaking theoretical generalization should be preceded by empirical generalization, this is not the case in reality partly because case studies are rarely conducted for the purpose of empirical generalization.

As indicated by Figure 5.2, there is an intricate relationship between theory building and theory testing, although it is rare that a case study would aim at achieving both at the same time. An objective of theoretical generalization is to build new theories or revise existing theories, from which hypotheses can be

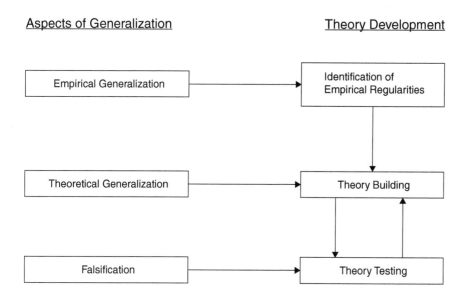

Figure 5.2 Contributions of case studies toward theory development

derived for theory testing by future studies. In addition to theory building, a case study may be carried out for the purpose of testing an existing theory. Cases that contradict the hypotheses derived from the theory constitute a result of falsification, which helps establish the boundary conditions of the theory. Persistent discovery of disconfirming cases by further studies nevertheless can lead to the revision or even refutation of the theory. In other words, theory building is a prerequisite for theory testing because without a theory, there is nothing to test. At the same time, results of theory testing will strengthen or weaken the empirical foundation of a theory and may even overturn the theory.

Notes

1 It is beyond the scope of this chapter to review the debate. In addition to the references cited, interested readers may also refer to Seddon and Scheepers (2015), who summarize and comment on the positions of both sides of the debate.

2 Chapter 7 discusses historiography, another qualitative research method, and the generalizability of its results.

3 I abhor the idea that qualitative researchers should have a definition of generalization different from that of quantitative researchers or that different philosophical perspectives should have different definitions of generalization. This will result in not only chaos but also communication breakdown. The concept of generalization has a rather commonly agreed definition in logic. This definition, which loosely speaking refers to inferring from what is less general to what is more general, should be adopted by all researchers regardless of their methodological or philosophical orientation.

4 The term "external validity" has been defined in various ways during the last three decades. For example, Cook and Campbell (1979: 37) defined it rather imprecisely as "the approximate validity with which we can infer that the presumed causal relationship can be generalized to and across alternate measures of the cause and effect and across different types of persons, settings, and times." Later Cronbach (1982) developed an elaborate notional system that covers four dimensions: unit of analysis, treatment, outcome, and setting. Using the system, he distinguished between internal and external validity.

5 It has never been my intention to dismiss the valuable contributions to case study research made by the following scholars, who inadvertently misconceive the concept of generalization. Rather, through discussing these misconceptions, I expect that the methodological foundation of case study research would be further strengthened.

6 The definition of analytic generalization is even more confusing in the fourth edition of Yin's book. In one place, he states: "In analytical generalization, the investigator is striving to generalize a particular set of results to some broader theory" (Yin 2009: 43). This statement is in line with the meaning of theoretical generalization, which concerns theory building. However, in another place, he considers analytic generalization a mode of generalization "in which a previously developed theory is used as a template with which to compare the empirical results of the case study" (Yin 2009: 38). This is not generalization. Rather, it is theory testing: the testing of the previously developed theory by the results of the case study. Generalization is one kind of induction whereas theory testing is based on deductive reasoning.

7　Space constraints do not allow me to discuss the debates about the principle of the uniformity of nature, first invoked by Mill (1925 [1843]), as a solution to Hume's problem of induction. Interested readers may refer to Brennan (1961).

8　A plausible explanation for mistaking inductive analogy for generalization is the casual usage of the latter in our daily life. For example, when the U.S. military invaded Iraq in 2003, someone might predict (accurately) that American soldiers would be caught in a quagmire based on the experience of the Vietnam War. One possible reaction might be something like, "Oh, you can't generalize from the Vietnam War to the current war in Iraq." While this kind of misuse may be forgivable in our everyday conversations, it is not in academic writings. Unfortunately the concept of naturalistic generalization is widely shared, as evidenced by the large number of citations. Simons's (2015) concept of situated generalization, for example, is based on naturalistic generalization.

9　It should not be difficult to imagine the catastrophic implications of denying the possibility of generalization in the natural sciences. For example, people would hesitate to take any drugs if the effects of chemicals tested in the laboratory are not generalizable to the same chemicals that are used to produce drugs. In short, the natural sciences are simply impossible without generalization. That is why Hume's problem of induction occupies such an important position in philosophy. Interested readers may refer to Chattopadhyaya (1991) for a comprehensive treatment of the problem and its various solutions proposed by generations of philosophers.

10　Unlike the natural sciences, there are few law-like phenomena to be discovered in the social sciences (Numagami 1998). As mentioned, it is not realistic to expect that all relevant data will be consistent with the prediction of a theory even if the theory is correct (Lieberson 1992). However, that does not imply that management theories are immune from falsification. While a single disconfirming case cannot falsify a theory, cumulative disconfirming evidence will cast doubt on the validity of the theory and may contribute to its eventual refutation.

11　Ruzzene (2012) introduces the concept of comparability and proposes that the representativeness (or typicality) of a case should be based on the result of comparing the pertinent causal mechanisms between the case and the target case/cases. The higher the level of similarity, the more representative the case and thus the more generalizable its findings. A problem is that Ruzzene fails to clearly delineate the procedure of comparison. Moreover, when researchers assess the representativeness of a case, is it that they would consciously or unconsciously engage in some kind of comparison? In other words, Ruzzene may inadvertently just recommend what some researchers have been doing.

References

Bengtsson, B. and Hertting, N. 2014. Generalization by mechanism: Thin rationality and ideal-type analysis in case study research. *Philosophy of the Social Sciences*, 44: 707–732.

Bhaskar, R. 1978. *A realist theory of science* (2nd ed.). Hassocks, England: Harvester Press.

Bitektine, A. 2008. Prospective case study design: Qualitative method for deductive theory testing. *Organizational Research Methods*, 11: 160–180.

Brady, H. E., Collier, D. and Seawright, J. 2006. Towards a pluralistic vision of methodology. *Political Analysis*, 14: 353–368.

Brennan, J. G. 1961. *A handbook of logic* (2nd ed.). New York: Harper and Brothers.

Bromiley, P. and Johnson, S. 2005. Mechanisms and empirical research. In D. J. Ketchen Jr. and D. D. Bergh (Eds.), *Research methodology in strategy and management*, Vol. 2: 15–29. Amsterdam, NL: Elsevier.

Buckley, P. J. and Chapman, M. 1997. The perception and measurement of transaction costs. *Cambridge Journal Economics*, 21: 127–145.

Buckley, P. J. and Chapman, M. 1998. The management of cooperative strategies in R&D and innovation programmes. *International Journal of the Economics of Business*, 5: 369–381.

Bunge, M. 1997. Mechanism and explanation. *Philosophy of the Social Sciences*, 27: 410–465.

Cambridge dictionary of philosophy (2nd ed.). 1999. Cambridge, England: Cambridge University Press.

Cavaye, A. L. M. 1996. Case study research: A multi-faceted research approach for IS. *Information Systems Journal*, 6: 227–242.

Chalmers, A. F. 1999. *What is this thing called science?* (3rd ed.). Maidenhead, England: Open University Press.

Chattopadhyaya, D. P. 1991. *Induction, probability, and skepticism*. Albany, NY: State University of New York Press.

Chreim, S., Williams, B. E. and Hinings, C. R. 2007. Interlevel influences on the reconstruction of professional role identity. *Academy of Management Journal*, 50: 1515–1539.

Cohen, M. R. and Nagel, E. 1934. *An introduction to logic and scientific method*. New York: Harcourt, Brace and World.

Cook, T. D. and Campbell, D. T. 1979. *Quasi-experimentation: Design and analysis issues for field settings*. Boston, MA: Houghton Mifflin.

Copi, I. M. and Cohen, C. 1990. *Introduction to logic* (8th ed.). New York: Macmillan.

Cronbach, L. J. 1975. Beyond the two disciplines of scientific psychology. *American Psychologist*, 30: 116–127.

Cronbach, L. J. 1982. *Designing evaluations of educational and social programs*. San Francisco, CA: Jossey-Bass.

Danermark, B., Ekstrm, M., Jakobsen, L. and Karlsson, J. C. 2002. *Explaining society: Critical realism in the social sciences*. London: Routledge.

Danis, W. M. and Parkhe, A. 2002. Hungarian-Western partnerships: A grounded theoretical model of integration processes and outcomes. *Journal of International Business Studies*, 33: 423–455.

David, R. J. and Han, S.-K. 2004. A systematic assessment of the empirical support for transaction cost economics. *Strategic Management Journal*, 25: 39–58.

Davis, F. D. 1989. Perceived usefulness, perceived ease of use, and user acceptance of information technology. *MIS quarterly*, 13: 319–340.

de Rond, M. and Bouchikhi, M. 2004. On the dialectics of strategic alliances. *Organization Science*, 15: 56–69.

Denzin, N. K. 1983. Interpretive interactionism. In G. Morgan (Ed.), *Beyond methods: Strategies for social research*: 129–146. Beverly Hills, CA: Sage.

Eisenhardt, K. M. 1989. Building theories from case study research. *Academy of Management Review*, 14: 532–550.

Eisenhardt, K. M. and Bourgeois III, L. J. 1988. Politics of strategic decision making in high-velocity environments: Toward a midrange theory. *Academy of Management Journal*, 31: 737–770.

Eisenhardt, K. M. and Graebner, M. E. 2007. Theory building from cases: Opportunities and challenges. *Academy of Management Journal*, 50: 25–32.

Ferner, A., Almond, P. and Colling, T. 2005. Institutional theory and the cross-national transfer of employment policy: The case of "workforce diversity" in US multinationals. *Journal of International Business Studies*, 36: 304–321.

Filtzer, D. 2002. *Soviet workers and de-Stalinization: The consolidation of the modern system of Soviet production relations, 1953–1964.* Cambridge, England: Cambridge University Press.

Firestone, W. A. 1993. Alternative arguments for generalizing from data as applied to qualitative research. *Educational Researcher*, 22(4): 16–23.

Flyvbjerg, B. 2006. Five misunderstandings about case-study research. *Qualitative Inquiry*, 12: 219–245.

Gefen, D. and Straub, D. W. 1997. Gender differences in the perception and use of e-mail: An extension to the technology acceptance model. *MIS Quarterly*, 21: 389–400.

Gensler, H. 2001. *Introduction to logic.* London: Routledge.

Gephart Jr., R. P. 2004. Qualitative research and the *Academy of Management Journal. Academy of Management Journal*, 47: 454–462.

Gerring, J. 2004. What is a case study and what is it good for? *American Political Science Review*, 98: 341–354.

Gerring, J. 2007. *Case study research: Principles and practices.* Cambridge, England: Cambridge University Press.

Gibbert, M. 2006. Munchausen, black swans, and the RBV: Response to Levitas and Ndofor. *Journal of Management Inquiry*, 15: 145–151.

Gibbert, M., Ruigrok, W. and Wicki, B. 2008. What passes as a rigorous case study? *Strategic Management Journal*, 29: 1465–1474.

Gobo, G. 2004. Sampling, representativeness and generalizability. In C. Seale, G. Gobo, J. F. Gubrium and D. Silverman (Eds.), *Qualitative research practice*: 405–426. London: Sage.

Goetz, J. P. and LeCompte, M. D. 1984. *Ethnography and qualitative design in education research.* Orlando, FL: Academic Press.

Gomm, R., Hammersley, M. and Foster, P. 2000. Case study and generalization. In R. Gomm, M. Hammersley and P. Foster (Eds.), *Case study: Key issues, key texts*: 98–115. London: Sage.

Greenwood, R. and Suddaby, R. 2006. Institutional entrepreneurship in mature fields: The big five accounting firms. *Academy of Management Journal*, 49: 27–48.

Guba, E. G. and Lincoln, Y. S. 1982. Epistemological and methodological bases of naturalistic enquiry. *Education Communication and Technology Journal*, 30: 233–252.

Hägg, I. and Hedlund, G. 1979. "Case studies" in accounting research. *Accounting, Organizations and Society*, 4: 135–143.

Halkier, B. 2011. Methodological practicalities in analytical generalization. *Qualitative Inquiry*, 17: 787–797.

Hambrick, D. C. 2007. The field of management's devotion to theory: Too much of a good thing. *Academy of Management Journal*, 50: 1346–1352.

Hamilton, D. 1981. Generalization in the educational sciences: Problems and purposes. In T. S. Popkewitz and B. R. Tabachnick (Eds.), *The study of schooling: Field based methodologies in educational research and evaluation*: 227–241. New York: Praeger.

Harrison, D. and Easton, G. 2004. Temporally embedded case comparison in industrial marketing research. In S. Fleetwood and S. Ackroyd (Eds.), *Critical realist applications in organisation and management studies*: 194–210. London: Routledge.

Helfat, C. E. 2007. Stylized facts, empirical research and theory development in management. *Strategic Organization*, 5: 185–192.

Hillebrand, B., Kok, R. A. W. and Biemans, W. G. 2001. Theory-testing using case studies: A comment on Johnston, Leach, and Liu. *Industrial Marketing Management*, 30: 651–657.

Hofstede, G. 1980. *Culture's consequences: International differences in work related values*. London: Sage.

Hurley, P. 2003. *A concise introduction to logic*. Belmont, CA: Wadsworth.

Johnson, P., Buehring, A., Cassell, C. and Symon, G. 2006. Evaluating qualitative management research: Towards a contingent criteriology. *International Journal of Management Reviews*, 8: 131–156.

Klein, H. K. and Myers, M. D. 1999. A set of principles for conducting and evaluating interpretive field studies in information systems. *MIS Quarterly*, 23: 67–94.

Kochan, T. and Rubinstein, S. 2000. Toward a stakeholder theory of the firm: The Saturn partnership. *Organization Science*, 11: 367–386.

La Porte, T. R. and Consolini, P. M. 1991. Working in practice but not in theory: Theoretical challenges of "high reliability organizations". *Journal of Public Administration Research and Theory*, 1: 19–47.

Lee, A. S. 1989. Case studies as natural experiments. *Human Relations*, 42: 117–137.

Lee, A. S. and Baskerville, R. L. 2003. Generalizing generalizability in information systems research. *Information Systems Research*, 14: 221–243.

Lee, A. S. and Baskerville, R. L. 2012. Conceptualizing generalizability: New contributions and a reply. *MIS quarterly*, 36: 749–761.

Leonard-Barton, D. 1990. A dual methodology for case studies: Synergistic use of a longitudinal single site with replicated multiple sites. *Organization Science*, 1: 248–266.

Levy, D. L. 1995. International sourcing and supply chain stability. *Journal of International Business Studies*, 26: 343–360.

Lieberson, S. 1992. Einstein, Renoir, and Greeley: Some thoughts about evidence in sociology. *American Sociological Review*, 57: 1–15.

Lincoln, Y. S. and Guba, E. G. 1985. *Naturalistic inquiry*. Beverly Hills, CA: Sage.

Lincoln, Y. S. and Guba, E. G. 2000. The only generalization is: There is no generalization. In R. Gomm, M. Hammersley and P. Foster (Eds.), *Case study: Key issues, key texts*: 27–44. London: Sage.

Lucas, J. W. 2003. Theory-testing, generalization, and the problem of external validity. *Sociological Theory*, 21: 236–253.

MacIntyre, A. 2007. *After virtue: A study in moral theory* (3rd ed.). Notre Dame, IN: University of Notre Dame Press.

Maguire, S., Hardy, C. and Lawrence, T. 2004. Institutional entrepreneurship in emerging fields: HIV/AIDS treatment advocacy in Canada. *Academy of Management Journal*, 47: 657–679.

Manicas, P. T. 2006. *A realist philosophy of social science*. Cambridge, England: Cambridge University Press.

Maxwell, J. A. 1992. Understanding and validity in qualitative research. *Harvard Educational Review*, 62: 279–300.

Mill, J. S. 1925 [1843]. *A system of logic*. London: Longmans, Green and Co.

Mintzberg, H. 2005. Developing theory about the development of theory. In K. G. Smith and M. A. Hitt (Eds.), *Great minds in management: The process of theory development*: 355–372. Oxford, England: Oxford University Press.

Mitchell, J. C. 1983. Case and situation analysis. *Sociological Review*, 31: 187–211.

Mjøset, L. 2009. The contextualist approach to social science methodology. In D. Byrne and C. C. Ragin (Eds.), *The Sage handbook of case-based methods*: 39–68. London: Sage.

Nagel, E. 1979. *The structure of science: Problems in the logic of scientific explanation*. Indianapolis, IN: Hackett Publishing.

Numagami, T. 1998. The infeasibility of invariant laws in management studies: A reflective dialogue in defense of case studies. *Organization Science*, 9: 2–15.

Orlikowski, W. J. and Baroudi, J. J. 1991. Studying information technology in organizations: Research approaches and assumptions. *Information Systems Research*, 2: 1–28.

Perrow, C. 1999. *Normal accidents: Living with high-risk technologies* (2nd ed.). Princeton, NJ: Princeton University Press.

Piekkari, R., Welch, C. and Paavilainen, E. 2009. The case study as disciplinary convention: Evidence from international business journals. *Organizational Research Methods*, 12: 567–589.

Roberts, K. H. 1989. New challenges in organization research: High reliability organizations. *Organization and Environment*, 3: 111–125.

Rousseau, D. M. and Fried, Y. 2001. Location, location, location: Contextualizing organizational research. *Journal of Organizational Behavior*, 22: 1–13.

Runde, J. and de Rond, M. 2010. Evaluating causal explanations of specific events. *Organization Studies*, 31: 431–450.

Ruzzene, A. 2012. Drawing lessons from case studies by enhancing comparability. *Philosophy of the Social Sciences*, 42: 99–120.

Sagan, S. D. 1993. *The limits of safety: Organizations, accidents, and nuclear weapons*. Princeton, NJ: Princeton University Press.

Sayer, A. 1992. *Method in social science: A realist approach* (2nd ed.). London: Routledge.

Schofield, J. W. 1990. Increasing the generalizability of qualitative research. In E. W. Eisner and A. Peshkin (Eds.), *Qualitative inquiry in education: The continuing debate*: 201–232. New York: Teachers College Press.

Schwandt, T. A. 1997. *Qualitative inquiry*. Thousand Oaks, CA: Sage.

Seddon, P. B. and Scheepers, R. 2015. Generalization in IS research: A critique of the conflicting positions of Lee & Baskerville and Tsang & Williams. *Journal of Information Technology*, 30: 30–43.

Sharp, K. 1998. The case for case studies in nursing research: The problem of generalization. *Journal of Advanced Nursing*, 27: 785–789.

Siggelkow, N. 2007. Persuasion with case studies. *Academy of Management Journal*, 50: 20–24.

Simons, H. 2015. Interpret in context: Generalizing from the single case in evaluation. *Evaluation*, 21: 173–188.

Stake, R. E. 1978. The case study method in social inquiry. *Educational Researcher*, 7(2): 5–8.

Stake, R. E. 1994. Case studies. In N. K. Denzin and Y. S. Lincoln (Eds.), *Handbook of qualitative research*: 435–454. Thousand Oaks, CA: Sage.

Stake, R. E. 1995. *The art of case study research*. Thousand Oaks, CA: Sage.

Stake, R. E. and Trumbull, D. J. 1982. Naturalistic generalizations. *Review Journal of Philosophy and Social Science*, 7: 1–12.

Steinmetz, G. 2004. Odious comparisons: Incommensurability, the case study, and "small N's" in sociology. *Sociological Theory*, 22: 371–400.

Stoecker, R. 1991. Evaluating and rethinking the case study. *Sociological Review*, 39: 88–112.

Straub, D. W. 1994. The effect of culture on IT diffusion: E-mail and FAX in Japan and the US. *Information Systems Research*, 5: 23–47.

Tsang, E. W. K. and Williams, J. N. 2012. Generalization and induction: Misconceptions, clarifications, and a classification of induction. *MIS Quarterly*, 36: 729–748.

Tsoukas, H. 1989. The validity of idiographic research explanations. *Academy of Management Review*, 14: 551–561.

Walton, J. 1992. Making the theoretical case. In H. S. Becker and C. Ragin (Eds.), *What is a case? Exploring the foundations of social inquiry*: 121–137. Cambridge, England: Cambridge University Press.

Welch, C., Plakoyiannaki, E., Piekkari, R. and Paavilainen-Mäntymäki, E. 2013. Legitimizing diverse uses for qualitative research: A theoretical analysis of two management journals. *International Journal of Management Reviews*, 15: 245–264.

Williams, J. N. and Tsang, E. W. K. 2015. Classifying generalization: Paradigm war or abuse of terminology. *Journal of Information Technology*, 30: 18–29.

Williams, M. 2000. Interpretivism and generalisation. *Sociology*, 34: 209–224.

Williamson, O. E. 1975. *Markets and hierarchies: Analysis and antitrust implications*. New York: Free Press.

Williamson, O. E. 1985. *The economic institutions of capitalism*. New York: Free Press.

Wilson, R. T. and Amine, L. S. 2009. Resource endowments, market positioning, and competition in transitional economies: Global and local advertising agencies in Hungary. *International Marketing Review*, 26: 62–89.

Winer, R. S. 1999. Experimentation in the 21st century: The importance of external validity. *Journal of the Academy of Marketing Science*, 27: 349–358.

Wynn Jr., D. and Williams, C. K. 2012. Principles for conducting critical realist case study research in information systems. *MIS Quarterly*, 36: 787–810.

Yin, R. K. 2009. *Case study research: Design and methods* (4th ed.). Thousand Oaks, CA: Sage.

Yin, R. K. 2010. Analytic generalization. In A. J. Mills, G. Durepos and E. Wiebe (Eds.), *Encyclopedia of case study research*, Vol. 1: 20–22. Thousand Oaks, CA: Sage.

Yin, R. K. 2014. *Case study research: Design and methods* (5th ed.). Thousand Oaks, CA: Sage.

Zachariadis, M., Scott, S. and Barrett, M. 2013. Methodological implications of critical realism for mixed-methods research. *MIS Quarterly*, 37: 855–879.

6 Replication
An ignored necessity

> It was a success story that Japan sorely needed: a young, talented and beautiful researcher developed a cheap and simple way to grow versatile stem cells . . . Intrigued by researcher Haruko Obokata's breakthrough, other scientists tried but failed to replicate her results. Peer-review websites accused her of falsifying data and doctoring images, and supervisors were accused of lax management. Obokata, 30, was forced to retract her scientific papers, and the government-sponsored research center where she worked launched a formal investigation. The matter took a darker turn this week when Obokata's supervisor and mentor, Yoshiki Sasai, a noted scientist in his own right, was found hanging from a stairway railing at his office.
>
> (Spitzer 2014)

This tragic incident shocked the community of stem cell research worldwide.[1] Yet it nicely illustrates a brute fact – "Replication is at the heart of science" (Cumming 2008: 286). Replication serves as "a kind of demarcation criterion between science and nonscience" (Braude 1979: 42). As a noted statistician well says, "the scientist begins to believe that (s)he is winning when (s)he gets reproducible results from several experiments done under various conditions, perhaps with different instruments at different sites etc." (Nelder 1986: 113). In many natural sciences the replication of empirical findings is a common practice. On the other hand, replications are less common in the social sciences in general and management in particular.

Table 6.1 lists 14 studies of replication research in business disciplines. The studies conclude that replications have not been sufficiently conducted for verification and generalization purposes and that more should be done. In the instances where replications were undertaken, their results often conflict with, or at best partially support, the original findings. Management researchers sometimes accept the findings of a single uncorroborated study whose validity may later turn out to be doubtful. For instance, the conflict resolution findings of Lawrence and Lorsch's (1967) landmark work have been widely accepted and disseminated. However, when Fry et al. (1980) tried to replicate the findings in a managerial sample, their result seriously questions the validity of Lawrence and Lorsch's scale for measuring conflict resolution modes.

Table 6.1 Studies of replication research in business disciplines

Study	Disciplines and journals investigated	Period	Amount of replicated studies	Results of replicated and original studies		
				Consistent	Partially consistent	Inconsistent
Brown and Coney (1976)[a]	All articles published in three marketing journals	1971–1975	13 (2.8%) out of 465 articles	Not available		
Reid et al. (1981)	All advertising articles published in three annual conference proceedings and 10 journals	1977–1979	30 (6.0%) out of 501 articles	40.0%	20.0%	40.0%
Zinkhan et al. (1990)	Systematic samples of experiment and survey articles published in four marketing journals	1975–1984	13 (4.9%) out of 263 articles	23.1%	30.7%	46.2%
Hubbard and Vetter (1991)	Random samples of empirical articles published in four finance journals	1969–1989	55 (9.9%) out of 555 articles	20.0%	20.0%	60.0%
Hubbard and Vetter (1992)	Random samples of empirical articles published in three economics journals	1965–1989	92 (9.8%) out of 942 articles	19.6%	15.2%	65.2%
Hubbard and Armstrong (1994)	Random samples of empirical articles published in three marketing journals	1974–1989	20 (2.4%) out of 835 articles	15.0%	25.0%	60.0%
Fuess (1996)	All articles published in the Quarterly Journal of Business and Economics	1984–1994	62 (22.5%) out of 275 articles	30.8%	34.6%	34.6%

Study	Description	Years	Replications			
Hubbard and Vetter (1996)	Random samples of empirical articles published in 18 journals in the areas of accounting, economics, finance, management, and marketing	1970–1991	266 (6.2%) out of 4,270 articles (ranging from 2.9% in marketing to 9.7% in finance)	27.1%	24.4%	45.5%
Hubbard and Vetter (1997)	Random samples of empirical articles published in 12 finance journals	1975–1994	144 (10.1%) out of 1,423 articles	16.0%	29.1%	54.9%
Hubbard et al. (1998)	Random samples of empirical articles published in nine management journals	1976–1995	37 (5.3%) out of 701 articles	29.7%	43.3%	27.0%
Darley (2000)	All empirical articles published in three marketing journals	1986–1995	22 (2.3%) out of 970 articles	31.8%	22.7%	45.5%
Evanschitzky et al. (2007)[b]	All empirical articles published in three marketing journals	1990–2004	16 (1.2%) out of 1,389 articles	43.8%	31.3%	24.9%
Evanschitzky and Armstrong (2010)[c]	All empirical articles published in two forecasting journals	1996–2008	78 (8.4%) out of 929 articles	35.3%	45.1%	19.6%
Park et al. (2015)	All empirical articles published in four advertising journals	1980–2012	82 (2.9%) out of 2,856 articles	53.7%	39.0%	7.3%

a The original replication estimate of 2.2% was based on all articles published in the three marketing journals. Hubbard and Lindsay (2013) re-calculated the 2.8% estimate based on empirical studies only.

b This is an extension of Hubbard and Armstrong's (1994) survey of replications published in three marketing journals. The authors included two more journals but did not report the extent of support shown by the 25 (2.5%) replications published in these two journals.

c For 27 of the 78 replications, there was insufficient information for the authors to judge the degree of support for the original study. Accordingly the percentages are based on the remaining 51 articles.

Despite repeated calls for more replication research over the decades, these calls seem to have fallen on deaf ears. In the case of marketing, for example, Evanschitzky et al. (2007) replicated Hubbard and Armstrong's (1994) survey of replications published in leading marketing journals during the period from 1974–1989 by extending it to the period from 1990–2004. They found that the proportion of replications dropped by half from 2.4 percent to 1.2 percent over the two periods. This is a far-from-satisfactory situation if members of the business disciplines regard themselves as conducting scientific research. As discussed in the next two sections, there are some philosophy-based challenges to replication research in addition to more practical obstacles. This chapter classifies replications into six types, highlights its epistemic significance, and discusses its role in theory development.

Why are replications seldom published in journals?

To answer this question, it is natural to start with journal editors, who serve as gatekeepers. Neuliep and Crandall (1990) surveyed editors of social and behavioral science journals. Among the 79 valid responses, only four indicated that as editorial policy, replications were explicitly encouraged for submission. Most of the editors responded that a study that demonstrates some new effect was more important than a study that replicates or fails to replicate an already existing effect. Neuliep and Crandall (1990: 87) conclude that "editors discourage replications and do not allot many pages to them."

Pursuant to Neuliep and Crandall's (1990) study, Madden et al. (1995) solicited journal editors' perceptions of their disciplines' attitudes toward replication research. They conducted two studies. The sample of the first study consisted of journals randomly selected from the social and natural sciences while the sample of the second study was essentially a census of all marketing, advertising, and related journals. They found that editors in the second study deemed that replications lacked creativity, that novelty was prized more than "mere" replications, and that something new must be in a manuscript for it to be publishable. Interestingly, the same editors also "seem to express *guilt* arising from the belief that *real* science requires a discrete ritual of replication of published works" (p. 84). In short, one major reason for the undervaluing of replication is that originality and creativity are highly valued by social scientists, but a focus on replications seems to be antithetical to these virtues.

Recently Easley et al. (2013) replicated Madden et al.'s (1995) two studies. For the first study, a comparison of results between the original and replicated surveys indicates a shift in attitudes among social science editors toward replication such that they are getting closer to their natural science counterparts. For the second study, a comparison between the two surveys indicates more emphasis on the use and value of replication in academic research. Ironically the above-mentioned Evanschitzky et al.'s (2007) analysis of replications published in marketing journals shows a significant decrease over the years.

In addition to editors, authors are also responsible for the paucity of replications, which may be the result of few replications being submitted to journals. Lack of prestige is one plausible reason deterring replication research (Earp and Trafimow 2015). Few researchers would want to be seen by their peers and in particular promotion and tenure committees as merely repeating others' work, and worse still they may be "looked down on as bricklayers and not advancing knowledge" (Makel et al. 2012: 537). Accordingly researchers, especially junior ones, would hesitate to spend time conducting replications.

For both the lukewarm attitude of journal editors toward publishing replications and the hesitation of authors to conduct and submit replications, concerns about novelty lie at the heart of the problem. Davis's (1971) popular article titled "That's Interesting! Towards a Phenomenology of Sociology and a Sociology of Phenomenology," which many social science researchers probably read during their doctoral training, has contributed to developing a research culture that places an extraordinarily high value on novelty, as exemplified by this comment from the editors of the *Academy of Management Journal*: "Like many other top journals, *AMJ* also emphasizes novelty in topic choice" (Colquitt and George 2011: 432–435).[2] Pillutla and Thau's (2013) analysis of citation patterns of his article interestingly shows that the largest number of citations (41.7 percent) appeared in management journals. More importantly, among the citations that appeared in editorials, management journals shared an even higher proportion (46.2 percent). Daft and Lewin's (1990: 5–6) comment represents a typical view:

> Murray Davis observed that theories perceived as "interesting" disagreed with the taken-for-granted world of their audience. Interesting research reported contrarian findings, disconfirmed established theories and challenged accepted assumptions. By contrast theories considered dull tended to fit the established mindset. The lesson is that researchers should try to develop theories and gather data that disconfirm existing views.

Management editors and authors' obsession with "interesting" theories and "counterintuitive" findings is unfounded because such attributes have little epistemic significance. Einstein's theory of relativity replaced Newtonian mechanics not because it was more interesting, counterintuitive, or novel, but simply because it had greater explanatory power, period (see Boyd 1985 for a realist discussion of explanatory power). Another noteworthy finding of Pillutla and Thau's (2013) analysis is that none of the citations of Davis's (1971) article were in traditional natural science journals. In this respect there is something that social scientists – in particular management researchers – can learn from their natural science counterparts.

A deeper, philosophical reason for the paucity of replications may be related to how researchers understand the nature of science. The emphasis on replication is part of the received view of positivism, which proposes that the goal of all sciences is the search for invariable laws of the form "whenever *F*, *G*" where

F and *G* represent types of events – e.g., "whenever the temperature of water is 100 °C, it will boil." For positivists, it also means that *F* causes *G* because causality is *just* a constant conjunction of events. The importance of replication lies in verifying or falsifying general laws: we bring about event *F* and then observe whether *G* follows. If it does, the law in question is verified; otherwise it is falsified.

The aforementioned picture looks like a reasonable account of physics, but whether replicability of findings should be deemed essential in social science is controversial. Hermeneuticists are philosophers who contend that the principle of replicability should not be imposed on the social sciences because they consider social science observations to be unique in nature (Bleicher 1982; Dilthey 1976; Winch 1958). The principle of replicability would become a straitjacket that impedes rather than enhances the advance of social science. Therefore social scientists are torn between two forces. On one hand, they may be swayed by the ideal of positivist science and the desire to attain similar prestige as that held by natural scientists. On the other hand, they may be swayed by the insights of hermeneuticists and repelled by the epistemic imperialism of positivists. Moreover, their research tends to suggest that invariable laws are almost impossible to come by in social science (Rosenberg 2008). The positivist ideal seems impractical.

Moreover, an ambivalent attitude toward replication seems to exist. In practice, replication is undervalued. In recent decades, positivism, even as an account of the *natural* sciences, has been widely discredited (see Brown 1977; Feyerabend 1978; Hanson 1958; Kuhn 1962; Polanyi 1957). If the search for general laws in social science is deemed impractical, the significance of replication, which is previously associated with the verification or falsification of general laws, is naturally thrown into doubt. However, that the positivist emphasis on replication still has lingering influence is seen from the guilt of the editors expressed in Neuliep and Crandall's (1990) survey mentioned earlier. This situation is far from satisfactory. While many social scientists still feel that replication is important, this feeling is not reflected in actual practice and seems to lack theoretical justification once the positivist ideal is abandoned. If we overreact to the demise of positivism by denying any need for objective testing, say, by replication, there is the danger of landing on relativism, which denies the possibility of objective truth. This chapter propounds a way out of this predicament through a critical realist treatment, which can help researchers steer a course between the Scylla of crude empiricism and the Charybdis of relativism.

Is replication possible in the social sciences?

As discussed, the absence of general laws in social science casts doubt on the value of replication. A more fundamental issue concerns whether replication is in fact possible. There is a nagging suspicion that replication is neither possible in, nor relevant for, social science research. The objectors often emphasize that replication presupposes the performance of experiments or studies under exactly identical conditions. They go on to claim that while this is possible in the natural sciences where experiments are conducted under controlled conditions, it is not possible in the social sciences because no two social situations can be exactly identical (Machlup 1994; Mill 1936). Kaplan (1964) shrewdly points out that the question "whether experimentation in behavioral science is worthwhile, or even possible, is beclouded by the vagueness of the term 'experiment' " (p. 161). If replication is interpreted in a strict sense, replicating experiments is also impossible in the natural sciences because it is impossible to impose exactly identical conditions when repeating an experiment. For example, the color of an instrument, the size of a beaker, the time of performing the experiment, the relational properties of the event of experimentation (i.e., its properties vis-à-vis other events), and so on are rarely identical. So even in the "hardest" science (i.e., physics), complete closure is not possible. The best we can do is to control for the conditions that are plausibly regarded to be relevant. Moreover, physics is only *a* branch of natural science. Many natural sciences, for instance, astronomy, geology, evolutionary biology, are also not "hard" sciences if possibility of replication in a strict sense is taken as the standard. Thus a more modest concept of replication is called for.

Kaplan's (1964) concept of experimentation is helpful: "Experimentation . . . consists in making observations in circumstances so arranged or interpreted that we have justification for analyzing out the factors relevant to our particular inquiry" (p. 162). The dichotomy between natural and social sciences is an over-simplification. Achievability of replication is a matter of degree. Admittedly, replication is, in general, more achievable in the natural sciences (more so in physics and less so in evolutionary biology). However, if most social conditions which are likely to be relevant are controlled for, we can say that a replication has been performed in the social sciences. Of course, many social constructs are so fluid that it is quite impossible to control for most of the relevant conditions. Here the argument is only that, to a significant extent, replication in many cases is feasible, not that it is possible in every situation. It is implausible to deny that two studies can sometimes be repeated under similar conditions: while no two social situations are exactly identical, no two social conditions are entirely dissimilar either. The claim that replication is always impossible is as implausible as the claim that replication is always possible.

Kaplan (1964) has also discussed other objections. He deems superficial the argument that the behavioral scientist cannot experiment because his or her subject matter does not lend itself to manipulation. This argument "underestimates both the recalcitrance of physical materials and the docility of human subjects" (p. 163). In response to the argument from the perpetual variability of social phenomena, he replies:

> It is perfectly true that the facts studied in behavioral science are in a perpetual state of change, but so are the facts studied in any other science. What we need for knowledge is not permanence but persistence, not the

absolutely unchanging but rather changes sufficiently slow or limited for
patterns to be recognizable.

(pp. 166–167)

There is still another crucial challenge to face. Largely owing to the work of
Feyerabend (1978), Hanson (1958), and Kuhn (1962), researchers are aware
that observations are not entirely free from the influence of theories. Even
apparently simple observations may hide "natural interpretations" (Feyerabend
1978). This raises doubts about how far a replication is an objective assessment
of the original study since observations, which are supposed to be neutral arbiters
of different theories, are themselves "contaminated" by theories. Building on
Kuhn's (1962) argument, some researchers propose the thesis that different
theoretical frameworks are incommensurable (Doppelt 1978; McKinley and
Mone 1998), as discussed in chapter 4. This issue is complicated. This section
can only briefly describe two main reasons why theory-ladenness of observation
does not destroy the value of replication.

First, it is necessary to distinguish between low-level and higher-level observations. "While observation is never theory-free, it does not follow that many (or
most) observations are such that people from a wide variety of quite different
theoretical frames will be in total disagreement about the facts of the case"
(Phillips 1992: 69). In fact, there are many situations where different frameworks
are likely to arrive at similar observations. This is particularly so for low-level
observations, such as "the number of hierarchical levels inside an organization,"
"the nationalities of the partners of an international joint venture," or "the steps
involved in a work procedure." A low-level observation is more objective in the
sense that a researcher's observation transcends his or her personal or theoretical
biases. Admittedly, in the case of higher-level observations, such as the measurement of transaction cost or agency cost, there might well be disagreement
between different theoretical perspectives. It does not imply that there is no
hope for observers steeped in different theories to enter into fruitful discussion,
criticism, and evaluation. It is because, at a lower level of observation, there
might well be some overlap of terminology between the theories, and this would
serve as a basis for communication. Moreover, there is always the possibility
that the observers can share, at least temporarily, each other's frameworks (Phillips 1992).

Second, the theory which leads us to inquire about a measured construct
need not be the same theory used in its measurement (Pawson 1989). Following this line of argument, Hunt (1994) develops a realist theory of empirical
testing. He distinguishes between two types of theories – explanatory and
measurement. Explanatory theories are the theories being tested by a process
involving observations whereas measurement theories are the ones that are
assumed, explicitly or implicitly, in the process of testing the explanatory theories.
He also splits the term "observations" into "percepts" and "data." Percepts,
the immediate results of perceptual discrimination and recognition (e.g., the
checkmarks on a survey questionnaire), become data (e.g., the scores of a certain

construct) only after being interpreted with the aid of measurement theories. Provided that explanatory theories do not prejudge the test by biasing measurement theories, data can be used to test the explanatory theories. The idea is that while complete neutrality is impossible, pair-wise neutrality is often possible. For instance, all the five constructs in Bedeian and Armenakis's (1981) model of the effects of role conflict and ambiguity on job-related attitudes are measured by instruments developed from other studies. Walsh's (1988) measurement of belief structures in his replicated study discussed below was borrowed from personality research.

Finally, while observations are theory-laden, they are not immune from criticism. The theory implicit in observations can be drawn out and tested. If the findings of a study withstand criticism, they can be "accepted" tentatively (Andersson 1994). Hence theory-ladenness does not mean the end of rational discussion and critical scrutiny.

In summary, these claims are controversial, and many complicated methodological questions, if space allows, should be thoroughly dealt with. Yet the current discussion is sufficient to show that the case for the impossibility of replication in social science is not incontrovertible. In view of the fact that replications have been actually performed by social scientists, it is justified to adopt the attitude of "the backwoodsman who, asked whether he believed in baptism, replied, 'Believe in it? Man, I've seen it done!' " (Kaplan 1964: 166). Since people use the term "replication" to refer to studies of very different natures, the next section clarifies the concept and classifies replications into six types.

A classification of replications

Replication is in essence "a method of verification of a scientific finding by repeating a certain procedure" (Schmidt 2009: 92). As noted by Rosenthal (1990: 5), "replications are possible only in a relative sense." Strictly speaking, the *same* study can never be repeated by a different researcher, or even by the same researcher (Brogden 1951). Both subjects and researchers will change with the passage of time (Rosenthal and Rosnow 1984). The critical realist views replication as an attempt to confirm the structures and mechanisms identified in the original study under similar contingent conditions. In its simplest form, replication involves doing the same study again in order to retest the same hypotheses, or explore the same issues, in the same way. The term, however, has also been used to refer to cases where the repeated study is conducted on a different population of subjects, employs a different method of data collection, uses a different method of data analysis, and so on.

Bahr et al. (1983) observed, from an examination of articles in the *Social Science Citation Index*, that "replication" was a term employed to describe studies that differed widely in terms of time, place, subjects, and research methods. This somewhat chaotic situation has not been improved over the decades. Confusion may be created when "replication" is used to refer to a great variety of studies. For example, Eden (2002: 842) claims that "most *AMJ* articles include at least partial replication, albeit not *exact* and, of course, not labeled 'replication research.' " Although a replication often differs from its related original study in some respects, as shown by the following classification, the two should share a certain degree of resemblance in terms of hypotheses, data, measurement, analysis, and so on; otherwise the term "replication" loses its meaning. Based on this standard, few *AMJ* articles can be regarded as replications.[3]

As there are different ways of repeating a study, a classification of replications facilitates the communication of replication research. Brown and Coney (1976) distinguish between two types of replication: (1) replication and (2) replication with extension. This crude distinction is probably the most commonly adopted classification in the literature although other classifications have since been proposed (e.g., Fuess 1996; Hendrick 1990; Lindsay and Ehrenberg 1993; Mittelstaedt and Zorn 1984; Reid et al. 1981; Schmidt 2009). The classification presented below is more detailed and covers a wider scope than the existing ones.[4]

Assumptions

The classification here is based on two assumptions. First, a replication uses the same research method as the original study; for example, if the original study is a case study, the replication should also be a case study. Since different research methods reflect different core ontological assumptions, basic epistemological stances, and assumptions about human nature (Morgan and Smircich 1980), it would be more appropriate to consider empirical studies using different research methods to test the same theory as distinct studies rather than replications.[5] Second, a replication is assumed to be carried out at a time after the original study has been completed. This assumption rules out intrastudy replication that examines "the reproducibility of results within the same study executed by the same investigators" (Park et al. 2015: 119). In organizational behavior studies, for example, researchers sometimes conduct multiple experiments to examine whether the main effect holds in different contexts. An intrastudy replication is, in fact, a specific research method and not a replication in the usual sense of the term.

This classification does not distinguish a replication that is conducted by the same researchers who completed the original study from one that is not. A replication conducted by researchers who are not associated with the original study is normally regarded as more objective (Monroe 1992; Rosenthal 1990) because the biases of previous researchers are avoided. In fact, replication is often seen as a means of checking these biases (Bryman 1988; Kidder and Judd 1986).

Types of replication

Replications are classified into six types along two dimensions (Table 6.2). The first dimension concerns whether a replication employs the same method of measuring constructs and analyzing data. Sometimes a replication may vary the

Table 6.2 Types of replication

	Same measurement and analysis	*Different measurement and/or analysis*
Same data set	Checking of analysis	Reanalysis of data
Same population	Exact replication	Conceptual extension
Different population	Empirical generalization	Generalization and extension

way of measuring certain constructs and/or use a different statistical method to analyze the findings. The second dimension is about the source of data. Instead of repeating the original study from beginning to end, a replication may be just conducted on the data generated or employed by the study. An alternative is to collect data again either from the same population or a population different from the one used by the original study. For simplicity's sake, the term "population" here also refers to the context in which a theory is tested. A replication may be conducted in a context different from that of the original study but within the same population of subjects. Suppose an empirical study and its replication test a certain organizational learning theory in the marketing and production domains, respectively, of the same firm. In this case, the two studies are treated as involving two different populations. A combination of the two dimensions produces six different types of replication as described in the following discussion.

Checking of analysis

In spite of the rigorous review process adopted by many academic journals, errors of data analysis are not rare in published articles. In this type of replication, researchers employ exactly the same procedures as a past study to analyze the latter's data set; it is popular in such disciplines as economics and finance, in which research is mainly based on publicly available databases. Its purpose is to check whether the investigators of the original study committed any errors in the process of analyzing the data. For instance, in July 1982, the *Journal of Money, Credit and Banking* adopted an editorial policy of requesting from its authors the programs and data used in their articles and making these materials available to other researchers upon request. Dewald et al. (1986) attempted to replicate the published results for a number of the submitted data sets. Their results suggest that "inadvertent errors in published empirical articles are a commonplace rather than a rare occurrence" (pp. 587–588).

A more recent example is Bakker and Wicherts's (2011) examination of the misreporting of statistical results in psychology journals. Based on a sample of 281 empirical articles published in 2008, they found that about 18 percent of statistical results were incorrectly reported and about 15 percent of the articles "contained at least one statistical conclusion that proved, upon recalculation, to be incorrect; that is, recalculation rendered the previously significant result insignificant, or vice versa" (p. 666). Error rates were generally lower in high-impact than low-impact journals. Since the former are likely to have more stringent reviews of manuscripts, this finding suggests a crucial gatekeeping function of the review process. An alternative explanation is that authors who submit their manuscripts to high-impact journals prepare the manuscripts more carefully than those submitting their works to low-impact journals. Bakker and Wicherts (2011) provide no information for assessing the relative plausibility of these two explanations because it is outside the scope of their research.

Reanalysis of data

Unlike the checking of analysis, this type of replication uses different procedures to reanalyze the data of a previous study. The aim is to assess whether and how the results are affected by the specific ways of measuring constructs or the particular techniques of analyzing data. Quite often the replication uses more powerful statistical techniques that were not available when the original study was conducted. An excellent example is provided by Franke and Kaul (1978), who reanalyzed the data of the seminal Hawthorne experiments conducted in the 1920s and 1930s at Western Electrics's Hawthorne plant. They used time-series econometric techniques, which were developed in the years after the experiments had been completed. Their results do not support the contention of the original researchers of the experiments that the so-called "Hawthorne effect" – a subject's behavior during the course of an experiment being altered by the subject's awareness of participating in the experiment – existed. Using a data set that is more comprehensive than Franke and Kaul's (1978), Jones's (1992) analysis also leads to the conclusion that there is essentially no evidence of the Hawthorne effect, which occupies a central role in the methodology of experimental design.

A prerequisite for conducting the two replication types – checking of analysis and reanalysis of data – is the availability of the original studies' data sets.[6] As mentioned, since 1982 the *Journal of Money, Credit and Banking* has adopted an editorial policy of making the programs and data used in its published articles publicly available. Other journals follow suit. For example, official journals of the American Economics Association that publish empirical research have a similar policy regarding the availability of data and materials. The American Sociological Association also has a policy that requires researchers to make their data available after publishing their works.[7] Some sociologists are not satisfied. For example, Freese (2007) advocates for a more transparent policy in which "authors use independent online archives to deposit the maximum possible information for replicating published results at the time of publication and are explicit about the conditions of availability for any necessary materials that are not provided" (p. 153). The management discipline seems to have lagged behind in this respect.

Exact replication

This is the case where a previous study is repeated on the same population by using basically the same procedures. The objective is to keep the contingent conditions as similar as possible to those of the previous study. In order to avoid the complications associated with the test-retest effect, a different sample of subjects is usually used. The main purpose is to assess whether the findings of a past study are reproducible or just "one-off" results. As such, this type of replication is "particularly suitable early in a program of research to establish quickly and relatively easily and cheaply whether a new result can be repeated at all" (Lindsay and Ehrenberg 1993: 221). If the findings are successfully replicated, the replication lends support to the internal validity of the study as well as the validity and reliability of the measuring instrument, if any, used in the study. On the other hand, a failed replication casts doubt on the robustness of the original findings and suggests that further research on the topic probably will not yield fruitful outcomes.

Exact replications are seldom published partly because of the belief that conducting such replications "largely is a waste of time" (Hubbard 2016: 112). Even among those who appreciate the value of exact replications, they are often regarded as a lesser form of replication: "useful as they may be, exact replications do not represent replication at its best" (Eden 2002: 842). Since different types of replication serve different functions, it makes little sense to claim that one type is better or worse than others. A discipline needs all of them to ensure its healthy development.

A caveat is that exact replication may not be feasible for some studies. In social psychology, Stroebe and Strack (2014: 62) argue that "faithfully replicating the original conditions of an experiment does not guarantee that one addresses the same theoretical construct as in the original study." For example, Dijksterhuis and van Knippenberg's (1998) study found that participants primed with a category of persons who are considered highly intelligent (e.g., professor) performed better on a trivial task than participants primed with a less intelligent category (e.g., hooligan). Even if the words "professor" and "hooligan" are accurately translated, they may not invoke similar perceptions of intelligence in other cultures. The failure of an exact replication in this case should not cast doubt on the original study because the priming words fail to operationalize the intended theoretical construct. That said, such situations are not common in quantitative management research, and even in social psychology, not every study has this problem.

Hinings and Lee's (1971) study is among the few examples of exact replication in management. They replicated the Aston study of organization structure on a smaller sample of nine manufacturing organizations by using the same measuring instruments and interviewing procedures. Both studies drew their samples from companies operating in the English Midlands. Overall, Hinings and Lee's findings show that the Aston results are reproducible. A caveat is that Hinings was a key researcher of the Aston program of organizational analysis and was heavily involved in the early empirical work that constituted the Aston study (see Greenwood and Devine 1997). As such, the replication might have been affected by the methodological biases, if any, of the program.

Conceptual extension

A conceptual extension involves employing procedures different from those of the original study and drawing a sample from the same population. The differences may lie in the way of measuring constructs, structuring the relationships among constructs, analyzing data, and so forth. In spite of these differences, the replication is based on the same theory as the original study. The findings may lead to a revision of the theory.

Walsh (1988) replicated Dearborn and Simon's (1958) study of selective perception in the identification of company problems. Walsh's experimental procedures were rather different from those of the original study. The results do not support Dearborn and Simon's argument that functional experience selectively channels the perceptions of managers when they solve complex problems.

This inconsistency of results prompted Beyer et al. (1997) to carry out another conceptual extension. They first examined the experimental procedures of both studies and suspected that some crucial procedural differences might account for the inconsistent results. Dearborn and Simon's respondents were asked to identify the most important problem facing the company in a case whereas Walsh's respondents were asked to identify as many problems as they considered important. Since the first method restricted respondents to a more limited observational goal (Dweck and Leggett 1988) than the second, it is likely that managers exhibited more selective perceptions in the first study than in the second. Moreover, Beyer et al. believed that when Walsh asked respondents about their belief structures before they analyzed the case, the resulting priming effects (Fiske 1993) became a confounding factor, which was absent in the original study by Dearborn and Simon, who did not measure belief structures. Based on these two considerations, Beyer et al. developed and tested a more comprehensive model than the ones employed by the two previous studies. The model postulates different mechanisms of how functional experience affects selective perception.

This example clearly illustrates how one study builds on another. Reliable cumulative knowledge is generated and leads to a refinement of the structures and mechanisms concerned. The fact that the two subsequent studies are replications of the first provides the continuity that facilitates this theory development process. The example also shows the advantage of having more than one replication conducted on the same original study. If a single replication fails to support the results of the original study, we can never be sure that the failure to replicate is due to the non-replicability of the original study or to the inexactness of the replication procedure. Rosenthal (1990) thus recommends that at least two replications of the original study should be carried out. Preferably one of these replications is as similar as possible to the original study and the other at least moderately dissimilar.

Empirical generalization

By repeating a past study on a different population, an empirical generalization tests how far the results of the study are generalizable to another population (see chapter 5 for a discussion of the different types of generalization). The research procedures of the original study are closely followed. Whether a replication should be regarded as an exact replication or an empirical generalization depends on how the populations of the original study and the replication are specified. The importance of this type of replication is growing because the applicability of management theories developed in one culture to other cultures has been questioned (Hofstede 1993; Rosenzweig 1994; Tsui et al. 2007).

Some years ago, I replicated Bettman and Weitz's (1983) study of self-serving attributions (see Tsang 2002). Their study tested the theory of self-serving bias in attribution of causality by conducting a content analysis of the Letters to Shareholders in 181 U.S. corporate annual reports published in 1972 and 1974. I closely followed their coding method and analyzed the Letters to Shareholders in 208 Singapore corporate annual reports published in 1985 and 1994. I also used exactly the same statistical analysis. My objective was to investigate whether their findings were generalizable to companies in Singapore, a predominantly Chinese society. Note that Bettman and Weitz (1983) is one of the three important studies of causal reasoning in corporate annual reports published in *Administrative Science Quarterly*, a top management journal, at around the same time. The other two are Salancik and Meindl (1984) and Staw et al. (1983). Despite the significance of these studies, mine is probably the first ever replication conducted on any of them.

The results of my study identified the general self-serving pattern of attributions found in Bettman and Weitz's study. Yet a major difference was that the data of their study did not unequivocally support either the motivational or informational explanation for the existence of self-serving attributions whereas the data of my replication clearly supported the latter explanation. My finding was consistent with the evidence emerging from the cross-cultural psychological research about East Asians' greater sensitivity to situational influences when they engage in causal attributions (Choi et al. 1999). The replication contributes empirically to the theory of self-serving bias by showing that cross-cultural differences in sensitivity to situational influences could be a significant moderating factor and that caution should be taken when generalizing findings in this domain cross-culturally.

More recently, my colleague and I replicated Barkema and Vermeulen's (1998) study of international expansion by Dutch firms based on a comparable data set of Singapore firms (see Tsang and Yamanoi 2016). We found that the authors misinterpreted their regression coefficients for hypothesis testing and that only two of their four hypotheses were in fact tested. For these two hypotheses, one was supported in neither their study nor ours, while the other was supported in their study but not ours. For the remaining two hypotheses (that were not tested in their study), we found partial support for one of them. To summarize, Barkema and Vermeulen (1998) claimed that all four hypotheses were supported whereas only one was partially supported in our replication.

Our experience of conducting this replication indicates that when a study is scrutinized for the purpose of replication, there will be a much higher chance of discovering errors made by the authors of the study than when the study is read casually for the purpose of literature review. While this outcome sounds commonsensical, it highlights the error discovery function of replication that has been neglected by management researchers. A side effect of this function is that if replication is regularly conducted in our field, researchers will be under greater pressure to ensure that their data analysis and interpretation of results are error free. This in turn will improve the quality of the literature on which future research is based.

Generalization and extension

This is a popular type of replication in management. Compared with the original study, a generalization and extension employs different research procedures and draws a sample from a different population of subjects. As argued by Rosenthal (1990), the more imprecise the replication, the greater the benefit to the external validity of the original finding if its results support the finding. On the other hand, if the results fail to support the original finding, it is difficult to tell whether that lack of support stems from the instability of the finding or from the imprecision of the replication. By contrast, in the case of exact replication, a failure to reproduce the original finding indicates that the former is a more likely explanation.

Klenke-Hamel and Mathieu (1990) repeated Bedeian and Armenakis's (1981) study of the effects of role conflict and role ambiguity on tension, job satisfaction, and propensity to leave. Using different construct labeling and measurement, they collected data from four different populations – blue-collar, staff, engineering, and university faculty employees – whereas Bedeian and Armenakis only used a sample of nurses. Their results indicated that the Bedeian and Armenakis model yielded a reasonable fit for staff employees only, but not for the other three samples.

Some of the constructs were measured in such a different way in Klenke-Hamel and Mathieu's study that Bedeian et al. (1992) seriously question whether the study is a valid replication or "a test of a different conceptual model" (p. 1096). For instance, the construct "tension" was measured in Bedeian and Armenakis's study by a nine-item scale developed by Lyons (1971) for tapping job-related tension. In contrast, Klenke-Hamel and Mathieu used a 20-item version of Goldberg's (1971) General Mental Health Questionnaire, which was developed specifically to detect psychiatric disturbance. In an attempt to extend the Bedeian and Armenakis model, Klenke-Hamel and Mathieu introduced employee personal characteristics (gender, education, age, and marital status) into the model and found that these variables improved the fit, depending on the specific sample. However, Bedeian et al. (1992) raise the concern about possible interactions of such variables with sampling because the composition of the samples with respect to personal characteristics could influence results in unknown ways. Owing to these as well as other problems, they challenge that the replication "contains concerns which may render its findings suspect" (p. 1093).

In line with management journal editors' preference for novelty (see Colquitt and George 2011), generalization and extension is likely to be their most favorable type of replication because, among the six types, generalization and extension includes the largest amount of variation. In an *AMJ* editorial, Eden (2002: 842) maintains that "the *less* similar a replication is to an original study, the greater its potential contribution." Klenke-Hamel and Mathieu's (1990) replication indicates that the sequel "and the more difficult it will be to identify the reasons for a failure to replicate" should be added to his statement.

The epistemic significance of replication

Existing articles about replication (e.g., Brown and Gaulden 1982; Hubbard et al. 1998; Lindsay and Ehrenberg 1993; Schmidt 2009) usually focus on the issues of reliability, internal validity, and external validity (or generalizability) only. Instead of summarizing these discussions, this section elaborates on the epistemic significance of predictive power shown by the first replication. Although replications do not lead to conclusive verification or falsification of theories, they do help to support or discredit theories.

Accommodation and prediction

Suppose a management researcher develops a theory from the result of a single empirical study. Later, another researcher conducts an exact replication and tests the hypotheses generated from the theory. All the hypotheses are well supported; that is, the replication arrives at findings very similar to those of the first study under very similar contingent conditions. What purposes does this replication serve? Although Lindsay and Ehrenberg (1993) state that the first replication is "the most dramatic" (p. 220), they focus on the generalization function of the replication, which is lacking in this particular case. The traditional view rarely goes beyond the comment that the result of this exact replication enhances confidence in the internal validity of the first study as well as the validity and reliability of the measurement instrument, if any, used in the study. Nevertheless, the first replication of a study on which a theory is based has other significant epistemic value.

In this hypothetical case, the first researcher constructs the theory to fit the available evidence obtained from the empirical study. Somewhat similar to the case of HARKing (Hypothesizing After the Results are Known) discussed in chapter 4, this is an example of accommodation. When the study is repeated by the second researcher, hypotheses derived from the theory are put to the test. Since the hypotheses are well supported, the theory is successful in making a prediction. The argument is that "a theory deserves more inductive credit when data are predicted than when they are accommodated" (Lipton 1991: 133). This argument is intuitively appealing. When Dmitri Mendeleev constructed a theory of the periodic table to account for all the 60 known elements, the scientific community was only mildly impressed. In contrast, when he went on to use his theory to predict the existence of two unknown elements that were later independently discovered, the Royal Society awarded him a Davy Medal (Maher 1988).

Why does prediction have a special value over accommodation? Lipton (1991) puts forward the fudging explanation mentioned in chapter 4. When data need to be accommodated, there is a motive to fudge a theory to make the accommodation. That is, by looking at the data, the researcher knows the result that the theory has to generate, and he or she may do whatever it takes to arrive at it. With special clauses to deal with particular accommodations, the theory may become more like an arbitrary conjunction than a unified explanation. Another issue is that a theory that is compatible with most of the background beliefs of a discipline is more credible than a theory that contradicts many of them. The need for accommodation may force the researcher to construct a theory that fits poorly into the background. In short, the act of fudging may weaken a theory. On the other hand, in the case of prediction, the theory comes into existence before the data and fudging is out of the question. "So there is reason to suspect accommodations that does not apply to predictions, and this makes predictions better" (Lipton 1991: 140).

Miller (1987) similarly argues that "when a hypothesis is developed to explain certain data, this can be grounds for a charge that its explanatory fit is due to the ingenuity of the developer in tailoring hypotheses to data, as against the basic truth of the hypothesis" (p. 308). However, if the hypothesis is subsequently supported in replications, this charge is not relevant because the "ingenuity in the investigators implies nothing about the presence of the alleged regularity in the world" (pp. 193–194).

An exact replication producing confirmatory results is a prediction inferred from the hypothesized validity of the original study. Therefore, a confirmatory replication obtained under suitable conditions should provide a theory with a quantum leap in credibility. The first replication of an empirical study on which a theory is based seems to play a far more significant role than what is usually recognized.

Verification and falsification of theories

The critical realist does not claim that replication can provide conclusive verification or falsification of theories (Bhaskar 1998; Keat and Urry 1982). The main objective of a replication is to examine the structures and mechanisms identified in the original study under similar contingent conditions. Since management studies are rarely conducted under conditions of closure, it is difficult to ascertain the nature of contingencies in which structures and mechanisms are located. Thus, the failure of a replication to confirm previous findings does not mean a conclusive falsification (see Popper 1959).

For the sake of discussion, let us assume that both the original study and its replication are error free in terms of research procedure and data analysis. One explanation for the failure of replication is that the structures and mechanisms as postulated in the theory are inaccurate; in this case, we have a true falsification. However, another possible explanation is that, in the replicated study, there is a different set of contingencies which either modifies the postulated mechanisms or invokes previously inactive countervailing mechanisms. This results in a different set of events being observed. For instance, Wiersema and Bird (1993) tested demography theory in Japanese firms. They examined the effects of the composition of top management teams on team turnover and found that demographic effects were significant correlates of team turnover. In addition, these findings were substantially stronger than those of comparable studies previously conducted in the U.S. (e.g., Jackson et al. 1991; Wagner et al. 1984; Wiersema and Bantel 1993). Wiersema and Bird (1993) argue that the very different ethnological context in Japan modifies the mechanisms that account for top management turnover in the U.S. context.

Although replication cannot yield certain conclusions, it does not follow that it is not desirable to conduct replicated studies or that replication has no epistemic significance. When a replication successfully confirms the findings of the original study, it provides *at least some* support for the theory concerned. If the two studies are far apart in time, the replication supports the temporal validity of the theory as well. When numerous replications in diverse circumstances are repeatedly successful, it is highly likely that the theory has hit upon some real structure or mechanism in the social world, barring an alternative nonrealist explanation of this success. For example, Hofstede's (1980) study of cultural dimensions using a sample of IBM employees has been replicated many times on samples of various characteristics. The differences predicted by Hofstede's dimensions are largely confirmed (Søndergaard 1994), which suggests that these dimensions reflect some real national cultural differences.

When the findings that support a theory repeatedly fail to be replicated, it is more reasonable to regard them as the result of chance factors or idiosyncrasies of the context rather than the manifestation of real structures or mechanisms. The difficulty of interpreting replication results calls for a more cautious approach. The significance of a replication should be considered within the context of related studies and relevant factors, rather than in isolation.

Among the four types of replication shown in the lower part of Table 6.2, it is advisable to start testing a theory by means of an exact replication where the contingent conditions are closest to those of the original study. If different findings are obtained, it is easier to locate the exact reasons for the difference (see Feynman 1985). Once the contingent conditions are confirmed to be very similar, the difference in findings probably lies in the way structures and mechanisms are postulated in the theory. On the other hand, if a generalization and extension study is employed instead, the differences in research procedures, as well as the populations from which samples were drawn, introduce so many new variables in the repeated study that it may be difficult to identify the reasons for the disconfirmation (Lindsay and Ehrenberg 1993). Klenke-Hamel and Mathieu's (1990) replication of the Bedeian and Armenakis (1981) study is a good example. A generalization and extension study seems more appropriate after the empirical foundation of a theory has been well established through exact replication, conceptual extension, and empirical generalization. This order of conducting replications enables researchers to better account for disconfirmation of previous findings, if any. Unfortunately, many replications in management are of the generalization and extension type, whereas exact replications are rare.

The complementarity of quantitative research and qualitative research discussed in chapter 4 can also be seen in relation to replication. Quantitative research is often preoccupied with establishing law-like relationships between organizational variables, or between organizational and environmental variables, through investigating large numbers of organizations (Bryman 1988). Accordingly this approach neglects the wider contexts within which these relationships are observed; contextual characteristics are useful for identifying the relevant contingent conditions under which these relationships occur. If the findings of a replication contradict those of the original study, it may be difficult to assess how far this is due to the different contingencies present in the two studies. For example, one factor that accounts for the difficulty in comparing the results of Bedeian and Armenakis (1981) and Klenke-Hamel and Mathieu (1990) is that both studies used questionnaire surveys to collect data from individual subjects and collected little information about the characteristics of the organizations in which the subjects worked. These contextual characteristics might affect how the model manifested itself.

While qualitative research is often criticized by quantitative researchers for "the difficulty of carrying out replications of its findings" (Bryman 1988: 38), interestingly it helps researchers interpret the findings of a repeated study. By trying to understand events in their context, qualitative researchers throw light on the specific contingent conditions under which the postulated mechanisms operate (Tsoukas 1989). This, in turn, helps compare the findings of a replication with those of the original study. For example, Martinko and Gardner (1990) replicated Mintzberg's (1973) influential study of managerial work. The former used school principals as subjects whereas the latter used CEOs. Both studies employed structured observation to collect data. In spite of the similarities between the findings, there are also key differences which stem from the contextual characteristics of a school principal's job.

Limitations of replication and the value of innovative studies

Despite their functions, replications do have limitations: replicability does not mean conclusive verification; failure to be replicable does not mean conclusive falsification. Hence, there is the danger of relying too much on replicable findings since they may turn out to be invalid. Furthermore, replication cannot replace innovative studies because, by itself, it usually provides neither new concepts for analysis nor original approaches for attacking problems. A more detailed comparison of the two is offered below.

Innovative studies contribute to theory development by introducing new concepts or extending the explanatory domain of a theory to interesting and important phenomena. Some well-known theories and perspectives in management were in fact generated from such path-breaking innovative studies as Hofstede (1980), Lawrence and Lorsch (1967), Mintzberg (1973) and Pfeffer (1972), the Aston study, and the Hawthorne experiments. These benefits of innovative studies are summarized and compared with those of replications in Table 6.3.

The table also indicates the shortcomings of the two types of study. The evidence provided by a single innovative study can be rather flimsy and is subject to the idiosyncrasies of the context in which the study was conducted. To strengthen the evidence, replications are needed, for the best empirical test of the reliability of evidence is provided by replication (Sidman 1960). Carrying out a replication, however, runs the risk of repeating studies that are so poorly designed and/or executed that they were not worth doing in the first place. The researcher should therefore carefully examine how far significant theoretical contributions have been made by an original study and consider whether it is worth replicating. Useful advice in this matter can be found in Sutton and Staw

Table 6.3 Innovative studies versus replications

	Innovative study	Replication
Merits	• Bringing in new concepts	• Detecting errors, if any, committed by researchers of the original study
	• Extending a theory's explanatory domain	• Determining the reliability and validity of the original study
	• Inspiring the development of new theories	• Increasing the credibility of a theory through successful prediction
		• Throwing light on the structures, mechanisms, and contingent conditions investigated by the original study
Limitations	• Possibility of relying on flimsy empirical evidence	• Possibility of repeating poor studies
		• Little likelihood of generating new theories
		• Perceived to be lacking imagination and creativity

(1995) and Whetten (1989). An additional means of evaluating the impact of an original study is the number of citations attracted by that study (see Baird and Oppenheim 1994; Colquitt and Zapata-Phelan 2007; Tahai and Meyer 1999). In addition to impactful studies, researchers may also consider studies that can rule out competing theories (Lamal 1990).

As the main objective of replication is to confirm previous findings, its results rarely lead to new theories or perspectives. Accordingly replication is often perceived to be lacking imagination and creativity (Madden et al. 1995). Yet two types of replication – conceptual extension along with generalization and extension – do frequently introduce new concepts or conceptual relations that help to develop theories. For example, in repeating Monteverde and Teece's (1982a) study of vertical integration, Walker and Weber (1984) brought the comparative production costs between buyer and supplier into their analysis. They found these costs to be the strongest predictor of make-or-buy decisions.

Moreover, when a replication produces inconsistent findings and the researcher tries to provide an explanation or adjust the model accordingly, such a task demands not only analytical power but also some creativity. For example, the failure of Walsh's (1988) replication to confirm Dearborn and Simon's (1958) evidence of selective perception in problem identification prompted Beyer et al. (1997) to develop and test a model for explaining the discrepancy. In addition, investigators of the original study may defend their findings and engage in constructive dialogue with the replicators (e.g., Geringer 1998; Glaister and Buckley 1998a, b). This activity helps clarify not only theoretical but also methodological issues.

An innovative study obviously offers more intellectual excitement than a seemingly mundane replication. Yet the latter has an indispensable role in theory development. Replication should not be emphasized to the detriment of other methods and approaches, but it should be given a more prominent place in researchers' methodological toolbox. One more reason for this proposal is that emphasis on replication will contribute to establishing a long-term pattern of knowledge accumulation built on a more solid foundation.

Replication and knowledge accumulation

The growth of knowledge in a subject is a cumulative process in which new insights are added to the existing stock of knowledge. The field of management research is said to be fragmented (Engwall 1995; Whitley 1984; Zald 1996) and, as pointed out in chapter 4, dotted with an amazing variety of theories (Koontz 1961, 1980). Unlike the natural sciences, management lacks a coherent body of knowledge. While the fragmented state is likely to continue (see Cannella and Paetzold 1994; Zald 1996), the present state of knowledge accumulation can be improved through encouraging more replications. A multifocal pattern of knowledge accumulation is proposed below and compared with the scattered pattern commonly found in management. Each pattern is illustrated by the empirical studies of a topic during its early stage of development.

Scattered pattern

The main characteristics of the scattered pattern are that empirical studies are rarely replicated and can differ greatly in terms of research method, measurement instrument, definition of key constructs, population of subjects, nature of phenomenon investigated, and so forth. The empirical body of knowledge formed under this pattern consists of scattered bits and pieces.

The scattered pattern is present in many streams of management research. An excellent example is organizational learning – an area with a proliferation of research studies since the early 1990s (Crossan and Guatto 1996). Table 6.4 shows some of the major empirical studies. It is obvious that a great variety of research methods have been employed; studies have been conducted in various national cultures and types of organization. Moreover, researchers define organizational learning differently (Tsang 1997) and use different ways to measure key constructs. Most of the studies do not build upon previous ones, and their findings are isolated and fragile. The lack of replication leads to a fragmented and dispersed literature with no sense of continuity. It is not clear whether the findings of these studies are reflections of real structures and mechanisms or, in the words of Popper (1959), mere isolated coincidences. These uncorroborated studies, even though routinely accompanied by statistically significant results, provide a weak foundation for theory development (Glaister and Buckley 1998b). On the positive side, we do find some innovative studies among them. For example, Brown and Duguid (1991) bring in a fresh perspective for studying organizational learning by introducing the concept of communities-of-practices. Hamel (1991) provides one of the first attempts to analyze inter-partner collaborative dynamics from an organizational learning point of view.

Without proper replications, sweeping generalization of research results should be avoided. In the case of organizational learning, Argyris (1990), who bases his theory on his years of research and consulting experience with Western companies, claims that the organizational defensive pattern identified by him "is generic to *all* human organizations, including private and public organizations, trade unions, voluntary organizations, universities and schools, as well as families" (p. 63, emphasis added). Nevertheless, he has not supported this law-like statement with empirical evidence. Even if we assume that the organizational defensive pattern is valid in other cultures, the form of expression may vary because of different contingent conditions. For example, the Chinese are very concerned with face (Ho 1976; Hu 1944), and face dynamics has pervasive and significant influences on organizational behavior in Asia (Kim and Nam 1998; Leung et al. 2014). Given that a main purpose of using organizational defenses is face-saving, we would expect that organizational defensive routines are more entrenched and complicated in Chinese than in Western organizations. How

Table 6.4 Scattered pattern of knowledge accumulation

Study	Research method	Organization	Country	Nature of phenomenon investigated
Brown and Duguid (1991)	Ethnography	Service technicians in a large corporation	U.S.	Learning and innovation generated in the context of communities-of-practice in which people work
Hamel (1991)	Case study	International strategic alliances	Europe and Japan	Dynamics of inter-partner learning in the context of international strategic alliances
Carley (1992)	Simulation	N/A	N/A	Impacts of personnel turnover on an organization's ability to learn and on its ultimate performance
Cook and Yanow (1993)	Ethnography	Flute-making workshops	U.S.	Learning through activities involving organizational cultural artifacts
Fiol (1994)	Analysis of a detailed log of communications	A new-venture team in a financial institution	U.S.	Collective processes of negotiating toward shared understanding of new and diverse information
Chang (1995)	Analysis of secondary data	Electronic manufacturing firms	Japan and U.S.	Learning behavior exhibited by the sequential entry processes of Japanese electronic manufacturers into the U.S.
Inkpen and Crossan (1995)	Case study	International joint ventures	Japan, Canada and U.S.	Integration of experiences learned in joint ventures at the North American parent firm level
Simonin (1997)	Questionnaire survey	Strategic alliances	U.S.	How firms learn from their strategic alliances
Kim (1998)	Longitudinal case study	Hyundai Motor	Korea	Effects of proactively constructed internal crises on organizational learning
Lane and Lubatkin (1998)	Expert evaluation and questionnaire survey	Pharmaceutical-biotechnology R&D alliances	Various	Role played by partner characteristics in the success of interorganizational learning

Note: Illustrated by studies of organizational learning.

far our expectation is correct can only be confirmed by repeating Argyris's study in Chinese organizations.

Some researchers may think that the problem can be dealt with by meta-analysis. Since meta-analysis attempts to establish the reproducibility of results by comparing and synthesizing existing findings from various studies, a clear overview of a research topic, such as organizational learning, can still be gained despite that the studies are scattered. While this argument has some merit, it has at least three limitations. First, meta-analysis cannot be conducted on the results of qualitative research such as case studies. Second, meta-analysis integrates research results with respect to a specific phenomenon (Easley et al. 2000). For example, Zhao et al.'s (2004) meta-analysis is concerned with empirical findings with respect to transaction-cost-related factors in affecting the ownership-based entry mode choice. When studies investigate a variety of phenomena, such as those listed in Table 6.4, there may not be a sufficient number of studies for any phenomenon to warrant a meta-analysis. Finally, according to the "garbage in, garbage out" principle, the quality of a meta-analysis depends a great deal on the quality of the studies that it covers, and replication is one essential way to check the quality of a study.

Instead of treating meta-analysis as a substitute for replication, it makes more sense to envision a symbiotic relationship between the two (Allen and Preiss 1993). On the one hand, Schmidt (1992) argues that meta-analysis can prevent the misallocation of scarce research resources by indicating when further research on certain phenomena is no longer worthwhile. Meta-analysis can also show which kind of further research is most fruitful (Eden 2002). On the other hand, the supply of well-designed and competently conducted studies, including replications, as data is required for conducting meta-analysis.

Multifocal pattern

During the initial stage of theory development, empirical studies are concentrated in only a few focal areas with regular replications. When existing focal areas have been well researched, studies are gradually carried out in new focal areas in order to further test a theory's explanatory power. The accumulation of replications in a focal area refines the structures and mechanisms postulated by a theory and provides a more in-depth understanding of the contingent conditions related to that area.

An example is offered by the investigation of vertical integration in transaction cost economics (TCE). Table 6.5 shows some major empirical studies in the focal area of vertical integration with respect to manufacturing industries. Some of the studies are in the form of generalization and extension. For instance, Hennart's (1988) study builds on Stuckey's (1983) and extends it to the tin industry. The studies together offer stronger empirical evidence for the transactional determinants of vertical integration than either does alone.

A prominent feature, revealed in Table 6.5, is the large proportion of studies conducted on the American automobile industry. It is clear that later studies

Table 6.5 Multifocal pattern of knowledge accumulation

Study	Research method	Organization	Country	Nature of phenomenon investigated
Monteverde and Teece (1982a)	Case study	Ford and General Motors	U.S.	Effects of transaction cost considerations surrounding the development and deepening of human skills on vertical integration
Monteverde and Teece (1982b)	Case study	An automobile supplier	U.S.	Relationship between quasi-vertical integration and appropriable quasi rents generated by transaction-specific physical assets
Stuckey (1983)	Analysis of secondary data	Aluminum producers	Various	Division of activities among firms in the international aluminum industry
Masten (1984)	Case study	An aerospace system	U.S.	Factors affecting the internal and external procurement of supplies in the aerospace industry
Walker and Weber (1984)	Case study	A large automobile manufacturer	U.S.	Influence of transaction costs on decisions to make or buy components
Walker and Weber (1987)	Case study	A large automobile manufacturer	U.S.	Elaborating on the findings of Walker and Weber (1984) with new data
Hennart (1988)	Analysis of secondary data	Aluminum and tin producers	Various	Whether Williamson's theory of vertical integration holds for the upstream stages of the aluminum and tin industries
Klein (1988)	Historiography	General Motors and Fisher Body	U.S.	Factors leading to the acquisition of Fisher Body by General Motors
Langlois and Robertson (1989)	Historiography	Automobile manufacturers	U.S.	Determinants of the levels of vertical integration during the early decades of the American automobile industry
Masten et al. (1989)	Case study	Chrysler, Ford and General Motors	U.S.	Relative influence of transaction-specific investments in physical versus human capital on the pattern of vertical integration

Note: Illustrated by studies of vertical integration in manufacturing industries as one focus.

build upon earlier ones, resulting in an accumulation of coherent knowledge. A good example is offered by the Monteverde and Teece (1982a, b) studies discussed in chapter 3. In one of the first systematic efforts to test a contractual interpretation of vertical integration, Monteverde and Teece (1982a) examined the effects of asset specificity, defined here as specialized human skills or "applications engineering effort," on the decision to produce auto components in-house or to buy them from outside suppliers. They found that applications engineering effort was a statistically significant determinant of vertical integration. In another study, Monteverde and Teece (1982b) investigated the phenomenon of quasi-vertical integration: "the ownership by a downstream firm of the specialized tools, dies, jigs, and patterns used in the fabrication of components for larger systems" (p. 321). They found a statistically significant positive relationship between the appropriable quasi rents associated with a given component and the occurrence of quasi integration.

These two studies suggest that human, rather than physical, assets play a more influential role in decisions to vertically integrate; quasi integration may be sufficient where transaction-specific investments reside in physical capital. To test this difference in the roles of specific physical and human assets, Masten et al. (1989) replicated Monteverde and Teece (1982a, b) and obtained an affirmative result. In yet two other studies, Walker and Weber (1984, 1987) focused on uncertainty and comparative production costs as determinants of vertical integration.

These five studies have enriched our knowledge of the structures and mechanisms associated with vertical integration in the American automobile industry. It should be noted that all the five studies adopted very similar research methods. They used a list of automobile components, supplied by their case companies and coded as made or bought, as the dependent variable. In fact, this method was also employed by Masten's (1984) study of make-or-buy decisions with respect to procurement in the aerospace industry.

Knowledge may grow by extension in a multifocal pattern whereby a relatively full explanation of a focal area is carried over to an explanation of adjoining areas (see Kaplan 1964). In TCE, for example, research efforts were extended from studying vertical integration in manufacturing industries to studying forward integration into marketing and distribution (e.g., Acheson 1985; Anderson and Schmittlein 1984; John and Weitz 1988). The extension of knowledge in a multifocal pattern is facilitated by the fact that when a theory is tested in several focal areas, a set of common constructs is likely to be involved. Such a set, in the case of TCE, includes asset specificity, site specificity, opportunism, and various kinds of uncertainty. Thus, new focal areas benefit from the construct measurements developed in old areas because the reliability and validity of these measurements are checked and improved by the replications conducted in the old areas.

By comparing knowledge accumulated in several focal areas, the explanatory power of a theory with respect to these areas is clearly demonstrated; some theories are good at explaining certain phenomena but not others. This facilitates the identification of the boundary beyond which a theory is unlikely to hold (see Dubin 1969). Knowledge about the boundary of a theory is especially vital when the theory is put into practice.

An integration

While Glaser and Strauss (1967) are right to point out that "accurate evidence is not so crucial for generating theory" (p. 30), accurate evidence is essential for further developing a theory so that it will better reflect real structures and mechanisms. The main advantage of the multifocal pattern is that by means of repeating past studies systematically, empirical evidence generated from several focal areas can be compared and contrasted. This may lead to further refinement of the theory concerned and helps identify its boundary.

Compared with the scattered pattern, the body of knowledge produced under the multifocal pattern is more coherent and rests on a more solid empirical foundation. However, since studies in the scattered pattern cover a wider range of phenomena, a broader spectrum of managerial implications can be generated. Moreover, the scattered pattern will promote a more adequate representation of complexity and freedom of inquiry (Mone and McKinley 1993).

Popper (1962) has characterized scientific discovery as a cycle of conjectures and refutations. Without bold and imaginative conjectures, no scientific theories can be generated and no scientific breakthroughs are possible. Without attempts at refutation (i.e., critical testing of theories), we cannot separate a search for truth from wild conjectures, and no scientific progress is possible. Both conjectures and testing, creativity and rigor, are needed. Similarly, the scattered and the multifocal patterns of research need to be integrated. Without the former, we may be stuck with solid but infertile theories. Without the latter, we may be swamped by a plethora of creative yet unsubstantiated theories. Under an integrated pattern, seminal studies are replicated and, at the same time, innovative studies are encouraged.

Conclusion

Since the principle of replicability is often regarded as the most important criterion of genuine scientific knowledge (Rosenthal and Rosnow 1984), the infrequent attempts at replication in management are a critical issue that has to be addressed. A root of this problem is probably the ambivalent attitude of social scientists toward replication. There is a tension between positivism, which exalts the importance of replication, on the one hand and several philosophical perspectives that dismiss the role of replication on the other. This dichotomy exists not only among different social scientists but even within an individual scientist. This chapter shows that critical realism can reconcile these polar views and gives an appropriate role to replication in theory development.

The common objections against the feasibility of replication are far from conclusive. Since confusion may arise when people use "replication" to refer to studies of very different natures, the prior discussion clarifies the concept and classifies replications into six types. In contrast to existing discussions of replication, which focus mainly on the issues of reliability and internal and external validity, this chapter highlights the epistemic significance of the first replication of a study on which a theory is based. A confirmatory replication may provide a theory with a quantum leap of credibility because of its success in making a prediction. Since management studies are rarely conducted under conditions of closure, failure of a replication should not be treated as a conclusive falsification of the theory concerned. Although qualitative research methods have a lower degree of replicability than quantitative ones, they provide a better understanding of the specific contingent conditions under which postulated mechanisms operate. This helps researchers locate the reasons for disconfirmation of previous findings, if any.

The multifocal pattern of knowledge accumulation should be integrated with the scattered pattern. The integrated pattern has distinct advantages in terms of providing a more solid empirical foundation for theory development. While the scattered pattern is already common in management research, the multifocal pattern will emerge only after a replication tradition has been established. Over the past decades, a number of valuable suggestions have been put forward to cultivate such a tradition (e.g., Brown and Coney 1976; Dewald et al. 1986; Hubbard 2016; King 1995; Singh et al. 2003). Yet it is unclear how seriously researchers and especially journal editors have considered these suggestions. While the limitations of replication and its complementarity with innovative studies should be recognized, the development of the management discipline may have come to a stage where researchers need to address this question: in the process of encouraging more innovative studies, have we inadvertently downplayed the role of replication?

Notes

1 Another notable example is the "discovery" of cold fusion in nuclear physics by Martin Fleischmann and Stanley Pons in their 1989 experiment. Their result was subsequently rejected because other scientists failed to replicate it (Taubes 1993).
2 A caveat is that for conceptual papers, such as those published in the *Academy of Management Review*, there should be a certain degree of novelty; otherwise the paper is just a rehash of the literature and does not deserve to be published.
3 Eden's (2002) claim suggests that he may regard studies of the same topic as replications. For instance, a study of how corporate governance affects firm performance is at least a partial replication of previous studies of this topic. However, this notion of replication is too broad to be consistent with the literature.
4 This classification first appeared in my earlier paper (Tsang and Kwan 1999), on which this chapter is based. Raymond Hubbard, who has extensively surveyed published replications in various business journals and is a staunch advocate of replication, adopted the classification in his recent book *Corrupt Research: The Case for Reconceptualizing Empirical Management and Social Science*.
5 Singh et al. (2003) propose the concept of good-enough replication – "one that conscientiously follows as closely as possible, the stated methodology of the original study pertaining to design, procedure, data collection, analysis, and reporting of

results" (p. 538). A good-enough replication can be based on a research method different from that of the original study (see their example on pp. 538–539). As such, they run the risk of over-stretching the domain of replication.

6   When my co-authors and I worked on our article that discusses different statistical models of analyzing count-based dependent variables (Blevins et al. 2015), we asked the authors of several published articles that employ the basic Poisson model to provide us the data sets so that we could reanalyze the data using a different model and compare the results. However, we received not even one data set at the end.

7   The exact wording of the related policy statement is:

> Sociologists make their data available after completion of the project or its major publications, except where proprietary agreements with employers, contractors, or clients preclude such accessibility or when it is impossible to share data and protect the confidentiality of the data or the anonymity of research participants (e.g., raw field notes or detailed information from ethnographic interviews).
> (https://us.sagepub.com/en-us/nam/american-sociological-review/journal201969#submission-guidelines)

References

Acheson, J. M. 1985. The Maine lobster market: Between market and hierarchy. *Journal of Law, Economics, and Organization*, 1: 385–398.

Allen, M. and Preiss, R. 1993. Replication and meta-analysis: A necessary connection. *Journal of Social Behavior and Personality*, 8(6): 9–20.

Anderson, E. and Schmittlein, D. C. 1984. Integration of the sales force: An empirical examination. *Rand Journal of Economics*, 15: 385–395.

Andersson, G. 1994. *Criticism and the history of science: Khun's, Lakatos's and Feyerabend's criticisms of critical rationalism*. Leiden, the Netherlands: E. J. Brill.

Argyris, C. 1990. *Overcoming organization defenses*. Needham Heights, MA: Simon and Schuster.

Bahr, H. M., Caplow, T. and Chadwick, B. A. 1983. Middletown III: Problems of replication, longitudinal measurement, and triangulation. *Annual Review of Sociology*, 9: 243–264.

Baird, L. M. and Oppenheim, C. 1994. Do citations matter? *Journal of Information Science*, 20: 2–15.

Bakker, M. and Wicherts, J. M. 2011. The (mis)reporting of statistical results in psychology journals. *Behavior Research Methods*, 43: 666–678.

Barkema, H. G. and Vermeulen, F. 1998. International expansion through start-up or acquisition: A learning perspective. *Academy of Management Journal*, 41: 7–26.

Bedeian, A. G. and Armenakis, A. A. 1981. A path-analytic study of the consequences of role conflict and ambiguity. *Academy of Management Journal*, 24: 417–424.

Bedeian, A. G., Mossholder, K. W., Kemery, E. R. and Armenakis, A. A. 1992. Replication requisites: A second look at Klenke-Hamel and Mathieu (1990). *Human Relations*, 45: 1093–1105.

Bettman, J. R. and Weitz, B. A. 1983. Attributions in the board room: Causal reasoning in corporate annual reports. *Administrative Science Quarterly*, 28: 165–183.

Beyer, J. M., Chattopadhyay, P., George, E., Glick, W. H., dt ogilvie and Pugliese, D. 1997. The selective perception of managers revisited. *Academy of Management Journal*, 40: 716–737.

Bhaskar, R. 1998. *The possibility of naturalism: A philosophical critique of the contemporary human sciences* (3rd ed.). New York: Routledge.

Bleicher, J. 1982. *The hermeneutic imagination: Outline of a positive critique of scientism and sociology.* London: Routledge and Kegan Paul.

Blevins, D. P., Tsang, E. W. K. and Spain, S. M. 2015. Count-based research in management: Suggestions for improvement. *Organizational Research Methods*, 18: 47–69.

Boyd, R. 1985. Observations, explanatory power, and simplicity: Toward a non-Humean account. In P. Achinstein and O. Hannaway (Eds.), *Observation, experiment, and hypothesis in modern physical science*: 47–94. Cambridge, MA: MIT Press.

Braude, S. E. 1979. *ESP and psychokinesis: A philosophical examination.* Philadelphia, PA: Temple University Press.

Brogden, W. J. 1951. Animal studies of learning. In S. S. Stevens (Ed.), *Handbook of experimental psychology*: 568–612. New York: Wiley.

Brown, H. I. 1977. *Perception, theory and commitment: The new philosophy of science.* Chicago, IL: University of Chicago Press.

Brown, J. S. and Duguid, P. 1991. Organizational learning and communities-of-practice: Toward a unified view of working, learning, and innovation. *Organization Science*, 2: 40–57.

Brown, S. W. and Coney, K. A. 1976. Building a replication tradition in marketing. In K. L. Bernhardt (Ed.), *Marketing 1776–1976 and beyond*: 622–625. Chicago, IL: American Marketing Association.

Brown, S. W. and Gaulden, C. F. J. 1982. Replication and theory development. In C. W. Lamb and P. M. Dunne (Eds.), *Theoretical developments in marketing*: 240–243. Chicago, IL: American Marketing Association.

Bryman, A. 1988. *Quantity and quality in social research.* London: Unwin Hyman.

Cannella, A. A. J. and Paetzold, R. L. 1994. Pfeffer's barriers to the advance of organizational science: A rejoinder. *Academy of Management Review*, 19: 331–341.

Carley, K. 1992. Organizational learning and personnel turnover. *Organization Science*, 3: 20–46.

Chang, S. J. 1995. International expansion strategy of Japanese firms: Capability building through sequential entry. *Academy of Management Journal*, 38: 383–407.

Choi, I., Nisbett, R. E. and Norenzayan, A. 1999. Causal attribution across cultures: Variation and universality. *Psychological Bulletin*, 125: 47–63.

Colquitt, J. A. and George, G. 2011. Publishing in *AMJ* – part 1: Topic choice. *Academy of Management Journal*, 54: 432–435.

Colquitt, J. A. and Zapata-Phelan, C. P. 2007. Trends in theory building and theory testing: A five-decade study of the *Academy of Management Journal*. *Academy of Management Journal*, 50: 1281–1303.

Cook, S. D. N. and Yanow, D. 1993. Culture and organizational learning. *Journal of Management Inquiry*, 2: 373–390.

Crossan, M. and Guatto, T. 1996. Organizational learning research profile. *Journal of Organizational Change Management*, 9(1): 107–112.

Cumming, G. 2008. Replication and p intervals: p values predict the future only vaguely, but confidence intervals do much better. *Perspectives on Psychological Science*, 3: 286–300.

Daft, R. L. and Lewin, A. Y. 1990. Can organization studies begin to break out of the normal science straitjacket? An editorial essay. *Organization Science*, 1: 1–9.

Darley, W. K. 2000. Status of replication studies in marketing: A validation and extension. *Marketing Management Journal*, 10: 121–132.

Davis, M. S. 1971. That's interesting! Towards a phenomenology of sociology and a sociology of phenomenology. *Philosophy of the Social Sciences*, 1: 309–344.

Dearborn, D. C. and Simon, H. A. 1958. Selective perception: A note on the departmental identifications of executives. *Sociometry*, 21: 140–144.

Dewald, W. G., Thursby, J. G. and Anderson, R. G. 1986. Replication in empirical economics: The *Journal of Money, Credit and Banking Project*. *American Economic Review*, 76: 587–603.

Dijksterhuis, A. and van Knippenberg, A. 1998. The relation between perception and behavior, or how to win a game of Trivial Pursuit. *Journal of Personality and Social Psychology*, 74: 865–877.

Dilthey, W. 1976. *Selected writings*. Cambridge, England: Cambridge University Press.

Doppelt, G. 1978. Kuhn's epistemological relativism: An interpretation and defense. *Inquiry*, 21: 33–86.

Dubin, R. 1969. *Theory building*. New York: Free Press.

Dweck, C. S. and Leggett, E. L. 1988. A social-cognitive approach to motivation and personality. *Psychological Review*, 95: 256–273.

Earp, B. D. and Trafimow, D. 2015. Replication, falsification, and the crisis of confidence in social psychology. *Frontiers in Psychology*, 6: 621.

Easley, R. W., Madden, C. S. and Dunn, M. G. 2000. Conducting marketing science: The role of replication in the research process. *Journal of Business Research*, 48: 83–92.

Easley, R. W., Madden, C. S. and Gray, V. 2013. A tale of two cultures: Revisiting journal editors' views of replication research. *Journal of Business Research*, 66: 1457–1459.

Eden, D. 2002. Replication, meta-analysis, scientific progress, and *AMJ's* publication policy. *Academy of Management Journal*, 45: 841–846.

Engwall, L. 1995. Management research: A fragmented adhocracy? *Scandinavian Journal of Management*, 11: 225–235.

Evanschitzky, H. and Armstrong, J. S. 2010. Replications of forecasting research. *International Journal of Forecasting*, 26: 4–8.

Evanschitzky, H., Baumgarth, C., Hubbard, R. and Armstrong, J. S. 2007. Replication research's disturbing trend. *Journal of Business Research*, 60: 411–415.

Feyerabend, P. 1978. *Against method*. London: Verso.

Feynman, R. P. 1985. *"Surely you're joking, Mr. Feynman!": Adventures of a curious character*. New York: W. W. Norton and Company.

Fiol, C. M. 1994. Consensus, diversity, and learning in organizations. *Organization Science*, 5: 403–420.

Fiske, S. T. 1993. Social cognition and social perception. *Annual Review of Psychology*, 44: 155–194.

Franke, R. H. and Kaul, J. D. 1978. The Hawthorne experiments: First statistical interpretation. *American Sociological Review*, 43: 623–643.

Freese, J. 2007. Replication standards for quantitative social science: Why not sociology? *Sociological Methods and Research*, 36: 153–172.

Fry, L. W., Kidron, A. G., Osborn, R. N. and Trafton, R. S. 1980. A constructive replication of the Lawrence and Lorsch conflict resolution methodology. *Journal of Management*, 6: 7–19.

Fuess Jr., S. M. 1996. On replication in business and economics research: The QJBE case. *Quarterly Journal of Business and Economics*, 35(2): 3–13.

Geringer, J. M. 1998. Assessing replication and extension. A commentary on Glaister and Buckley: Measures of performance in UK international alliances. *Organization Studies*, 19: 119–138.

Glaister, K. W. and Buckley, P. J. 1998a. Measures of performance in UK international alliances. *Organization Studies*, 19: 89–118.

Glaister, K. W. and Buckley, P. J. 1998b. Replication with extension: Response to Geringer. *Organization Studies*, 19: 139–154.

Glaser, B. G. and Strauss, A. L. 1967. *The discovery of grounded theory*. New York: Aldine de Gruyter.

Goldberg, D. P. 1971. *The detection of psychiatric illness by questionnaire*. Oxford, England: Oxford University Press.

Greenwood, R. and Devine, K. 1997. Inside Aston: A conversation with Derek Pugh. *Journal of Management Inquiry*, 6: 200–208.

Hamel, G. 1991. Competition for competence and inter-partner learning within international strategic alliances. *Strategic Management Journal*, 12(Summer Special Issue): 83–103.

Hanson, N. R. 1958. *Patterns of discovery*. Cambridge, England: Cambridge University Press.

Hendrick, C. 1990. Replications, strict replications, and conceptual replications: Are they important? *Journal of Social Behavior and Personality*, 5(4): 41–49.

Hennart, J.-F. 1988. Upstream vertical integration in the aluminum and tin industries: A comparative study of the choice between market and intrafirm coordination. *Journal of Economic Behavior and Organization*, 9: 281–299.

Hinings, C. R. and Lee, G. L. 1971. Dimensions of organization structure and their context: A replication. *Sociology*, 5: 83–93.

Ho, D. Y.-F. 1976. On the concept of face. *American Journal of Sociology*, 81: 867–884.

Hofstede, G. 1980. *Culture's consequences*. Beverly Hills, CA: Sage.

Hofstede, G. 1993. Cultural constraints in management theories. *Academy of Management Executive*, 7(1): 81–94.

Hu, H. C. 1944. The Chinese concepts of "face". *American Anthropologist*, 46: 45–64.

Hubbard, R. 2016. *Corrupt research: The case for reconceptualizing empirical management and social science*. Thousand Oaks, CA: Sage.

Hubbard, R. and Armstrong, J. S. 1994. Replications and extensions in marketing: Rarely published but quite contrary. *International Journal of Research in Marketing*, 11: 233–248.

Hubbard, R. and Lindsay, R. M. 2013. From significant difference to significant sameness: Proposing a paradigm shift in business research. *Journal of Business Research*, 66: 1377–1388.

Hubbard, R. and Vetter, D. E. 1991. Replications in the finance literature: An empirical study. *Quarterly Journal of Business and Economics*, 30(4): 70–81.

Hubbard, R. and Vetter, D. E. 1992. The publication incidence of replications and critical commentary in economics. *American Economist*, 36(1): 29–34.

Hubbard, R. and Vetter, D. E. 1996. An empirical comparison of published replication research in accounting, economics, finance, management, and marketing. *Journal of Business Research*, 35: 153–164.

Hubbard, R. and Vetter, D. E. 1997. Journal prestige and the publication frequency of replication research in the finance literature. *Quarterly Journal of Business and Economics*, 36(4): 3–14.

Hubbard, R., Vetter, D. E. and Little, E. L. 1998. Replication in strategic management: Scientific testing for validity, generalizability, and usefulness. *Strategic Management Journal*, 19: 243–254.

Hunt, S. D. 1994. A realistic theory of empirical testing: Resolving the theory-ladenness/objectivity debate. *Philosophy of the Social Sciences*, 24: 133–158.

Inkpen, A. C. and Crossan, M. M. 1995. Believing is seeing: Joint ventures and organization learning. *Journal of Management Studies*, 32: 595–618.

Jackson, S. E., Brett, J. F., Sessa, V. I., Cooper, D. M., Julin, J. A. and Peyronnin, K. 1991. Some differences make a difference: Individual dissimilarity and group heterogeneity as correlates of recruitment, promotions, and turnover. *Journal of Applied Psychology*, 76: 675–689.

John, G. and Weitz, B. A. 1988. Forward integration into distribution: An empirical test of transaction cost analysis. *Journal of Law, Economics, and Organization*, 4: 337–355.

Jones, S. R. 1992. Was there a Hawthorne effect? *American Journal of Sociology*, 98: 451–468.

Kaplan, A. 1964. *The conduct of inquiry: Methodology for behavioral science*. New York: Harper and Row.

Keat, R. and Urry, J. 1982. *Social theory as science* (2nd ed.). London: Routledge and Kegan Paul.

Kidder, L. H. and Judd, C. M. 1986. *Research methods in social relations* (5th ed.). New York: Holt, Rinehart and Winston.

Kim, J. Y. and Nam, S. H. 1998. The concept and dynamics of face: Implications for organizational behavior in Asia. *Organization Science*, 9: 522–534.

Kim, L. 1998. Crisis construction and organizational learning: Capability building in catching-up at Hyundai Motor. *Organization Science*, 9: 506–521.

King, G. 1995. Replication, replication. *PS: Political Science and Politics*, 28: 444–452.

Klein, B. 1988. Vertical integration as organized ownership: The Fisher Body-General Motors relationship revisited. *Journal of Law, Economics, and Organization*, 4: 199–213.

Klenke-Hamel, K. E. and Mathieu, J. E. 1990. Role strains, tension, and job satisfaction influences on employees' propensity to leave: A multi-sample replication and extension. *Human Relations*, 43: 791–807.

Koontz, H. 1961. The management theory jungle. *Academy of Management Journal*, 4: 174–188.

Koontz, H. 1980. The management theory jungle revisited. *Academy of Management Review*, 5: 175–187.

Kuhn, T. S. 1962. *The structure of scientific revolutions*. Chicago, IL: University of Chicago Press.

Lamal, P. A. 1990. On the importance of replication. *Journal of Social Behavior and Personality*, 5(4): 31–35.

Lane, P. J. and Lubatkin, M. 1998. Relative absorptive capacity and interorganizational learning. *Strategic Management Journal*, 19: 461–477.

Langlois, R. N. and Robertson, P. L. 1989. Explaining vertical integration: Lessons from the American automobile industry. *Journal of Economic History*, 49: 361–375.

Lawrence, R. R. and Lorsch, J. W. 1967. *Organization and environment*. Boston, MA: Harvard University Press.

Leung, K., Chen, Z., Zhou, F. and Lim, K. 2014. The role of relational orientation as measured by face and renqing in innovative behavior in China: An indigenous analysis. *Asia Pacific Journal of Management*, 31: 105–126.

Lindsay, R. M. and Ehrenberg, A. S. C. 1993. The design of replicated studies. *American Statistician*, 47: 217–228.

Lipton, P. 1991. *Inference to the best explanation*. London: Routledge.

Lyons, T. F. 1971. Role clarity, need for clarity, satisfaction, tension, and withdrawal. *Organizational Behavior and Human Performance*, 6: 99–110.

Machlup, F. 1994. Are the social sciences really inferior? In M. Martin and L. C. McIntyre (Eds.), *Readings in the philosophy of social science*: 5–19. Cambridge, MA: MIT Press.

Madden, C. S., Easley, R. W. and Dunn, M. G. 1995. How journal editors view replication research. *Journal of Advertising*, 24(4): 77–87.

Maher, P. 1988. Prediction, accommodation, and the logic of discovery. In A. Fine and J. Lepin (Eds.), *Philosophy of science association 1988*: 273–285. East Lansing, MI: Philosophy of Science Association.

Makel, M. C., Plucker, J. A. and Hegarty, B. 2012. Replications in psychology research: How often do they really occur? *Perspectives on Psychological Science*, 7: 537–542.

Martinko, M. J. and Gardner, W. L. 1990. Structured observation of managerial work: A replication and synthesis. *Journal of Management Studies*, 27: 329–357.

Masten, S. E. 1984. The organization of production: Evidence from the aerospace industry. *Journal of Law and Economics*, 27: 403–417.

Masten, S. E., Meehan, J. W. J. and Snyder, E. A. 1989. Vertical integration in the U.S. auto industry. *Journal of Economic Behavior and Organization*, 12: 265–273.

McKinley, W. and Mone, M. A. 1998. The re-construction of organization studies: Wrestling with incommensurability. *Organization*, 5: 169–189.

Mill, J. S. 1936. *A system of logic*. London: Longman.

Miller, R. W. 1987. *Fact and method: Explanation, confirmation and reality in the natural and social sciences*. Princeton, NJ: Princeton University Press.

Mintzberg, H. 1973. *The nature of managerial work*. New York: Harper and Row.

Mittelstaedt, R. A. and Zorn, T. S. 1984. Econometric replication: Lessons from the experimental sciences. *Quarterly Journal of Business and Economics*, 23(1): 9–15.

Mone, M. A. and McKinley, W. 1993. The uniqueness value and its consequences for organization studies. *Journal of Management Inquiry*, 2: 284–296.

Monroe, K. B. 1992. On replications in consumer research: Part I. *Journal of Consumer Research*, 19(1): Preface.

Monteverde, K. and Teece, D. J. 1982a. Supplier switching costs and vertical integration in the automobile industry. *Bell Journal of Economics*, 13: 207–213.

Monteverde, K. and Teece, D. J. 1982b. Appropriate rents and quasi-vertical integration. *Journal of Law and Economics*, 25: 321–328.

Morgan, G. and Smircich, L. 1980. The case for qualitative research. *Academy of Management Review*, 5: 491–500.

Nelder, J. A. 1986. Statistics, science and technology. *Journal of the Royal Statistical Society*, Series A, 149: 109–121.

Neuliep, J. W. and Crandall, R. 1990. Editorial bias against replication research. *Journal of Social Behavior and Personality*, 5(4): 85–90.

Park, J. H., Venger, O., Park, D. Y. and Reid, L. N. 2015. Replication in advertising research, 1980–2012: A longitudinal analysis of leading advertising journals. *Journal of Current Issues and Research in Advertising*, 36: 115–135.

Pawson, R. 1989. *A measure for measures: A manifesto for empirical sociology*. London: Routledge.

Pfeffer, J. 1972. A resource dependence perspective on interorganizational relations. *Administrative Science Quarterly*, 17: 382–394.

Phillips, D. C. 1992. *The social scientist's bestiary: A guide to fabled threats to, and defenses of, naturalistic social science*. Oxford, England: Pergamon.

Pillutla, M. M. and Thau, S. 2013. Organizational sciences' obsession with "that's interesting!": Consequences and an alternative. *Organizational Psychology Review*, 3: 187–194.

Polanyi, M. 1957. *Personal knowledge*. London: Routledge and Kegan Paul.

Popper, K. 1959. *The logic of scientific discovery*. London: Hutchison.

Popper, K. 1962. *Conjectures and refutations*. New York: Basic Books.

Reid, L. N., Soley, L. C. and Wimmer, R. D. 1981. Replication in advertising research: 1977, 1978, 1979. *Journal of Advertising*, 10(1): 3–13.

Rosenberg, A. 2008. *Philosophy of social science* (3rd ed.). Boulder, CO: Westview.

Rosenthal, R. 1990. Replication in behavioral research. *Journal of Social Behavior and Personality*, 5(4):1–30.

Rosenthal, R. and Rosnow, R. L. 1984. *Essentials of behavioral research: Methods and data analysis*. New York: McGraw-Hill.

Rosenzweig, P. M. 1994. When can management science research be generalized internationally? *Management Science*, 40: 28–39.

Salancik, G. R. and Meindl, J. R. 1984. Corporate attributions as strategic illusions of management control. *Administrative Science Quarterly*, 29: 238–254.

Schmidt, F. L. 1992. What do data really mean? Research findings, meta-analysis, and cumulative knowledge in psychology. *American Psychologist*, 47: 1173–1181.

Schmidt, S. 2009. Shall we really do it again? The powerful concept of replication is neglected in the social sciences. *Review of General Psychology*, 13: 90–100.

Sidman, M. 1960. *Tactics of scientific research*. New York: Basic Books.

Simonin, B. L. 1997. The importance of collaborative know-how: An empirical test of the learning organization. *Academy of Management Journal*, 40: 1150–1174.

Singh, K., Ang, S. H. and Leong, S. M. 2003. Increasing replication for knowledge accumulation in strategy research. *Journal of Management*, 29: 533–549.

Søndergaard, M. 1994. Hofstede's consequences: A study of reviews, citations and replications. *Organization Studies*, 15: 447–456.

Spitzer, K. 2014. Science scandal triggers suicide, soul-searching in Japan. *Time*, August 8 (http://time.com/3091584/japan-yoshiki-sasai-stem-cells-suicide-haruko-obokata/).

Staw, B. M., McKechnie, P. I. and Puffer, S. M. 1983. The justification of organizational performance. *Administrative Science Quarterly*, 28: 582–600.

Stroebe, W. and Strack, F. 2014. The alleged crisis and the illusion of exact replication. *Perspectives on Psychological Science*, 9: 59–71.

Stuckey, J. A. 1983. *Vertical integration and joint ventures in the aluminum industry.* Cambridge, MA: Harvard University Press.

Sutton, R. I. and Staw, B. M. 1995. What theory is not. *Administrative Science Quarterly*, 40: 371–384.

Tahai, A. and Meyer, M. J. 1999. A revealed preference study of management journals' direct influences. *Strategic Management Journal*, 20: 279–296.

Taubes, G. 1993. *Bad science: The short life and weird times of cold fusion.* New York: Random House.

Tsang, E. W. K. 1997. Organizational learning and the learning organization: A dichotomy between descriptive and prescriptive research. *Human Relations*, 50: 73–89.

Tsang, E. W. K. 2002. Self-serving attributions in corporate annual reports: A replicated study. *Journal of Management Studies*, 39: 51–65.

Tsang, E. W. K. and Kwan, K.-M. 1999. Replication and theory development in organizational science: A critical realist perspective. *Academy of Management Review*, 24: 759–780.

Tsang, E. W. K. and Yamanoi, J. 2016. International expansion through start-up or acquisition: A replication. *Strategic Management Journal*, forthcoming.

Tsoukas, H. 1989. The validity of idiographic research explanations. *Academy of Management Review*, 14: 551–561.

Tsui, A. S., Nifadkar, S. S. and Ou, A. Y. 2007. Cross-national, cross-cultural organizational behavior research: Advances, gaps, and recommendations. *Journal of Management*, 33: 426–478.

Wagner, W., Pfeffer, J. and O'Reilly III, C. A. 1984. Organizational demography and turnover in top management groups. *Administrative Science Quarterly*, 29: 74–92.

Walker, G. and Weber, D. 1984. A transaction cost approach to make-or-buy decisions. *Administrative Science Quarterly*, 29: 373–391.

Walker, G. and Weber, D. 1987. Supplier competition, uncertainty, and make-or-buy decisions. *Academy of Management Journal*, 30: 589–596.

Walsh, J. P. 1988. Selectivity and selective perception: An investigation of managers' belief structures and information processing. *Academy of Management Journal*, 31: 873–896.

Whetten, D. A. 1989. What constitutes a theoretical contribution? *Academy of Management Review*, 14: 490–495.

Whitley, R. 1984. The fragmented state of management studies: Reasons and consequences. *Journal of Management Studies*, 21: 331–348.

Wiersema, M. F. and Bantel, K. A. 1993. Top management team turnover as an adaptation mechanism: The role of the environment. *Strategic Management Journal*, 14: 485–504.

Wiersema, M. F. and Bird, A. 1993. Organizational demography in Japanese firms: Group heterogeneity, individual dissimilarity, and top management team turnover. *Academy of Management Journal*, 36: 996–1025.

Winch, P. 1958. *The idea of a social science.* London: Routledge and Kegan Paul.

Zald, M. N. 1996. More fragmentation? Unfinished business in linking the social sciences and the humanities. *Administrative Science Quarterly*, 41: 251–261.

Zhao, H., Luo, Y. and Suh, T. 2004. Transaction cost determinants and ownership-based entry mode choice: A meta-analytical review. *Journal of International Business Studies*, 35: 524–544.

Zinkhan, G. M., Jones, M. Y., Gardial, S. and Cox, K. K. 1990. Methods of knowledge development in marketing and macromarketing. *Journal of Macromarketing*, 10(2): 3–17.

7 Historiography
A neglected research method

More than two decades ago Goodman and Kruger (1988: 315) argued that "historiography can make significant contributions to variable selection and evaluation, theory building, and hypothesis generation" for management research.[1] Several years later Kieser (1994) asked, "Why does organization theory need historical analyses?" and proposed a few suggestions for performing historical analyses. At approximately the same time Zald (1993: 519) called for "the development of a historically informed organizational theory." Despite such urges, historiography is seldom used by mainstream management researchers, and empirical studies based on historiography rarely appear in leading management journals.

Related to the issue of adopting historiography as a research method is how history matters in management studies. Path dependence is probably the most prominent concept through which history makes itself felt in management studies. For example, using the case of the Bertelsmann book club in Germany, Schreyögg et al. (2011) illustrate the theory of organizational path dependence which connects business history with organization theory. Building on the concept of path dependence, Booth (2003) discusses how counterfactual analysis deepens our historical understanding of strategy, technology, and organization. Organizational cultures are also generally perceived as historically based. However, expectations that the concept of culture would make management research more historical and offer theoretical relevance for business history have not been fulfilled.

Recently Greenwood and Bernardi (2014) lament that history's relevance for management studies still remains far from commonly accepted. More specifically, Bell and Taylor (2013) argue with supporting evidence that historiography is apparently excluded from management research methods textbooks. Business historians further claim to experience isolation and marginalization within the management research community. Such claims of exclusion consist of four interrelated elements:

(1) that historical research is not well acknowledged in scholarly debates; (2) that history is not well represented at conferences; (3) that there are very few established lectureships that require historical research or

teaching as part of the post; and (4) that history is poorly represented in the textbooks that contribute to forming the next generation of researchers in our field.

(Bell and Taylor 2013: 127)

Adding to the above exclusion claims is that historiography is seldom covered in a typical doctoral course in research methodology. If our next generation of researchers is not exposed to historiography as a legitimate research method at the inception of their careers, how can we expect them to employ the method in the years to come? Historians usually do not provide a methodological justification for their work (Yates 2014). Decker (2013: 2) points out that "historians are not explaining their methodology, and in fact are missing a language and a format to do so that are compatible with the approach in social sciences." In contrast, qualitative researchers in management are expected to justify their methods in detail. This difference implies that it will be difficult for a typical historical writing to become accepted in mainstream management journals, as well as that the method of historical research must be explicitly incorporated into journal submissions.

It is necessary to discuss not only how history matters in management studies, but also how historiography matters as a research method. The latter is more fundamental in the sense that in order to promote historical studies, it is essential to show the merits of the method used to conduct these studies. Indeed, one major reason for historiography's exclusion from management research methods textbooks may be that the method is perceived as having "nothing distinctive or unique" (Bell and Taylor 2013: 129). In reflecting on the epistemological problem of representing the past, Rowlinson et al. (2014) devise four research strategies for organizational history. This chapter complements their contribution by discussing the general merits of historiography as well as its specific advantages relative to the traditional methods employed by management researchers. These advantages enable historical studies to uniquely contribute to theory development, which is one of the major criteria used by management journals to evaluate submissions (Hambrick 2007).

In line with the usual conception of history, historical studies here refer to studies of historical events using the method of historiography. For the sake of discussion, the chapter focuses on organizational history, which "draws upon concepts from organization theory and the wider social sciences and humanities" (Booth and Rowlinson 2006: 12) and is "an emerging field that crosses intellectual domains and continents" (Carroll 2002: 556). The defining qualities of a historical event are sequence, contingency, and singularity; the event is a "historically singular happening that takes place in a particular time and place and sequentially unfolds or develops through time" (Griffin 1992: 414). As Hammer (2008: 185) well says, "In history, our interests and our epistemic capacities typically lead us to give narratives." This chapter therefore excludes quantitative studies that primarily analyze longitudinal archival data such as studies in population ecology (e.g., Baum and Mezias 1992; Carroll and Delacroix

1982; Lomi 1995), although these studies do have a more substantial historical element than other management studies. Population ecologists neither use
historiography nor rely on source materials to conduct their analyses (Leblebici
2014). The method of analysis employed by a typical population ecology study
is much more similar to a management study that analyzes panel data (e.g.,
Barkema and Vermeulen 1998) than a historical study that constructs a narrative account of past events (e.g., Hassard 2012). Historical studies that take
into account the three aforementioned defining qualities of events are inevitably
qualitative in nature.

This chapter shows how historical studies contribute to theory development
in management by first examining the nature of theory. As discussed in chapter 2, two major functions are usually attributed to theory – explanation and
prediction (Hempel 1965). Kaplan (1964: 347) maintains that "if we look at
the explanations which actually occur in science as well as in everyday life, and
not only at what an ideal explanation would be or what all explanations are
'in principle,' it appears that we often have explanations without being able to
predict." Sayer (1992) similarly stresses the priority of explanation over prediction for theory development in social science because the validity of predictions
depends a great deal on *ceteris paribus* conditions which do not hold in open
systems where social phenomena occur. The chapter accordingly focuses on
the explanatory function of theory by discussing historical explanation from a
mechanism-based perspective.

The chapter uses the example of the vertical integration between General
Motors (GM) and Fisher Body in 1926 to illustrate the nature of historical
explanation and, more importantly, the merits of historical studies. This historical event is chosen because it is "the most commonly cited example of a
holdup problem solved by vertical integration" (Klein 2008: 442) and is thus
a classic example of market failure in the transaction cost economics (TCE)
literature. As an illustrative example, the GM–Fisher Body integration is better
than other well-known historical studies such as Chandler (1962, 1977) and
Pettigrew (1985) because it is a single event with a clear boundary and the facts
related to the event are more manageable within the length of a book chapter.
In addition to introducing historiography, this chapter also serves the purpose
of illustrating how the methodological issues discussed in chapters 2 to 6 can
be used to assess a research method, reflecting another practical aspect of the
discussions in these chapters.

The nature of historical explanation

"Mainstream historians could be characterized as having a pragmatically realist
approach" (Mutch 2014: 227) with the objective of discovering how certain
past events actually unfolded. Nevertheless, a historical study is "neither a regression of variables against time nor a mere record of events" (Calhoun 1998: 857).
It is conducted with the aim of explaining and not simply reporting. To explain
something is to provide an answer to the question, "Why?" (Megill 2007).

"The business of an historian is to make judgments and to establish causal relationships between facts; he must place them in some significant pattern in order and not simply be a reporter" (Canter and Schneider 1967: 19). There are several ways of framing historical explanation (see Glennan 2010; Tilly 2001; Topolski 1991). This chapter discusses two of them – the deductive-nomological (D-N) model and the mechanismic approach (see chapter 2) – that span across the natural and social sciences, corresponding respectively to Salmon's (1998) argument that scientific explanations take two general forms: appealing to a general law or a mechanism.

The defining characteristic of a historical explanation is that "it explains the occurrence of some *particular* event or state of affairs by describing how it came to be" (Glennan 2010: 251). In contrast, an ahistorical explanation treats an event as an example of a recurrent phenomenon and abstracts from the particulars associated with the event. In addition to the usual explanations given by historians, this defining characteristic covers some kinds of natural science explanations such as the formation of a certain geographical landscape or solar system. Nagel (1979) argues that although historians are concerned with explaining events that are unique and non-recurrent, they must abstract from the concrete occurrences they study and use common names or general descriptive terms in their narratives. As such, historians assume that there are various kinds of occurrences and that there are empirical regularities associated with each kind, differentiating one kind from other kinds. His argument helps to bridge the gap between the idiographic nature of historical explanations and the nomothetic nature of typical scientific explanations.

The deductive-nomological model and mechanismic explanation

The most notable attempt to include historical explanations under the general umbrella of scientific explanations is Hempel's (1942) application of his D-N model to historical studies. His approach "treats events as replicable and expects to find enduring regularities which can be codified in generalizations or even laws" (Sayer 2000: 144). Led by Dray (1957), the D-N model has been attacked especially in the late 1960s and 1970s.[2] Roberts (1996: 9) aptly summarizes the sentiment as: "ordinary historians find his model strange and irrelevant." A major objection is that historians do not in fact employ the model in their work, and another related objection is the difficulty of identifying any general laws of the type required by the model for explaining historical events (Murphey 1986). Moreover, as Nagel (1979: 574) observes, the model cannot explain "collective events that are appreciably complex," but such events are precisely the ones that historians deal with. Historians rarely seek to explain the occurrence of a complex event by explicitly subsuming it under one or more general laws (Roberts 1996). Therefore, this chapter focuses on the mechanismic approach.

As mentioned, sequence, contingency, and singularity are the defining qualities of historical events. An important criterion for evaluating a historical explanation is accordingly that each quality should be incorporated into the very logic of how events are explained (Griffin 1992). The mechanismic approach does a better job in this respect than the D-N model. Unlike the D-N model, which was introduced by a non-historian to historical studies, the mechanismic approach was advocated by Charles Tilly, a noted political scientist and historian. He started the so-called "mechanism movement" by proposing that social historical research should focus on the discovery of mechanisms and reorient explanations from episodes to processes. Mechanism-based accounts explain salient features of episodes by identifying within the episodes robust mechanisms of relatively general scope (Tilly 2001). A mechanism-based perspective is especially relevant to the GM-Fisher integration because the concept of mechanism, such as self-reinforcement mechanism (Klein 2000) and holdup mechanism (Klein 1988), is used in formulating the prevailing view of the integration discussed in a section below.

A mechanismic explanation for an event should describe the cogs and wheels of the causal process through which the event was brought about (Hedström and Ylikoski 2010). Typically mechanisms in general and social mechanisms in particular are unobservable (Kiser and Hechter 1991), and their descriptions are therefore bound to consist of constructs that do not appear in empirical data (Bunge 2004). This partly accounts for the fact that sometimes different explanations may be formulated for the same historical event as shown by the GM–Fisher Body integration.

Mechanisms studied in the natural sciences, such as the mechanism of a watch, an epidemic outbreak, a volcano eruption, or a solar eclipse, are often rather stable by nature. In contrast, a distinguishing characteristic of social mechanisms in historical studies is that the circumstances bringing together the various entities whose interactions gave rise to the event in question were ephemeral. Yet once historians have identified these circumstances they explain by showing how, given the circumstances, there was a likelihood or necessity for the event's occurrence (Glennan 2010). Historians attempt to tease out the causal nexus related to the event. Inquiries into the mechanisms concerned would facilitate their causal inference.

In this respect, Little (1991) connects mechanisms with causation by proposing that X is a cause of Y if and only if there is a mechanism connecting X with Y. That is, if we can identify a mechanism running from X to Y, then we may conclude that X is a cause of Y. Conversely, if we have some good reason to believe that there is no mechanism from X to Y, then we may conclude that X is not a cause of Y (Steel 2004). Explaining a historical event often includes a variety of mechanisms that link a number of prior events with the focal event. The explanation may also exclude an alleged linkage between a prior event and the focal event by showing that there is no good reason to believe that the events are connected by any mechanism with the aim of ruling out a causal relationship.

Another distinguishing characteristic of social mechanisms in historical studies is that these mechanisms are formed by human actions with underlying purposes and intentions. Max Weber, a founding father of sociology who is also viewed by some (e.g., Lustick 1996; McLemore 1984) as primarily a historian, offers some important insight on the implications of this characteristic. Historical agents envisage the outcomes they hope to achieve and work out the means of attaining them. That is what motivates them to act. Weber (1949) regards the motive driving an action as its cause. As shown by the discussion of the GM–Fisher Body integration below, the different explanations for the integration are to a certain extent based on different interpretations of the motives behind observable actions. Weber (1975) considers the interpretation of human actions as one form of causal analysis – "a historical 'interpretive' inquiry into motives is *causal* explanation in absolutely the same logical sense as the causal interpretation of any concrete natural process" (p. 194).

Since interpretive understanding enables the historian to identify the motives behind actions as well as the context of meaning in which the actions are embedded, the historian can trace the mechanisms that link cause and effect. Although Weber rarely uses the term "mechanism," a number of interesting social mechanisms can be identified in some of his major works such as his proposed connection between Protestant religious doctrine and capitalist economic system as pictorially represented by Figure 2 of Hedström and Swedberg (1996).

Idiographic explanation and nomothetic knowledge

Contrary to the claims of some critics, "historical research is not antithetical to theory and generalization" (Lipartito 2014: 285). A management scholar who adopts a historically informed methodology in fact contends that "the best historians don't shy away from abstractions and theory" (Murmann 2012: 92). Historians assume that there are various kinds of occurrences and that there are distinct empirical regularities associated with each kind. Similarly, Weber argues that causes and effects in historical studies must be described at a level of generality that allows them to be related to "rules of experience" (*Erfahrungsregeln*). Such rules are similar to imperfect empirical generalizations and are one form of nomothetic knowledge (Ringer 2002). These two arguments help bridge the gap between the idiographic nature of historical explanations and the nomothetic nature of organization theories that seek to cover categories of phenomena.

Weber (1968) further provides a description of the relationship between sociology and history that throws light on the relationship between management studies and organizational history: "sociology formulates type concepts and searches for general uniformities (*Regeln*) within the stream of events, in contrast to history, which aims at the causal analysis and causal attribution of individual actions, structures and personalities that have cultural significance" (p. 19). There is little difference between these two disciplines because "both for sociology in the present sense and for history the object of cognition is the subjective meaning (*Sinnzusammenhang*) of action" (p. 13). For Weber, sociology is a generalized form of the study of history (Roth 1976); the same comment is equally applicable to management studies and organizational history. The dichotomy between the two, which is based on the traditional idiographic-nomothetic distinction, is more apparent than real; instead there are elements of complementarity. On the one hand, theories created by management researchers may help organizational historians search for and construct explanations for specific events. On the other hand, such explanations may contribute to the development of management theories, as illustrated by the GM–Fisher Body integration discussed in the next section.

The General Motors–Fisher Body integration

This section first describes the prevailing view of the integration. Since there is a serious debate concerning the actual causes leading to the integration, the section then presents several different explanations of the event.[3] Before proceeding, it is necessary first to briefly summarize a few simple facts regarding the event that all parties of the debate would accept: in 1919 GM signed a supply contract with Fisher Body for closed auto bodies and acquired a 60 percent interest in the company. The contract included an exclusive dealing clause whereby GM would buy virtually all of its closed bodies from Fisher at a price set at cost plus 17.6 percent. In 1926 GM acquired the remaining 40 percent of the stock of Fisher Body, resulting in a vertical integration.

The prevailing view

Klein et al. (1978) were the first to use the event as a holdup example supporting the TCE arguments. The discussion of the event only constitutes a very small part of their article and can by no means be considered a historical analysis. The historical data used are sketchy. Many subsequent publications adopt Klein et al.'s (1978) interpretation, which has become the prevailing view. The following description of the event is based on their interpretation as supplemented by Klein's (1988) subsequent elaboration. In 1919 GM signed a 10-year contract with Fisher Body for the supply of largely metal closed auto bodies, which replaced the open and largely wooden bodies previously used to build automobiles. Based on this contract GM acquired a 60 percent interest in Fisher by purchasing 300,000 shares of newly issued Fisher common stock. The contract included an exclusive dealing clause whereby GM would buy substantially all of its closed bodies from Fisher as an incentive for the latter to make the required specific investments. This exclusive dealing clause significantly reduced the likelihood that GM would act opportunistically by demanding a lower purchase price after Fisher had made the specific production capacity investments. On the other hand, the clause created an opportunity for Fisher to take advantage of GM by setting a monopoly price for the bodies. The contract accordingly fixed the price that Fisher could charge GM. The price was set at cost plus 17.6 percent where cost excluded the interest paid on invested capital. Moreover, the contract stipulated that the price could be neither higher than the price Fisher charged other automakers for similar bodies nor higher than the average market price of similar bodies manufactured by companies other than Fisher. The contract also included provisions for compulsory arbitration in case disputes regarding price arose.

Over the next few years after the contract was signed, the market experienced a significant jump in the demand for automobiles as well as a significant shift from open bodies to the closed models supplied by Fisher, making it profitable for Fisher to hold up GM. Given the absence of a capital cost pass-through in the contract, GM found that the price charged by Fisher was too high due to a significant increase in body output per unit of capital employed and was very unhappy about it. "Fisher effectively held up General Motors by adopting a relatively inefficient, highly labor-intensive technology and by refusing to locate the body-producing plants adjacent to General Motors assembly plant" (Klein 1988: 202). GM claimed that having Fisher's plants close to its own was necessary for achieving production efficiency. However, it would require a large specific investment on the part of Fisher which was possibly appropriable. "By 1924, General Motors had found the Fisher contractual relationship intolerable and began negotiations for purchase of the remaining stock in Fisher Body, culminating in a final merger agreement in 1926" (Klein et al. 1978).

As discussed in chapter 2, causal claims can be interpreted as having a contrastive structure (Woodward 2003). The implicit contrastive question answered by Klein et al. (1978) is, "Why did GM acquire Fisher Body in 1926 rather than keeping the status quo?" and the related allomorph is, "GM *acquired* Fisher Body in 1926." The puzzle to be explained here is why GM did not keep Fisher Body as a legally separate entity. Although the alternative explanations presented below cite events that occurred at different times, the point of contention is not about the timing of the acquisition that corresponds to allomorph "GM acquired Fisher Body in *1926*." Rather, it is about the acquisition itself. The contrastive approach to explanation is especially relevant to historiography because the complexity of a historical event makes it impossible to explain all of the event's particularities in one go. Researchers are forced to focus on explaining certain aspects of the event only.

With the risk of over-simplification, Hempel's D-N model can be applied to frame the historical explanation given by Klein et al. (1978) for the acquisition of Fisher Body by GM:

1   If a firm finds itself trapped in a holdup situation by an opportunistic supplier and if its financial condition permits, the firm will attempt to acquire the supplier.
2   In the early 1920s, GM found itself trapped in a holdup situation by the opportunistic Fisher Body and GM was in good financial shape.
3   GM attempted to acquire Fisher Body and successfully did so in 1926.

Although the mechanismic approach also regards holdup as the cause, it explains the acquisition in a different manner as follows. There was a substantial increase in the demand for closed bodies during the years after signing the 10-year contract, making holdup a profitable option for Fisher Body. GM found that the price charged by Fisher was too high. Given the exclusive dealing clause, Fisher held up GM by employing a relatively inefficient, highly labor-intensive technology and refusing to locate its plants near GM's assembly plants for production efficiency. This led to a situation perceived by GM as "intolerable," resulting in the acquisition of Fisher Body. There are some implicit mechanisms connecting these events together. For example, Klein (2000: 127–130) describes in detail how the increase in demand for closed bodies would make it profitable for Fisher Body to hold up GM using the concept of the self-reinforcement mechanism. The exclusive dealing clause, which prevented GM from purchasing closed bodies elsewhere, made the holdup possible. Colocating the plants of both companies, as GM claimed, would improve GM's production efficiency, particularly in view of the relatively backward communication and data-processing technologies of the 1920s. In fact, Klein (1988) calls Fisher Body's two actions – employing a relatively inefficient technology and refusing to collocate plants – the "holdup mechanism" which "had the advantage, from Fisher's viewpoint, of increasing profitability since the contractually specified price formula set price equal to Fisher's 'variable cost' plus 17.6 percent, placing a 17.6 percent profit upcharge on Fisher's labor and transportation costs" (p. 202).

Alternative explanations

Although Klein et al.'s (1978) explanation is rather well received, there are different views concerning the reasons behind the integration. In particular, a major point of contention is whether Fisher Body did hold up GM and whether holdup was a critical cause of the integration. As covered in chapter 2, Runde and de Rond (2010) propose three broad criteria for evaluating causal explanations of specific events, the first two of which are: (1) the factors cited as causes were actually present and (2) such factors were causally effective in contributing to the occurrence of the event. In other words, the prevailing view is challenged with respect to these two criteria, especially the first one concerning whether the so-called holdup existed.

Coase (2000: 16) summarizes his objection as follows: "I believe that the prevailing view gives a completely false picture of the events leading to the acquisition of Fisher Body by General Motors. There was no holdup. The situation never became 'intolerable.' " He argues that the relationship between the two companies became much closer after signing the 1919 agreement. GM nominated 7 of the 14 directors, 2 of the 7 executive committee members, and 3 of the 5 finance committee members of Fisher Body. Moreover, in 1921 Fred Fisher, who founded Fisher Body with his five younger brothers, became a director of GM and, in 1922, was appointed a member of its executive committee. In 1924 Charles and Lawrence Fisher joined their elder brother on the board of directors and GM's executive committee. In the following year Lawrence Fisher became head of Cadillac, a key division of GM.

Since the Fisher brothers occupied senior positions in GM, it is highly implausible that they would engage in opportunistic behaviors that hurt the company's interests. The increasingly close relationship between the two companies leads Coase (2000: 25) to arrive at this conclusion: "From 1924 on, it seems to have been understood that ultimately Fisher Body would probably merge with General Motors." GM was anxious to acquire the remaining 40 percent of Fisher Body partly because it worried that the minority shareholding might fall into the hands of parties who were difficult to deal with. Coase (2000) also provides empirical evidence to show that contrary to Klein et al.'s (1978) claim, Fisher Body did not locate its plants far away from GM's. He argues that the 1919 agreement would be able to attenuate the asset specificity problem in a satisfactory way without the need for vertical integration. In short, he provides some good reasons against Klein et al.'s (1978) explanation but is somewhat brief in proposing an alternative one.

In contrast, Freeland (2000) provides an elaborated alternative explanation. He argues that GM's apprehension of losing the Fisher brothers' specialized human assets was the primary cause for the vertical integration. Before signing the 1919 agreement with Fisher Body, GM lacked both the knowledge and manufacturing facilities necessary for producing closed bodies and worried that closed bodies might become the industry trend. Its initial attempt to acquire knowledge of closed-body business by hiring four of the Fishers as employees failed because they preferred to work together in their family-run business. GM then turned to the strategy of procuring their services through acquiring an interest in Fisher Body, resulting in the 1919 agreement which also precluded others such as Ford from entering into an arrangement with Fisher.

Some provisions of the agreement were designed to secure the Fishers' human assets by providing powerful financial incentives to induce them to stay and manage the business. These provisions were set to expire on October 1, 1924. The issue of what would happen once the provisions expired arose as early as mid-1922 when Fred Fisher considered the possibility of a GM-Fisher merger. A study was commissioned to investigate this option. The merger idea failed to move forward likely due to the Fishers' preference to stay together as a unit and their resistance to see their family business completely disappear. Just before the expiry date GM devised a plan to ensure the Fishers' continued employment and align the interests of the two companies.

By November 1925 GM began negotiations to purchase Fisher Body. Freeland (2000) highlights four factors that drove the decision to integrate. First, increasing demand for closed bodies created strain over issues of plant location and financing expansion. Second, the shift to closed bodies made body styling a crucial element of GM's competition within the industry. GM accordingly sought to coordinate the design and engineering of bodies with those of chassis by carrying out both processes under the roof of a single company. Third, GM was also motivated to integrate for purely defensive reasons – to deprive its competitors of Fisher's products. Finally, the integration would eliminate GM's apprehension that either the Fishers or their partners might sell their shares to unfriendly parties, a reason also given by Coase (2000).

The final alternative explanation discussed here is the one proposed by Casadesus-Masanell and Spulber (2000), who argue that the need for more efficient coordination was the overarching reason for the integration. Specifically, they state four factors. First, the closed bodies manufactured by Fisher were of distinct quality and style, offering a competitive advantage to GM. The integration assured a supply of these bodies. Second, GM grew primarily by vertical and horizontal integration. By 1910 it obtained either a complete or controlling interest in more than 20 automobile and parts-manufacturing companies. The Fisher Body deal was therefore consistent with GM's pattern of growth and development. The next two factors are similar to those from Freeland (2000). Third, by making Fisher Body a division under the same roof GM could lower the cost of coordinating the production of bodies and assembly. Finally, in 1923 GM introduced the multidivisional structure and faced a shortage of managers who could lead within the new organizational form. The integration was a natural way to convince the Fisher brothers, who were very experienced managers, to dedicate all of their time and talents to GM.

Casadesus-Masanell and Spulber (2000) also cite historical events that challenge Klein et al.'s (1978) explanation. For example, they argue that the contractual relationship between GM and Fisher Body exhibited trust. Supporting pieces of evidence include GM cars showing a distinctive plate "Body by Fisher," GM investing an additional $4.5 million in Fisher Body during 1923, increasing involvement of the Fisher brothers in GM's top management, and so on. If the contractual relationship between these two companies did exhibit trust, then it is not likely that Fisher Body would engage in the so-called "holdup mechanism," and Klein et al.'s (1978) explanation would fall apart.

Merits of historiography

The prevailing view of the GM–Fisher Body integration is frequently used in academic discussions on contracting, vertical integration, and the theory of the firm in order to illustrate the economic implications of asset specificity and opportunism, as well as the failure of market contracts. It is also cited in many economics and business textbooks (Casadesus-Masanell and Spulber 2000). Why is this example so powerful? It is partly because the example concerns a historical event that occurred naturally as a result of actual business activities. From a practitioner's perspective, the event nicely connects abstract terms such as imperfect contracting, specific investment, opportunism, and holdup with concrete episodes. Unlike a typical empirical study that may involve convoluted logic and complex statistics, Klein et al.'s (1978) explanation of the event is relatively lucid. Academically, historical studies have at least two major advantages as discussed below. Table 7.1 summarizes the merits and limitations of historical studies covered in this and the next sections.

Table 7.1 Merits and limitations of historiography

Merits	Limitations
General	• Generalizability of results restricted by small sample size
• Enriching theoretical knowledge by examining causal mechanisms	• Research restricted by availability of relics that are finite and incomplete
• Offering "pre-theoretical" contexts for unbiased theory testing	• Lack of sampling controls over relics
Relative to case studies	
• Commonly accessible relics facilitating replication and avoiding post hoc storytelling	• Little chance of gaining access to historical actors, most of whom are long dead at the time of study
Relative to experiments	
• Enhancing the generalizability of results to the real world because historical events unfold within a natural setting free of any researcher manipulations	• Inference from relics subject to error and subjective judgment
Relative to analysis of archival data	
• Chronological sequence of events facilitating the identification of causal relationships	
• Investigating core assumptions	
• Avoiding post hoc hypothesis development	

Enriching theoretical knowledge

Fischer (1970) discusses five major functions of history, one of which is that history refines theoretical knowledge. Klein (2000) claims that Klein et al.'s (1978) explanation of the GM–Fisher Body integration illustrates the mechanism of a core TCE argument: the presence of specific investments creates a potential holdup problem that increases market contracting costs and, therefore, the incentive for vertical integration. Moreover, using the concepts of self-enforcement and court enforcement mechanisms, Klein (2000) explains in detail why it became profitable for Fisher Body to hold up GM after the contract had been renewed in October 1924. If the prevailing view is correct, the intricate theoretical issues covered in his discussion enrich TCE.

A historical event can do more than confirm or disprove a hypothesis; it may suggest new hypotheses (Moore 1958). Freeland's (2000) explanation illustrates this function of historical events. Unlike Klein et al. (1978) who emphasize the role played by physical assets in creating holdup, Freeland (2000) shifts his attention to human assets and examines the post-integration period. After the Fisher brothers sold their 500,000 shares of GM common stock to pay off their debts caused by the depression in 1931, they had few holdings in GM outside of their participation in the company's stock incentive plan. In 1933 the six Fishers demanded that GM grant them an option on 200,000 shares of GM common stock with an exercise price set at the then prevailing market price of $40 per share. When their demand was refused they threatened to collectively leave GM. In response to the threat GM eventually agreed to grant an option on 100,000 shares of GM common stock at $40 per share.

The Fisher brothers' ability to engage in a successful holdup was due to their specialized knowledge of the closed-body business and its management. After the integration the Fishers intentionally kept their division independent of GM with regard to its management so that others in GM were unfamiliar with the body portion of the business. As a result they continued to monopolize the knowledge and skills necessary for managing GM's body business. GM management worried that if they did not accede to the Fishers' demand, the brothers might leave and even seek employment with GM's competitors. GM executives therefore regarded the Fishers' threat as credible. Note that none of the mechanisms proposed by TCE to mitigate problems of human asset specificity – ownership of Fisher's physical assets, central control of its team labor contracts, monitoring and control mechanisms associated with GM's M-form structure, or the ability to exercise fiat and authority over employees of the Fisher Body Division (including the Fisher brothers) – seemed to be sufficient to curb this threat.

The GM–Fisher Body integration mainly attenuated the problems associated with physical asset specificity but also increased GM's vulnerability to the Fisher brothers' holdup rooted in their human asset specificity. The case supports Holmström and Roberts's (1998: 91) comment that "the theory of the firm, and especially work on what determines the boundaries of the firm, has become too narrowly focused on the holdup problem and the role of (physical) asset specificity." The factors shaping the boundary between firm and market can be more diverse, complex, and subtle than those taken into account by TCE. Freeland's (2000) analysis of the GM–Fisher Body integration leads him to this conclusion: "We have made much progress in explaining the role of physical assets and property rights in determining these boundaries. We are considerably more in the dark when it comes to issues of human assets and specialized knowledge" (p. 63). Freeland's argument points to some interesting new research directions for further developing TCE.

Offering "pre-theoretical" contexts

As discussed in chapter 4, management researchers' activities may change the beliefs and practices of managers, undermining the stability of the phenomena under investigation (Numagami 1998) and causing complications in interpreting theory testing results. In the natural sciences, self-fulfilling and self-defeating prophecies are not causes for concern. A theory of meteorite formation will not affect how meteorites are actually formed. In contrast, managers may alter their behaviors accordingly on learning the knowledge created by management researchers through education or other sources (Knights 1992). For example, managers who are shaped by the logic of TCE taught in the classroom tend to impose controls curbing opportunism. However, such controls may have the dysfunctional consequence of encouraging more difficult-to-detect opportunistic behaviors (Ghoshal and Moran 1996), fundamentally changing the phenomenon concerned.

By the same token, managers who have learned the functions of vertical integration tend to select this option whenever they perceive a probable holdup situation even though other governance structures may indeed be more efficient. In this case TCE is supported not because of its predictive power but due to its pervasive influence in management education. It reflects the so-called "performativity" phenomenon – a theory is empirically supported mainly because people believe it and operate according to it, not because it describes some independent reality (MacKenzie and Millo 2003). The results of such tests must be interpreted with extreme care.

By going back in time, historical events may have the unique advantage of being "pre-theoretical" (Ingram et al. 2012); that is, an event happened before the theory in question was created. This rules out the possibility of performativity. This point is best illustrated here by the GM–Fisher Body integration which took place in 1926, well before the publication of Coase's (1937) seminal work that started the stream of TCE research. If the TCE argument related to vertical integration is supported by the case, as Klein et al. (1978) claim, it is by no means due to the possibility that GM management had previously learned TCE and made the acquisition decision accordingly. This case therefore represents a direct and unbiased test of TCE.

Comparison with traditional research methods

In spite of their general merits, relatively few historical studies have been published in mainstream management journals, and few management researchers employ historiography as their preferred research method. A likely reason is that historical studies have some well-known limitations. For example, as one form of qualitative research, historical studies may be criticized on the grounds that their results are not generalizable to other settings because of the small-N problem – similar to case studies discussed in chapter 5 (Gerring 2007; Steinmetz 2004). There are also limitations specific to historical studies. Goldthorpe (1991: 213) argues that historians "can only know the past on the basis of what has physically survived from the past: that is, on the basis of the relic – or of what may be alternatively described as the residues, deposits or traces – of the past" and that relics are finite and incomplete. Given the haphazard circumstances by which relics are preserved, historians often lack any sampling controls over the relics they study (Bryant 1994). Unlike case study researchers or organizational ethnographers, organizational historians rarely have access to the subjective worlds of historical actors through interrogation because most of these people are long dead at the time of study (Rock 1976). Historians must interpret the relics left behind alone. Generally speaking "a historical fact is an inference from the relics" (Goldthorpe 1991: 213); inference is subject to error and subjective judgment. For example, in the debate concerning the GM–Fisher Body integration Coase (2006: 262) frankly admits that "the important difference between Klein and me was due to a difference in our perception of the facts."

Another reason for the marginalized position of historical studies is that historiography is less known among management researchers and is rarely covered in doctoral training as a research method. The following discussion addresses this problem by highlighting the advantages of historiography relative to three traditional research methods – case study, experiment, and analysis of archival data. It is clear that historiography has some unique benefits not shared by other research methods.

Case studies

If the term "case study" is used in a loose sense then examining the GM–Fisher Body integration can be considered a case study. Both Klein (2008) and Macher and Richman (2008) in fact classify the integration this way. However, Yin (2014: 16) defines a case study as "an empirical inquiry that investigates a contemporary phenomenon (the 'case') in depth and within its real-world context, especially when the boundaries between phenomenon and context may not be clearly evident." Since the GM–Fisher Body integration is not a contemporary phenomenon, the definition excludes it from the domain of case study research. Other than this temporal difference, there is some similarity shared by case study research and historiography. Both methods intensively investigate events that occurred in a real-life context based on data collected from a variety of sources.

A major difference stems from the fact that case researchers often interview individuals related to the focal events. For instance, Argyres (1996) interviewed managers, engineers, and chemists working in various divisions and at the corporate level of a California-based Fortune 500 firm during his case study of vertical integration decisions. On the other hand, historians rarely do so because the people they would want to interview are likely deceased. For example, when the GM–Fisher Body integration was first discussed by Klein et al. (1978), half a century had already lapsed. Yet Coase (2000) does mention that during his visit to the U.S. in 1931–1932, he asked a GM executive why the company acquired Fisher Body. He was told that it was to make sure that the body plants of Fisher Body were located near the GM assembly plants. This is the only sketchy interview data cited in the integration discussion by various scholars. Coase (2000) himself waited until 1996 before he began his investigation with the help of a research assistant.

While the opportunity to interview key actors is surely an advantage of case study research over historiography, it is not without deficiencies. Huber and Power (1985) cite four primary reasons that respondents provide inaccurate or biased information regarding organizational events in their retrospective reports – motivation to do so, perceptual and cognitive limitations, lacking crucial information concerning the event, and being questioned using an inappropriate data elicitation procedure. Some of these reasons are due to the fact that they are asked to provide the information in a research setting. For example, they may be motivated to provide inaccurate information in order to protect their company's reputation or their own careers. Another problem is that interview data cannot be readily checked by other researchers. Not revealing the identity of a case company is often a condition for gaining research access to the company. Argyres (1996: 131) admits that "the firm's anonymity makes direct replication of the study difficult." Putting aside the problem of research access, it is awkward for another researcher to go into the same company and ask the same questions even with a different group of respondents. Attempts at replicating interviews in another company may be complicated by the fact that the original interview protocol is often not well structured.

The relics used in historical studies avoid many of these problems. For instance, Klein et al.'s (1978) explanation is based on three documents – the 1919 agreement, a GM annual report, and a deposition from Alfred Sloan in *United States v. Du Pont & Co.* – all readily accessible by other researchers. Subsequent discussions of the case make use of additional documents such as contracts, letters, trial transcripts, and annual reports. The information contained in some of these documents such as trial transcripts is likely to be more accurate than that in the retrospective reports of case studies; there is a penalty for perjury whereas there is none for lying to a researcher. However, it is imperative that researchers "establish the *credibility* of a source, which involves assessing a source's trustworthiness or reliability in addressing the researcher's question" (Kipping et al. 2014: 314). For example, Sloan's deposition was given more than two decades after the GM–Fisher Body integration and therefore was subject to errors of recall. Moreover, the deposition was part of a high-stakes antitrust trial – "The government was attempting to demonstrate in this case that General Motors vertically integrated in order to get Fisher to purchase its glass requirements from DuPont" (Klein et al. 1978: 309). Sloan might not be motivated to reveal in court the true reason for the integration if that reason would put GM in an unfavorable legal position.

Another major difference between case studies and historical studies concerns data and source (Rowlinson et al. 2014). While case study researchers describe in detail how their data were collected, they may disclose little information regarding the data source due to the need to preserve anonymity. In contrast, credibility in history rests on replicability (Lipartito 2014). Historians are expected to practice source transparency by linking evidence back to specific relics (Kipping et al. 2014). Although the possibility that different historians may interpret the same relic differently should not be underestimated, the availability of a set of commonly accessible relics should help ease the job of replicating an original study. Given the crucial role played by replication in theory development (see chapter 6), historical studies possess a clear advantage here. A shared pool of raw data also facilitates discussions and debates, helping readers judge the evidence provided by each side of a debate. This issue is again well illustrated by the GM–Fisher Body integration. For instance, there is a debate regarding the effect of a specific legal agreement on Fisher Body's ability to hold up GM. There were provisions in the 1919 agreement designed to meet the Fisher brothers' demands for autonomy. The 300,000 shares of Fisher Body purchased by GM were placed in a voting trust managed by two representatives each from GM and Fisher. Since decisions made by the trust had to be approved unanimously by the four trustees, this arrangement prevented GM from using its majority ownership of 60 percent to control Fisher's internal operations. Engaging in a thought experiment (see De Mey and Weber 2003), Freeland (2000) argues that since the voting trust agreement was set to expire on October 1, 1924, after that date GM could easily have thwarted any attempt at holdup by exercising its voting right based on the 60 percent ownership. That is, the mechanism that linked GM's majority voting right and the prevention of a holdup attempt would be operative once the voting trust agreement expired. He uses this as one of three reasons to challenge Klein et al.'s (1978) explanation.

In response to Freeland's (2000) critique, Klein (2000) quotes the testimony of Sloan in the Du Pont case: "we could not adjust because we always had to respect the forty percent outstanding interests . . . we were bound by a contract in which the minority interest was outstanding, which we had to respect" (p. 120). Sloan admitted GM's inability to rescind the principle of upholding Fisher Body's autonomy reflected in the voting trust agreement. Moreover, Lawrence Fisher testified in the same court case that the management of Fisher Body maintained operating control after the expiration of the voting trust agreement in 1924. To summarize, Klein's (2000) argument is that the spirit of the voting trust agreement that supported Fisher Body's autonomy remained after its expiration. His argument is more convincing than Freeland's because the former is based on the testimonies of two key executives whereas the latter is simply an inference that after October 1, 1924, GM would exercise its voting right in order to prevent any holdup if needed. These testimonies cast doubt on the soundness of Freeland's reasoning. In other words, the alleged mechanism that would prevent a holdup attempt was not likely to be operative even after the expiry of the voting trust agreement.

A caveat is that Fisher Body's ability to maintain autonomy should not be simply interpreted as the prevailing view being more plausible than the alternative explanations. This issue of autonomy is only one element of the overall explanation. The evidence being in favor of Klein's (2000) argument instead suggests that Freeland (2000) inappropriately uses the voting trust agreement as a reason to challenge the prevailing view.

Experiments

Many mechanisms proposed through management theories consist of chains of causal links in which one event leads to another. Experiments throw light on these links by testing the effects of mechanisms under conditions similar to those of a closed system where "a constant conjunction of events obtains; i.e. in which an event of type a is invariably accompanied by an event of type b" (Bhaskar 1978: 70). Experiments are uncommon in management studies in general and in TCE research in particular. As an exception, Pilling et al. (1994) conducted an experiment with midlevel purchasing managers as subjects. They asked these managers to examine the effects of different levels of asset specificity, uncertainty, and frequency on transaction costs and relational closeness. One strength of their study is that they could vary the independent variable levels in a way that is not possible in a natural setting. Their results provide some insights into intermediate-range exchange relationships that fall between market-based transactions and vertical integration.

The most salient limitation of experiments is the questionable generalizability of their results to the real world (Croson et al. 2007). Closure conditions are rarely achievable in the social sciences as shown by the artificiality of laboratory experiments performed by social psychologists (Harré and Second 1972). In economics it is impossible to specify all the necessary initial conditions in a test situation, even in controlled experiments. These conditions can be large in number, are subject to change, and may not be independently observable (Caldwell 1984). More importantly, subjects may significantly change their behavior in response to an experimental setting. Experimental results may accordingly provide little useful information regarding how far the theory in question can accurately describe real-world phenomena. In contrast, historical events unfold in a natural setting free of any researcher manipulations. The GM–Fisher Body integration is an excellent example of such an event; the "naturalness" of historical evidence has an advantage in this respect (Bryant 1994).

However, historical studies face a generalizability problem of a different nature since their small sample sizes may limit the generalizability of their results to other settings. The GM–Fisher Body integration is admittedly just one historical event. Yet we have to distinguish between theory testing and theory building. Klein et al.'s (1978) explanation can be considered an attempt to test TCE with an affirmative result. Their intention is to show that the event supports the TCE argument concerning how market failure can be remedied by vertical integration. The generalizability of the event is therefore not a relevant issue here. In contrast, generalizability is a pertinent concern in theory building. Freeland's (2000) study suggests an opportunity for theory building with respect to how human asset specificity determines firm boundaries. Other things being equal, multiple historical events surely provide more compelling evidence than a single event because it can be difficult to separate the theoretical relationships found in an event, which are supposedly generalizable, from idiosyncrasies associated with the event itself.

Analysis of archival data

Analysis of archival data here refers to the use of statistical methods in analyzing either an existing database or a database compiled by researchers through a questionnaire survey.[4] This research method has an advantage over case study research and historiography in that it uses large samples and avoids the small-N problem. Since these samples consist of data that reflect actual phenomena, this research method overcomes the main limitation of experiments that the results are not generalizable to the real world. Yet archival data analysis has two main shortcomings, both of which are not shared by historical studies.

The first shortcoming is best summarized by Ghoshal and Moran's (1996) critique concerning the empirical research in TCE: "Even though an impressive number of empirical studies have found a positive relationship between asset specificity and internalization . . . correlation does not demonstrate causation" (p. 40). This problem is illustrated by Masten et al.'s (1989) study concerning the relative influence of transaction-specific investments in physical and human assets on vertical integration based on data obtained directly from Chrysler, Ford, and GM. Their sample consisted of 118 automobile components, each measured in terms of specialized technical know-how and two types of physical asset specificity. Their regression results indicate that investments in specialized technical know-how have a greater effect than those in specialized physical assets on the decision to vertically integrate. Since their results only display a set of correlational relationships among the focal variables, they throw little light on the mechanisms that connect these variables. Monteverde and Teece's (1982a, 1982b) earlier studies on the same topic using data of a similar nature suffer from exactly the same problem, as discussed in chapter 3.

On the other hand, historical studies have a clear strength in this respect. The temporal dimension plays a critical role in historical explanation since "all historical methods are, by definition, longitudinal" (Yates 2014: 274). Given the temporal precedence of causes, time is an essential element of causal mechanisms (Healey 1983). The different explanations of the GM–Fisher Body integration, whether supporting the holdup thesis or not, all involve some description of mechanisms consisting of a chronological sequence of events. For instance, Freeland's (2000) aforementioned argument is that after the expiry of the voting trust agreement on October 1, 1924, GM could legally defeat any holdup attempt. This argument consists of a chronological sequence of two key events with a clear causal relationship – the expiry of the voting trust agreement and the establishment of GM's majority voting right. Moreover, the implication is that given the occurrence of the second event, holdup should not be a reason for the integration that took place afterward in 1926. Klein (2000) challenges Freeland's argument in that the expiry of the voting trust agreement did not change GM's respect for Fisher Body's operational autonomy, as evidenced by the testimonies made by Sloan and Lawrence Fisher. Therefore, the mechanism linking GM's majority voting right and the prevention of a holdup attempt would not have occurred.

Moreover, through explicating causal mechanisms, historical studies throw light on the core assumptions of the theory concerned. The discussion of the GM–Fisher Body integration shows how the role of opportunism, which is a core TCE assumption, unfolded in the events leading to the integration. The prevailing view infers opportunism on the part of Fisher Body by extracting evidence from the related historical documents. In spite of the disputes concerning the accuracy of such inference, the case indicates the ability of historical studies to investigate core assumptions directly. In contrast, as argued in chapter 3, quantitative methods test reduced models that often exclude core assumptions.

Another shortcoming of analyzing archival data concerns HARKing (Hypothesizing After the Results are Known), as discussed in chapter 4. Leung's (2011) crude analysis of the mostly quantitative papers published in the *Academy of Management Journal* in 2009 indicates that this ethically questionable practice is by no means a rare phenomenon. The possibility of HARKing is ruled out in historical studies, which are not based on large samples. Yet it is possible that a variant of HARKing is present in historical studies (and also case studies) in the form of post hoc storytelling where researchers selectively present information related to a historical event that supports a theory-based story. This possibility is not negligible, as Kieser (1994: 610) cautions, "The identification of actual organizational problems and of their appropriate remedies is often not free of ideology." For example, Klein et al.'s (1978) explanation *could be* an outcome of a one-sided presentation of information with the intention of telling a classic holdup story. However, an important difference is that while there is little risk of being challenged for HARKing in quantitative data analysis, this is not so for post hoc storytelling in historical studies. In the former case, let us assume that a researcher who engages in HARKing properly executes all required statistical procedures. Accordingly, if other researchers replicate the study by following the same statistical procedures and based on the same database, they will arrive at exactly the same results. Although the results may be different if another database is used, this does not invalidate the previous results but instead indicates that they are not generalizable to the second database. Since the data are not collected under conditions of closure in both cases and are subject to diverse contingent influences, it is not surprising that the results of the original study are not replicable. When replications are undertaken in business disciplines, they often conflict with, or at best partially support, the original findings (Hubbard and Vetter 1996; Hubbard et al. 1998). Researchers who practice HARKing in quantitative studies face little risk of being contested as long as the data analysis is properly conducted.

The case of historical studies is very different. "Historians ought to be able to offer evidence and arguments for their historical claims, and to do so in a specific and not merely a vague, ostensive way" (Megill 2007: 85). Moreover, there is usually a set of commonly accessible relics to which historians can refer, and new relics may be discovered as time passes. Biased presentation of information is risky because different, or even contradictory, information is readily available to all who are interested in the focal event. A good example is the issue of whether or not Fisher Body refused to locate its plants close to GM's assembly plants. While Klein et al. (1978) assert Fisher Body's refusal without any supporting evidence, Klein (1988) cites Sloan's testimony in the Du Pont case for support. Coase (2000: 27–29) examines in detail Klein et al.'s (1978) claim and interprets the testimony as a dispute not about plant location, but about which company should put up the capital required for building the plants. He also shows that while Fisher Body did not build any body plants between 1919 and 1921, all of its eight body plants built during the period from 1922 to 1925 were constructed near GM plants. He therefore rejects this claim as "completely untrue." Without going into the details of the debate, it is interesting to note that Klein (2000: 111) retorts, "Coase misses five of the 14 body plants Fisher built or acquired during 1919–24." The exchange between Klein and Coase lucidly illustrates the risk of one-sided information presentation, which has the effect of discouraging its use in historical studies. This is actually an additional advantage of historical studies over case studies. Interview data collected by case researchers are not readily available to other researchers, and it is therefore difficult to judge how far the information presented in a case study is free of bias.

Conclusion

Historical studies are still a relatively rare species in mainstream management journals, and historiography is by no means a familiar method among management researchers. One plausible reason is that researchers are not cognizant of the desirable role that historiography can play in theory development. This chapter systematically discusses from a methodological perspective the general merits of historiography and its specific advantages relative to three traditional research methods – case study, experiment, and analysis of archival data – based on the GM–Fisher Body integration example.

Historiography enriches theoretical knowledge and may provide "pre-theoretical" contexts for theory testing. A major advantage over case studies is that the availability of a set of commonly accessible relics facilitates the work of replicating an original study. Historiography avoids a key limitation of experiments that research results may not be generalizable to the real world. Finally, compared with analysis of archival data, historiography has a clear strength of showing the mechanisms related to the focal event instead of simply presenting correlations among a set of variables. Moreover, historiography discourages biased presentation of information, which may be committed by case study researchers. In his review of the debate concerning the GM–Fisher Body integration, Coase (2006: 276) pinpoints a blind spot of economists:

> The fact of the matter is that economists commonly obtain their theories in the study of industrial organization (and probably elsewhere) as a result, not of examining what actually happened but by thinking about it. This was certainly the way in which the "classic example" of Fisher Body and GM was created and it led to the wrong answer.

The same warning is applicable to management researchers. Given their strengths, historical studies are in an excellent position to contribute to a solid empirical foundation for management theories.

To conclude, this chapter does not argue that historiography should be the dominant method of inquiry in management studies, particularly because theoretically interesting historical events can be hard to find. Rather, historical studies deserve to receive a commensurate level of attention from management researchers given the merits of historiography over traditional research methods.

Notes

1 Although the term "historiography" has several distinct meanings, I follow Goodman and Kruger (1988) and use it throughout this chapter to refer to research methods used by historians.
2 Recently Leuridan and Froeyman (2012) tried to revive the D-N model by reconceptualizing the notion of general laws using Woodward's (2003) theory of causation, which characterizes causation as "invariance under interventions." Only time can tell if their attempt will be successful in changing historians' attitude toward the model.
3 Owing to space limitations, I can only briefly highlight a few key points for each explanation with the risk of losing some pertinent details. Interested readers may refer to the original sources. After carefully reading the articles but without consulting the historical documents cited in these articles, I am of the opinion that the prevailing view's focus on holdup as a critical cause is simplistic and contradicts some of the evidence brought forward by the opposing camp. The multiple causes proposed by Freeland (2000) as well as Casadesus-Masanell and Spulber (2000) sound more plausible. Moreover, in a subsequent review of the debate, Coase (2006) highlights an important inconsistency in argument between Klein (2000) and Klein et al. (1978) – "Whereas we were told previously that GM found the contractual relations with Fisher Body 'intolerable' by 1924, we are now told that up to 1924 'the contract functioned well' " (p. 269) – that calls into question the credibility of the supporting evidence of the prevailing view.
4 I do not separately discuss questionnaire surveys because they are somewhat similar to analyses of traditional archival data such as Compustat. A main difference is that the data for the former are collected through surveys while those of the latter are extracted from existing databases. This difference does not affect my discussion of the relative advantages of historical studies.

References

Argyres, N. 1996. Evidence on the role of firm capabilities in vertical integration decisions. *Strategic Management Journal*, 17: 129–150.

Barkema, H. G. and Vermeulen, F. 1998. International expansion through start-up or acquisition: A learning perspective. *Academy of Management Journal*, 41: 7–26.

Baum, J. A. C. and Mezias, S. J. 1992. Localized competition and organizational failure in the Manhattan hotel industry, 1898–1990. *Administrative Science Quarterly*, 37: 580–604.

Bell, E. and Taylor, S. 2013. Writing history into management research. *Management and Organizational History*, 8: 127–136.

Bhaskar, R. 1978. *A realist theory of science* (2nd ed.). Hassocks, England: Harvester Press.

Booth, C. 2003. Does history matter in strategy? The possibilities and problems of counterfactual analysis. *Journal of Management History*, 41: 96–104.

Booth, C. and Rowlinson, M. 2006. Management and organizational history: Prospects. *Management and Organizational History*, 1: 5–30.

Bryant, J. M. 1994. Evidence and explanation in history and sociology: Critical reflections on Goldthorpe's critique of historical sociology. *British Journal of Sociology*, 45: 3–19.

Bunge, M. 2004. How does it work? The search for explanatory mechanisms. *Philosophy of the Social Sciences*, 34: 182–210.

Caldwell, B. J. 1984. Some problems with falsificationism in economics. *Philosophy of the Social Sciences*, 14: 489–495.

Calhoun, C. 1998. Explanation in historical sociology: Narrative, general theory, and historical specific theory. *American Journal of Sociology*, 104: 846–871.

Canter, N. F. and Schneider, R. I. 1967. *How to study history*. New York: Crowell.

Carroll, C. E. 2002. Introduction. *Journal of Organizational Change Management*, 15: 556–562.

Carroll, G. R. and Delacroix, J. 1982. Organizational mortality in the newspaper industries of Argentina and Ireland: An ecological approach. *Administrative Science Quarterly*, 27: 169–198.

Casadesus-Masanell, R. and Spulber, D. F. 2000. The fable of Fisher Body. *Journal of Law and Economics*, 43: 67–104.

Chandler Jr., A. D. 1962. *Strategy and structure: Chapters in the history of the industrial enterprise*. Cambridge, MA: MIT Press.

Chandler Jr., A. D. 1977. *The visible hand: The managerial revolution in American business*. Cambridge, MA: Harvard University Press.

Coase, R. H. 1937. The nature of the firm. *Economica*, 4: 386–405.

Coase, R. H. 2000. The acquisition of Fisher Body by General Motors. *Journal of Law and Economics*, 43: 15–31.

Coase, R. H. 2006. The conduct of economics: The example of Fisher Body and General Motors. *Journal of Economics and Management Strategy*, 15: 255–278.

Croson, R., Anand, J. and Agarwal, R. 2007. Using experiments in corporate strategy research. *European Management Review*, 4: 173–181.

Decker, S. 2013. The silence of the archives: Business history, post-colonialism and archival ethnography. *Management and Organizational History*, 8: 155–173.

De Mey, T. and Weber, E. 2003. Explanation and thought experiments in history. *History and Theory*, 42: 28–38.

Dray, W. H. 1957. *Laws and explanation in history*. Oxford, England: Oxford University Press.

Fischer, D. H. 1970. *Historians' fallacies: Toward a logic of historical thought*. New York: Harper Perennial.

Freeland, R. F. 2000. Creating holdup through vertical integration: Fisher Body revisited. *Journal of Law and Economics*, 43: 33–66.

Gerring, J. 2007. The case study: What it is and what it does. In C. Boix and S. C. Stokes (Eds.), *The Oxford handbook of comparative politics*: 90–122. Oxford, England: Oxford University Press.

Ghoshal, S. and Moran, P. 1996. Bad for practice: A critique of the transaction cost theory. *Academy of Management Review*, 21: 13–47.

Glennan, S. 2010. Ephemeral mechanisms and historical explanation. *Erkenntnis*, 72: 251–266.

Goldthorpe, J. H. 1991. The uses of history in sociology: Reflections on some recent tendencies. *British Journal of Sociology*, 42: 211–230.

Goodman, R. S. and Kruger, E. J. 1988. Data dredging or legitimate research method? Historiography and its potential for management research. *Academy of Management Review*, 13: 315–325.

Greenwood, A. and Bernardi, A. 2014. Understanding the rift, the (still) uneasy bedfellows of history and organization studies. *Organization*, 21: 907–932.

Griffin, L. J. 1992. Temporality, events, and explanation in historical sociology: An introduction. *Sociological Methods and Research*, 20: 403–427.

Hambrick, D. C. 2007. The field of management's devotion to theory: Too much of a good thing. *Academy of Management Journal*, 50: 1346–1352.

Hammer, C. 2008. Explication, explanation, and history. *History and Theory*, 47: 183–199.

Harré, R. and Second, P. F. 1972. *The explanation of social behavior*. Oxford, England: Basil Blackwell.

Hassard, J. S. 2012. Rethinking the Hawthorne Studies: The Western Electric research in its social, political and historical context. *Human Relations*, 65: 1431–1461.

Healey, R. A. 1983. Temporal and causal asymmetry. In R. Swinburne (Ed.), *Space, time and causality*: 79–103. Dordrecht, the Netherlands: Springer.

Hedström, P. and Swedberg, R. 1996. Social mechanisms. *Acta Sociologica*, 39: 281–308.

Hedström, P. and Ylikoski, P. 2010. Causal mechanisms in the social sciences. *Annual Review of Sociology*, 36: 49–67.

Hempel, C. G. 1942. The function of general laws in history. *Journal of Philosophy*, 39(2): 35–48.

Hempel, C. G. 1965. *Aspects of scientific explanation and other essays in the philosophy of science*. New York: Free Press.

Holmström, B. and Roberts, J. 1998. The boundaries of the firm revisited. *Journal of Economic Perspectives*, 12(4): 73–94.

Hubbard, R. and Vetter, D. E. 1996. An empirical comparison of published replication research in accounting, economics, finance, management, and marketing. *Journal of Business Research*, 35: 153–164.

Hubbard, R., Vetter, D. E. and Little, E. L. 1998. Replication in strategic management: Scientific testing for validity, generalizability, and usefulness. *Strategic Management Journal*, 19: 243–254.

Huber, G. P. and Power, D. J. 1985. Retrospective reports of strategic-level managers: Guidelines for increasing their accuracy. *Strategic Management Journal*, 6: 171–180.

Ingram, P., Rao, H. and Silverman, B. S. 2012. History in strategy research: What, why, and how? In S. J. Kahl, B. S. Silverman and M. A. Cusumano (Eds.), *Advances in strategic management*, Vol. 29: 241–273. Bingley, England: Emerald Group Publishing.

Kaplan, A. 1964. *The conduct of inquiry*. San Francisco, CA: Chandler Publishing.

Kieser, A. 1994. Why organization theory needs historical analyses – and how this should be performed. *Organization Science*, 5: 608–620.

Kipping, M., Wadhwani, R. D. and Bucheli, M. 2014. Analyzing and interpreting historical sources: A basic methodology. In M. Bucheli and R. D. Wadhwani (Eds.), *Organizations in time: History, theory, methods*: 305–329. Oxford, England: Oxford University Press.

Kiser, E. and Hechter, M. 1991. The role of general theory in comparative-historical sociology. *American Journal of Sociology*, 97: 1–30.

Klein, B. 1988. Vertical integration as organizational ownership: The Fisher Body-General Motors relationship revisited. *Journal of Law, Economics, and Organization,* 4: 199–213.

Klein, B. 2000. Fisher-General Motors and the nature of the firm. *Journal of Law and Economics,* 43: 105–141.

Klein, B., Crawford, R. G. and Alchian, A. A. 1978. Vertical integration, appropriable rents, and the competitive contracting process. *Journal of Law and Economics,* 21: 297–326.

Klein, P. G. 2008. The make-or-buy decision: Lessons from empirical studies. In C. Menard and M. M. Shirley (Eds.), *Handbook of new institutional economics*: 435–464. Berlin: Springer.

Knights, D. 1992. Changing space: The disruptive impact of a new epistemological location for the study of management. *Academy of Management Review,* 17: 514–536.

Leblebici, H. 2014. History and organization theory: Potential for a transdisciplinary convergence. In M. Bucheli and R. D. Wadhwani (Eds.), *Organizations in time: History, theory, methods*: 56–99. Oxford, England: Oxford University Press.

Leung, K. 2011. Presenting post hoc hypotheses as a priori: Ethical and theoretical issues. *Management and Organization Review,* 7: 471–479.

Leuridan, B. and Froeyman, A. 2012. On lawfulness in history and historiography. *History and Theory,* 51: 172–192.

Lipartito, K. 2014. Historical sources and data. In M. Bucheli and R. D. Wadhwani (Eds.), *Organizations in time: History, theory, methods*: 284–304. Oxford, England: Oxford University Press.

Little, D. 1991. *Varieties of social explanation: An introduction to the philosophy of social science.* Boulder, CO: Westview Press.

Lomi, A. 1995. The population ecology of organizational founding: Location dependence and unobserved heterogeneity. *Administrative Science Quarterly,* 40: 111–144.

Lustick, I. S. 1996. History, historiography, and political science: Multiple historical records and the problem of selection bias. *American Political Science Review,* 90: 605–618.

Macher, J. T. and Richman, B. D. 2008. Transaction cost economics: An assessment of empirical research in the social sciences. *Business and Politics,* 10: 1–63.

MacKenzie, D. and Millo, Y. 2003. Constructing a market, performing theory: The historical sociology of a financial derivatives exchange. *American Journal of Sociology,* 109: 107–145.

Masten, S. E., Meehan, J. W. J. and Snyder, E. A. 1989. Vertical integration in the U.S. auto industry. *Journal of Economic Behavior and Organization,* 12: 265–273.

McLemore, L. 1984. Max Weber's defense of historical inquiry. *History and Theory,* 23: 277–295.

Megill, A. 2007. *Historical knowledge, historical error: A contemporary guide to practice.* Chicago, IL: University of Chicago Press.

Monteverde, K. and Teece, D. J. 1982a. Appropriable rents and quasi-vertical integration. *Journal of Law and Economics,* 25: 321–328.

Monteverde, K. and Teece, D. J. 1982b. Supplier switching costs and vertical integration in the automobile industry. *Bell Journal of Economics,* 13: 207–213.

Moore Jr., B. 1958. *Political power and social theory: Six studies.* Cambridge, MA: Harvard University Press.

Murmann, J. P. 2012. Marrying history and social science in strategy research. In S. J. Kahl, B. S. Silverman and M. A. Cusumano (Eds.), *Advances in strategic management*, Vol. 29: 89–115. Bingley, England: Emerald Group Publishing.

Murphey, M. G. 1986. Explanation, cause, and covering laws. *History and Theory*, 25: 43–57.

Mutch, A. 2014. History and documents in critical realism. In P. K. Edwards, J. O'Mahoney and S. Vincent (Eds.), *Studying organizations using critical realism: A practical guide*: 223–240. Oxford, England: Oxford University Press.

Nagel, E. 1979. *The structure of science: Problems in the logic of scientific explanation*. Indianapolis, IN: Hackett Publishing.

Numagami, T. 1998. The infeasibility of invariant laws in management studies: A reflective dialogue in defense of case studies. *Organization Science*, 9: 2–15.

Pettigrew, A. M. 1985. *The awakening giant: Continuity and change in Imperial Chemical Industries*. Oxford, England: Basil Blackwell.

Pilling, B. K., Crosby, L. A. and Jackson, D. W. 1994. Relational bonds in industrial exchange: An experimental test of the transaction cost economic framework. *Journal of Business Research*, 30: 237–251.

Ringer, F. 2002. Max Weber on causal analysis, interpretation, and comparison. *History and Theory*, 41: 163–178.

Roberts, C. 1996. *The logic of historical explanation*. University Park, PA: Pennsylvania State University Press.

Rock, P. 1976. Some problems of interpretative historiography. *British Journal of Sociology*, 27: 353–369.

Roth, G. 1976. History and sociology in the work of Max Weber. *British Journal of Sociology*, 27: 306–318.

Rowlinson, M., Hassard, J. and Decker, S. 2014. Research strategies for organizational history: A dialogue between historical theory and organization theory. *Academy of Management Review*, 39: 250–274.

Runde, J. and de Rond, M. 2010. Evaluating causal explanations of specific events. *Organization Studies*, 31: 431–450.

Salmon, W. C. 1998. *Causality and explanation*. Oxford, England: Oxford University Press.

Sayer, A. 1992. *Method in social science: A realist approach* (2nd ed.). London: Routledge.

Sayer, A. 2000. *Realism and social science*. London: Sage.

Schreyögg, G., Sydow, J. and Holtmann, P. 2011. How history matters in organisations: The case of path dependence. *Management and Organizational History*, 6: 81–100.

Steel, D. 2004. Social mechanisms and causal inference. *Philosophy of the Social Sciences*, 34: 55–78.

Steinmetz, G. 2004. Odious comparisons: Incommensurability, the case study, and "small N's" in sociology. *Sociological Theory*, 22: 371–400.

Tilly, C. 2001. Mechanisms in political processes. *Annual Review of Political Science*, 4: 21–41.

Topolski, J. 1991. Towards an integration model of historical explanation. *History and Theory*, 30: 324–338.

Weber, M. 1949. *The methodology of the social sciences* (translated and edited by E. A. Shils and H. A. Finch). New York: Free Press.

Weber, M. 1968. *Economy and society* (edited by G. Roth and C. Wittich). New York: Bedminster.

Weber, M. 1975. *Roscher and Knies: The logical problems of historical economics* (translated by G. Oakes). New York: Free Press.

Woodward, J. 2003. *Making things happen: A theory of causal explanation.* New York: Oxford University Press.

Yates, J. 2014. Understanding historical methods in organization studies. In M. Bucheli and R. D. Wadhwani (Eds.), *Organizations in time: History, theory, methods*: 265–283. Oxford, England: Oxford University Press.

Yin, R. K. 2014. *Case study research: Design and methods* (5th ed.). Thousand Oaks, CA: Sage.

Zald, M. N. 1993. Organization studies as a scientific and humanistic enterprise: Toward a reconceptualization of the foundations of the field. *Organization Science*, 4: 513–528.

8   Looking ahead
To be, or not to be, a science

Throughout this book, I have an implicit assumption that management researchers regard their work as scientific activities, and my methodological suggestions are based on this assumption. Yet the previous chapters have highlighted that current research practices are sometimes inconsistent with certain norms of scientific research. Some examples of such norms are: replication is a cornerstone of empirical research (chapter 6); whether a theory is counterintuitive, interesting, or novel is irrelevant as far as its acceptability is concerned (chapter 6); negative findings (i.e., those that do not support a theory) carry equal, if not more, epistemic weight compared with positive findings (chapter 4); theories that have failed repeated empirical tests are abandoned (chapter 4); important discoveries, such as the discovery of penicillin, are treasured even if they cannot be explained by any existing theory or simply cannot be explained (chapter 2).[1] Such discrepancies are problematic only if my assumption is valid, but do management researchers really think that they are doing science?

Embracing the science label

Reflecting on the state of the management discipline from the 1920s to the early 1950s, Perrow (1994: 192) maintains that "there was widespread agreement that management was becoming a science." This "widespread agreement" has been reflected by the names of some leading academic journals such as *Administrative Science Quarterly*, *Management Science*, and *Organization Science*. In fact, one of the early works that formed the foundation of the subject – Taylor's (1911) *The Principles of Scientific Management* – has a title that reminds the reader of the scientific nature of its content. A similar emphasis is echoed in the lead article of the first issue of *Management Science*: "The Science of Managing is, like all true sciences, creating an expanding universe of concepts and principles" (Smiddy and Naum 1954: 31). Interestingly the term "true sciences" signifies the authors' anxiety that management may be erroneously regarded as a pseudoscience.

Given the remarkable progress and achievements of natural science since the scientific revolution during Renaissance, science is generally held in high regard. It is no wonder that a relatively new discipline such as management is eager to be perceived as a member of the prestigious "science club." In the domain of pedagogy, it is again easy to understand why the science label is desirable. A management theory surely sounds more authoritative and legitimate to students if they are told that it is the outcome of scientific research rather than other endeavors such as storytelling.

The tendency of many, if not most, management researchers to treat their discipline as a science is also reflected in the controversy aroused by Pfeffer's (1993) well-known methodological essay. Borrowing Kuhn's (1962) concept of paradigm, he cautions against theoretical and methodological pluralism and argues that researchers should attempt to reach some level of consensus, which is a critical precondition for advancing paradigm development in management and raising management's status relative to its peer disciplines such as economics.[2] None of the critiques of Pfeffer's argument challenge his presumption that management is a science. For example, Van Maanen's (1995) critique, which is probably the harshest, pinpoints that Pfeffer's view is "extraordinarily naive as to how science actually works" (p. 133), thus confirming the presumption.

Even management researchers who take a more radical postmodernist stance would like to embrace the science label by, for example, using the oxymoron "postmodern science" (Chia 1996, 2003). It is an oxymoron because scientific endeavors rely on confidence in the power of reason and the postmodernist movement can be described as "the counter-Enlightenment attack on reason" (Hicks 2011: 23). Generally speaking, science adopts a realist ontology and an objectivist epistemology whereas postmodernism adopts an anti-realist ontology and a social subjectivist epistemology.[3]

A predicament

The prior discussion suggests the existence of a predicament: while the management discipline claims, or aspires, to be scientific, some of its key practices are plainly not so. One possible response is to maintain that management is a science, but a different kind of science compared to natural science. As such, management researchers do not have to follow the latter's principles. There are signs along this line of argument in both Cannella and Paetzold's (1994) and Van Maanen's (1995) social constructivist critiques of Pfeffer's (1993) essay. For the former, "the test of publishability [of a research paper] should be coherent persuasiveness – an internal logic and cohesion capable of winning support" (Cannella and Paetzold 1994: 338). As to the latter, "putting theory in print is a literary performance; an activity involving the use of language whose methods are ways of writing through which certain identifiable reader responses are produced" (Van Maanen 1995).

Although Popper (1959) argues that what is to be called a "science" is a matter of convention, it does not follow that the science label can be used arbitrarily. In fact, as mentioned in chapter 4, Popper himself uses falsifiability as a criterion of demarcation between science and non-science.[4] Generally speaking, "to call a study a science implies that there is an empirical constraint on the acceptability of its statements, that the testing of its statements against the world is at least one strong criterion for the acceptance or rejection of those statements" (Thomas 1979: 2). Based on this criterion, assessing the quality of a piece of research is neither a popularity contest nor a literary evaluation, as the prior quotes of Cannella and Paetzold (1994) and Van Maanen (1995), respectively, seem to imply.[5]

It goes without saying that social science, to which management belongs, is different from natural science (see chapter 4). Yet it does not follow that social scientists should use completely different methods and follow completely different norms.[6] As Bhaskar (1998: 20) well says, "although, because social objects are irreducible to (and really emergent from) natural objects, and so possess qualitatively different features from them, they cannot be studied in the same way as them, they can still be studied 'scientifically.' " His point suggests that studies of either natural or social objects should follow a similar set of scientific norms, such as those mentioned earlier. Some of these norms in fact are concerned with the foundation of scientific knowledge. Consider, for example, replication. As Collins (1992: 18) comments:

> How do scientists establish that they have made a discovery that should be a new part of the public domain? Press scientists and in the last resort they will defend the validity of their claims by reference to the repeatability of their observations or the replicability of their experiments.

In brief, it is problematic to stretch the meaning of science to the extent that it accommodates unscientific practices. You can't have the cake and eat it too: if management researchers want to free themselves from the straightjacket of scientific norms, they should stop claiming that they are doing science. This leads to a second possible response to the predicament, which is to drop the science label altogether. Honesty is the best policy – if a discipline does not fit the domain of science, why not just say so?

Honesty is especially critical in the classroom. For instance, in natural science, empirical findings that are based on a single, or a couple, of studies, such as the case of versatile stem cells mentioned in chapter 6, are rarely taught as established research results – or are not even mentioned – in the classroom. How often do management instructors teach students findings of single uncorroborated – and perhaps novel – studies as if these were pieces of established scientific knowledge? Hubbard (2016) provides some examples of erroneous results based on such studies that have been taught in the classroom for decades. Telling students that management is a science, while knowing that it is not, is to tell a lie. Telling students that management is a science, while believing that it is (as proponents of the first response may do), is to tell a falsehood. Either way, it does more harm than good.[7]

Lastly, a third possible response, which I would recommend, is to live up to the scientific status that the discipline strives to achieve. In this case, management researchers should follow the norms of science. Needless to say, it would be very difficult, if ever possible, for subscribers to certain philosophical perspectives to do that. As mentioned, science is built on a realist ontology and an objectivist epistemology; any philosophical perspective, such as postmodernism, that holds an opposite ontological and/or epistemological position is *prima facie* inconsistent with science.[8]

There is some progress in the direction of complying with the norms of science. One development is the editorial changes at *Strategic Management Journal* mentioned in chapter 4. Another is the new journal, *Academy of Management Discoveries*, with the mission of promoting "exploratory empirical research of management and organizational phenomena that our theories do not adequately explain." While this is encouraging, a problem is that the journal is by no means close to the *Academy of Management Journal* in terms of reputation. Scholars who work toward their promotion and tenure are more likely to conduct research that aims at the latter than the former. On the whole, the progress is too slow and too little.

A concerted effort

It's high time the management research community tackled the predicament together through open, frank, and democratic discussions. If possible, the whole community may reach some kind of consensus as to whether the discipline should aspire to be a science *and* follow scientific norms. If not, the discipline may split into, say, two streams: one follows the path of science and the other a different path. The development of psychology versus parapsychology (Collins 1992) or astronomy versus astrology (Abramowicz 2011) may provide some insights in this respect. Though splitting the community may not be a desirable outcome, it is surely better than the current chaotic situation where research practices of all sorts are labeled as scientific, confusing such major stakeholders as students and managers.

To end this book, I would like to highlight a critical and penetrating comment made by Bertrand Russell about a century ago at the beginning of his book *Our Knowledge of the External World*: "Philosophy, from the earliest times, has made greater claims, and achieved fewer results, than any other branch of learning" (Russell 1972 [1914]: 13). If management researchers, including myself, lack a concerted effort to address the predicament, his comment – with "Philosophy" replaced by "Management" – may also be applicable to our discipline.

Notes

1 The fact that management is a young discipline is not an excuse for not following these norms. For example, a discipline does not have to be well established before replicated studies can be conducted. In fact, as a young discipline, it should welcome discoveries of important phenomena that fall outside the explanatory domain of its current theories.
2 While it is not my intention to review or participate in the debate surrounding Pfeffer's essay, I would like to point out that it is unfortunate for him to base his

argument on the muddled concept of paradigm (see chapter 1). First, the concept is not required for his argument. Like Pfeffer, I also caution against the proliferation of management theories in chapter 4, but I do it without using the concept. Second, the concept has led to unnecessary confusions. For example, in his critique of Pfeffer's essay, Perrow (1994) uses the words "paradigm" and "theory" interchangeably, as indicated by the terms "rational choice paradigm" and "rational choice theory." Such an oversight contributes nothing but chaos to the debate.

3 The incoherency associated with "postmodern science" is not surprising given the relativist stance of postmodernism. Relativist arguments often suffer from such inconsistency as "if the relativists say that beliefs have no objective validity then that belief itself has none" (Holcomb 1987: 467).

4 Mahoney (1993: 179) argues that "there is no meaningful way to separate science from non-science" and therefore the demarcation problem is a "pseudo-problem." An implication is that it is not meaningful to discuss whether management is a science. At the theoretical level, I am agnostic as to whether there is a meaningful way to distinguish science from non-science. My hunch is that the distinction is not likely to be either/or; that is, science and non-science are likely to be the ends of a continuum within which a discipline falls based on a set of criteria (see Dupré 1993; Kitcher 1993). At the logical level, whenever the word "science" is used, some sort of demarcation is presumed. There must be some features that distinguish science from non-science in order that the word can be used meaningfully. At the practical level, Resnik (2000: 249) astutely comments that the demarcation problem "is not merely a philosophical issue, however, since it has a significant bearing on practical policy questions and practical decisions." The fact is, "science" is a commonly used term in not only our daily lives but also academia. The problem discussed in this chapter is that many, if not most, management researchers claim that they are doing science (probably because the word "science" has far more positive connotations than "non-science" or "pseudoscience"). Yet some of their practices are simply inconsistent with established scientific norms. This predicament has practical implications and, regardless of whether the demarcation problem can be solved, has to be addressed.

5 I do agree with the view of Cannella and Paetzold (1994) and Van Maanen (1995) that management researchers should write in a coherent, persuasive, and eloquent manner. Yet these qualities should be of secondary importance compared with other aspects of scientific research such as soundness of method and quality of data. Like Van Maanen I am also a fan of Karl Weick. That said, I would opt for a clumsily composed theory if it offers greater explanatory power than one elegantly written by Weick.

6 Science originated from the study of natural phenomena. The term "social science" was later created to indicate that it is a kind of science different from natural science with the understanding that both share certain similarities in terms of methods and principles – i.e., share a certain degree of scientificity; otherwise a term without the science label, such as "social study," "social inquiry," or "social investigation," should be used instead.

7 These two types of persons are somewhat analogous to the ordinary and pompous fools mentioned in the explosive comment made by Feynman (1985), who was famous for his frank and direct character, on the participants of a multidisciplinary conference discussing the ethics of equality:

> Ordinary fools are all right; you can talk to them, and try to help them out. But pompous fools – guys who are fools and are covering it all over and impressing people as to how wonderful they are with all this hocus

pocus– THAT, I CANNOT STAND! An ordinary fool isn't a faker; an honest fool is all right. But a dishonest fool is terrible!

(p. 284)

8 I understand that my comment may arouse uproar among researchers who subscribe to these philosophical perspectives and that I may be accused of being "extraordinarily naive as to how science actually works" (Van Maanen 1995: 133). I always welcome others pointing out errors of my arguments and am prepared to engage in dialogues for settling intellectual disputes.

References

Abramowicz, M. A. 2011. Astronomy versus astrology. In J.-P. Lasota (Ed.), *Astronomy at the frontiers of science*: 285–307. Dordrecht, Netherland: Springer.

Bhaskar, R. 1998. *The possibility of naturalism: A philosophical critique of the contemporary human sciences* (3rd ed.). New York: Routledge.

Cannella, A. A. J. and Paetzold, R. L. 1994. Pfeffer's barriers to the advance of organizational science: A rejoinder. *Academy of Management Review*, 19: 331–341.

Chia, R. 1996. The problem of reflexivity in organizational research: Towards a postmodern science of organization. *Organization*, 3: 31–59.

Chia, R. 2003. Organization theory as a postmodern science. In H. Tsoukas and C. Knudsen (Eds.), *The Oxford handbook of organization theory*: 113–140. Oxford, England: Oxford University Press.

Collins, H. 1992. *Changing order: Replication and induction in scientific practice*. Chicago, IL: University of Chicago Press.

Dupré, J. 1993. *The disorder of things: Metaphysical foundations of the disunity of science*. Cambridge, MA: Harvard University Press.

Feynman, R. P. 1985. *"Surely you're joking, Mr. Feynman!": Adventures of a curious character*. New York: W. W. Norton and Company.

Hicks, S. R. C. 2011. *Explaining postmodernism: Skepticism and socialism from Rousseau and Foucault* (Expanded ed.). Loves Park, IL: Ockham's Razor Publishing.

Holcomb III, R. H. 1987. Circularity and inconsistency in Kuhn's defense of his relativism. *Southern Journal of Philosophy*, 25: 467–480.

Hubbard, R. 2016. *Corrupt research: The case for reconceptualizing empirical management and social science*. Thousand Oaks, CA: Sage.

Kitcher, P. 1993. *The advancement of science*. New York: Oxford University Press.

Kuhn, T. S. 1962. *The structure of scientific revolutions*. Chicago, IL: University of Chicago Press.

Mahoney, J. T. 1993. Strategic management and determinism: Sustaining the conversation. *Journal of Management Studies*, 30: 173–191.

Perrow, C. 1994. Pfeffer slips! *Academy of Management Review*, 19: 191–194.

Pfeffer, J. 1993. Barriers to the advance of organizational science: Paradigm development as a dependent variable. *Academy of Management Review*, 18: 599–620.

Popper, K. 1959. *The logic of scientific discovery*. London: Hutchison.

Resnik, D. B. 2000. A pragmatic approach to the demarcation problem. *Studies in History and Philosophy of Science*, 31: 249–267.

Russell, B. 1972 [1914]. *Our knowledge of the external world*. London: George Allen and Unwin.

Smiddy, H. F. and Naum, L. 1954. Evolution of a "science of managing" in America. *Management Science*, 1: 1–31.

Taylor, F. W. 1911. *The principles of scientific management.* New York: Harper and Brothers Publishers.

Thomas, D. 1979. *Naturalism and social science: A post-empiricist philosophy of social science.* Cambridge, England: Cambridge University Press.

Van Maanen, J. 1995. Style as theory. *Organization Science*, 6: 133–143.

Appendix
How philosophy contributes to research methodology

Although the number of philosophy-based discussions of methodological issues has been growing in the management literature, to my knowledge, there has not been any review of this stream of research. This appendix aims to achieve two objectives. First, it provides a systematic review of such articles published in leading management journals. Second, it offers suggestions for moving this research stream forward. To achieve the first objective, I searched nine management journals from their first issues until the end of 2015: *Academy of Management Review* (*AMR*), *Administrative Science Quarterly* (*ASQ*), *Journal of Applied Psychology* (*JAP*), *Journal of International Business Studies* (*JIBS*), *Journal of Management* (*JOM*), *Journal of Management Studies* (*JMS*), *Organization Science* (*OSc*), *Organization Studies* (*OSt*), and *Strategic Management Journal* (*SMJ*). All of them are commonly regarded as leading journals in the management field. I excluded the *Academy of Management Journal* because it only publishes empirical articles whereas virtually all philosophical discussions of research methodology are conceptual in nature. I also excluded the *International Journal of Management Reviews* because it is a reviews journal and does not publish articles that tackle specific methodological issues. I also searched *Organization* (*O*), which has a reputation of publishing philosophy-based articles, and *Organizational Research Methods* (*ORM*), which is a premier journal in the field of research methodology.

I searched these 11 journals using the word "philosophy." Such a liberal search resulted in a large number of hits for some of the journals. For example, there were 789 and 559 hits for *OSt* and *JMS* respectively. Based on my previous literature reviews in this stream of research, I also considered potentially relevant articles published in these journals that were not captured by the search word. I read through each of the shortlisted articles, starting from its abstract, to determine its relevance. The scope of this review is determined by two main criteria. First, the article has a substantial philosophical element underlying its core arguments, and second, it is concerned with specific methodological issues. As expected, most of the shortlisted articles fail to satisfy either or both of the criteria. For example, Lewis's (2000) discussion of how to study paradoxical tensions in organizations fails to satisfy the first criterion because it is mostly based on logic. Although logic is sometimes considered a branch of philosophy, here I adopt a narrower definition of philosophy and exclude logic. Another example, similar to the case of Lewis (2000), is Ketokivi and Mantere's (2010) examination of two inductive reasoning strategies – idealization and contextualization – that can be used when theoretical conclusions are drawn from empirical data. As to the second criterion, Calás and Smircich's (1999) work, for example, does not satisfy this criterion, although it satisfies the first one. The authors review the impact of postmodernism on organizational theorizing during the past decade and do not discuss specific methodological issues. Similarly, Tsang and Ellsaesser (2011) discuss how contrastive explanation can assist management researchers in creating, broadening, and deepening their theories through posing suitable contrastive questions. Although the discussion draws heavily on philosophy of science, it focuses on theory building rather than research methodology. As a further example, Tomkins and Simpson (2015: 1013) develop "the idea of caring leadership based on Heidegger's philosophy of care" and focus more on theory development than tackling any specific methodological issue.

Reading the abstracts alone resulted in eliminating most of the shortlisted articles. Articles that required further reading were in the hundreds. Table A.1 lists the 50 articles that have satisfied both criteria, their major methodological issues covered, the nature of their contributions, and the philosophical perspectives or philosophers that form the basis of their discussions. It does not include subsequent commentaries, if any, of these articles (e.g., Kwan and Tsang 2001) and the authors' responses (Mir and Watson 2001). Although I excluded books and book chapters in my review, this collection of journal articles has provided a fairly comprehensive picture of how philosophy has contributed to methodological discussions since the 1980s.

Of the 11 journals, *OSt* has published the largest number (16) of articles on this list, followed by *ORM*, which has 11 articles. Two journals – *JAP* and *JOM* – have not published any articles that fall within the current review. This finding is more surprising for a generalist journal like *JOM* than a heavily empirical-based journal like *JAP*. Methodological discussions published in the latter are usually related to statistical analysis, a typical example of which is the review of common method bias written by Podsakoff et al. (2003). As to the former, the article that is closest to the domain of this review is Locke's (2007) argument for inductive theory building, which is similar in nature to Ketokivi and Mantere's (2010) inductive reasoning strategies and is based more on logic than on philosophy. Another "near miss" is Singh et al.'s (2003) proposal of a re-conceptualization of replication studies to that of the so-called "good-enough replication." Their discussion builds heavily on Tsang and Kwan (1999), but unlike the latter, it draws little on philosophy, as clearly indicated by their cited references. The oldest article in the group is Whitley (1984), published in *JMS*. If we use the year 2000 to split the period 1984–2015 into two equal sub-periods, there are 13 articles published from 1984–1999 and 37 from 2000–2015, indicating a significant upward trend. An interesting observation is that 27 of the 50 articles are sole authored, a percentage that is much higher than that of management literature in general. The influence

Table A.1 Philosophical discussions of methodological issues in leading management journals

Author and Year	Journal	Methodological Issue	Nature of Contribution	Philosophical Perspective/Philosopher
Amis and Silk (2008)	ORM	Assessment of quality in qualitative research	Problem solving	Foundationalism, quasi-foundationalism, and nonfoundationalism
Astley (1985)	ASQ	Theory-ladenness of empirical research	Presenting an alternative approach	Not specified
Avenier (2010)	OSt	Generating and using knowledge about organizations	Creating a new approach	Constructivism
Brannick and Coghlan (2007)	ORM	Justifying insider academic research	Problem solving	Positivism, hermeneutics, and critical realism
Cederström and Spicer (2014)	O	Getting "real" about organizational discourse analysis	Presenting an alternative approach	Post-foundationalism
Chia (1995)	OSt	Comparing between modernist and postmodernist approaches to organizational analysis	Comparing approaches	Postmodernism
Chia and Holt (2006)	OSt	Reconceptualizing agency, action, and practice and how they interrelate in the process of strategizing	Comparing approaches	Heidegger
Cohen (2007)	OSt	Representations of organizational routines as patterns-in-variety	Problem solving	Dewey
Cox and Hassard (2005)	O	Re-presenting the concept of triangulation	Presenting an alternative approach	Postmodernism
Durand and Vaara (2009)	SMJ	Causal analysis in strategy research	Problem solving	Positivism, constructionism, realism, and pragmatism

(Continued)

Table A.1 (Continued)

Author and Year	Journal	Methodological Issue	Nature of Contribution	Philosophical Perspective/ Philosopher
Everett (2002)	ORM	Relational analysis, reflexivity, the role of the researcher, and methodological polytheism	Presenting an alternative approach	Bourdieu
Fairclough (2005)	OSt	Discourse analysis	Presenting an alternative approach	Critical realism
Farjoun et al. (2015)	OSc	Applying pragmatism to organization studies	Presenting an alternative approach	Pragmatism
Gill (2014)	ORM	Classifying and contrasting phenomenological methodologies	Comparing approaches	Phenomenology
Godfrey and Hill (1995)	SMJ	Dealing with unobservable constructs	Problem solving	Realism
Gray and Cooper (2010)	ORM	Identifying the limits of a theory	Presenting an alternative approach	Not specified
Harris et al. (2013)	AMR	Grafting, contextualizing, and repurposing representational models	Comparing approaches	Model-theoretic philosophy
Hassard (1994)	JMS	Five key concepts for postmodern organizational analysis – "representation," "reflexivity," "writing," "différance," and "de-centring the subject."	Presenting an alternative approach	Postmodernism
Herepath (2014)	OSt	Interplay of structure and agency in strategy formation and strategizing	Presenting an alternative approach	Critical realism
Holt and Mueller (2011)	OSt	Fixing meaning and the conditions of meaning	Presenting an alternative approach	Heidegger and Wittgenstein
Hoon (2013)	ORM	Meta-synthesis of qualitative case studies	Creating a new approach	Postpositivism

Citation	Journal	Description	Purpose	Paradigm
Hosking (2011)	*OSt*	Inquiry as a process of (re)constructing realities and relations	Presenting an alternative approach	Relational constructionism
Jeffcutt (1994)	*JMS*	Analyzing organizational culture and symbolism	Presenting an alternative approach	Postmodernism
Johnson and Duberley (2003)	*JMS*	Three generic forms of reflexivity, each with distinctive implications for management research	Comparing approaches	Critical theory, neo-empiricism, positivism, and postmodernism
Kilduff and Mehra (1997)	*AMR*	Reviving classic studies, attention to local knowledge, eclectic approach, and searching for paradox	Presenting an alternative approach	Postmodernism
Knights (1997)	*OSt*	Deconstructing dualisms in organizational analysis	Problem solving	Postmodernism
Leitch et al. (2010)	*ORM*	Validating interpretivist entrepreneurship research	Problem solving	Interpretivism
Lorino et al. (2011)	*OSt*	Non-representational approaches to studying organizational complexity	Creating a new approach	Pragmatism and dialogism
Martela (2015)	*OSt*	Applying pragmatism to organizational research	Presenting an alternative approach	Dewey
McKelvey (1997)	*OSc*	Framing a quasi-natural organization science for investigating phenomena consisting of idiosyncratic organizational microstates	Creating a new approach	Scientific realism
Miller (2009)	*OSt*	Assumptions in organizational risk research	Comparing approaches	Postmodernism
Miller (2015a)	*ORM*	Applying practical theology to organizational research	Presenting an alternative approach	Practical theology
Miller (2015b)	*OSt*	Agent-based modeling	Problem solving	Critical realism

(Continued)

Table A.1 (Continued)

Author and Year	Journal	Methodological Issue	Nature of Contribution	Philosophical Perspective/Philosopher
Miller and Tsang (2011)	SMJ	Theory testing	Problem solving	Critical realism
Mir and Watson (2000)	SMJ	Applying constructivism to strategic management research	Presenting an alternative approach	Constructivism
Powell (2001)	SMJ	The hypothesis that sustained superior performance arises from sustainable competitive advantages	Problem solving	Pragmatism
Prasad (2002)	ORM	Applying hermeneutics to management research	Presenting an alternative approach	Hermeneutics
Rosile et al. (2013)	ORM	Conceptualizing a storytelling diamond model as a metatheoretical and methodological tool that enables a deeper examination of storytelling inquiry	Creating a new approach	Various
Runde and de Rond (2010)	OSt	Causal explanations of specific events	Problem solving	Critical realism
Sandberg (2005)	ORM	Justifying research results produced by interpretive approaches	Problem solving	Phenomenology
Shotter (2005)	OSt	Understanding management processes, especially those related to unique persons and events	Presenting an alternative approach	Wittgenstein
Simpson (2009)	OSt	The practice turn in the field of organization studies	Presenting an alternative approach	Mead
Steffy and Grimes (1986)	AMR	Practical relations and dynamic interplay among organizational research, theory, technology, practice, praxis, and ideology	Presenting an alternative approach	Critical theory

Tsang (2006)	*SMJ*	Testing behavioral assumptions of a theory	Problem solving	Critical realism
Tsang and Kwan (1999)	*AMR*	The role played by replication in theory development and a classification of replications	Problem solving	Critical realism
Tsoukas (1989)	*AMR*	External validity of organizational explanations produced through idiographic research	Problem solving	Critical realism
Watson (2011)	*JMS*	Enhancing the potential for ethnography to play a more mainstream role in management research	Presenting an alternative approach	Pragmatism
Whitley (1984)	*JMS*	Epistemological barriers to management research as a scientific subject	Presenting an alternative approach	Critical realism
Welch et al. (2011)	*JIBS*	Methods of theorizing from case study findings	Comparing approaches	Positivism, interpretivism, and critical realism
Wicks and Freeman (1998)	*OSc*	Incorporating ethics into the mainstream of management research	Presenting an alternative approach	Pragmatism

of the "lonely" philosophical tradition seems evident here as philosophy is well-known for having mostly sole-authored works.

A set of heterogeneous contributions

Reflecting the rugged terrain of the discipline of philosophy, the 50 articles form a set of heterogeneous contributions in terms of the methodological issues covered, philosophical perspectives adopted, and style of presentation. This section attempts to provide some systematic review of this somewhat chaotic literature.

Philosophical perspectives adopted

The philosophical perspectives or philosophers listed in Table A.1 are the ones that authors either advocate or compare (if they do not express their preference for a particular perspective or philosopher). A number of the perspectives do not belong to the group of four compared in Table 1.1 of chapter 1. Yet most of them are closely related to a member of the group. For instance, both scientific realism (McKelvey 1997) and critical realism belong to the family of realism (Godfrey and Hill 1995). Constructivism (Avenier 2010), relational constructionism (Hosking 2011),[1] hermeneutics (Prasad 2002), interpretivism (Leitch et al. 2010), and phenomenology (Gill 2014; Sandberg 2005) are more closely associated with postmodernism than the other three members of the group, and postmodernists have drawn heavily on the thinking of Heidegger (Chia and Holt 2006) and Wittgenstein (Shotter 2005). Dewey (Cohen 2007; Martela 2015) and Mead (Simpson 2009) are key figures of pragmatism. Finally, foundationalism, quasi-foundationalism, nonfoundationalism (Amis and Silk 2008), and post-foundationalism (Cederström and Spicer 2014) refer to theories of epistemic justification. Foundationalism holds that knowledge rests ultimately on some secure foundation of basic beliefs such as mental states and immediate experience (O'Brien 2006). Its opposite, nonfoundationalism, denies such a foundation and maintains that truths are relative to the context in which they are constructed; quasi-foundationalism is between the two extremes. Amis and Silk (2008) associate foundationalism, quasi-foundationalism, and nonfoundationalism with positivism, neorealism, and postmodernism, respectively. By post-foundationalism, Cederström and Spicer (2014: 185) refer to the view that a discourse "can never be grounded on a stable foundation," somewhat similar to nonfoundationalism.

Perhaps because positivism is regarded as a popular perspective held by management researchers (Daft and Lewin 1990; Gephart 2004; Johnson and Duberley 2000), there may not be a perceived need to use this "default" perspective to solve a methodological problem or elaborate a methodological issue. The stress on novelty by journal editors, as discussed in chapter 6, reinforces this perception. As such, none of the articles are based on positivism alone, and positivism is included for the purpose of comparison (e.g., Brannick and Coghlan 2007;

Durand and Vaara 2009; Martela 2015). On the other hand, postmodernism and its associated perspectives as a group is the most popular choice. This is not surprising as the postmodern movement in the social sciences has tended to pick on positivism as representing modernism (Kilduff and Mehra 1997). Postmodernist management researchers may perceive the need to challenge the dominant positivist position in order to establish their foothold in the discipline.

It is advisable for authors to specify the philosophical perspectives that they adopt for supporting their arguments. This helps readers better understand their reasoning and the associated ontological and epistemological assumptions. There are two articles that do not specify the underlying perspective – Astley (1985) and Gray and Cooper (2010). The core thesis of Astley (1985: 513) is that "the body of knowledge that constitutes administrative science is a socially constructed product" and that "the knowledge of administrative science is not built from objective truths but is, instead, an artifact." This is squarely a social constructionist view. Astley might not be cognizant of the term, which emerged in the 1980s, when he wrote the article. However, his failure to cite Berger and Luckmann's (1967) *The Social Construction of Reality*, which introduced the term to sociology and started the development of the perspective (Elder-Vass 2012), is less forgivable.

To increase the coherence of the field of organization studies, Gray and Cooper (2010: 620) advocate "a strategy of pursuing failure by (a) identifying the tacit assumptions embedded in theories, (b) discovering the boundaries beyond which theories do not hold, (c) conducting competitive tests between theories, and (d) adopting research methods that seek to explain counterexamples." It is natural to associate the strategy with Popper's falsificationism as Gray and Cooper (2010: 625) themselves admit, "The best-known advocate for the strategy of pursuing failure is Popper (1959)." However, they criticize Popper's perspective by quoting Lakatos (1970: 116): "no experimental result can ever kill a theory: any theory can be saved from counterinstances either by some auxiliary hypothesis or by a suitable reinterpretation of its terms." Yet there is no indication that they subscribe to Lakatos's progressive research programs either. They also try to distance themselves from positivism: "Nor are we advocating a return to the kind of doctrinal logical positivism seen in early Wittgenstein (1922) and the strong form of verificationism (Ayer 1946)" (p. 637). It is perplexing as to which philosophical perspective they adopt or what perspective they have created for supporting their so-called "strategy of pursuing failure." Lacking a guiding perspective, there are signs of incoherence in their discussion. For example, on one hand, they provide a recommendation with a strong pragmatist flavor: "Maybe all we need are theories that are good enough to provide general guidance, inviting smart practitioners to choose what to adopt (and adapt) and what to reject based on their own needs" (p. 636). On the other hand, their strategy of pursuing failure is very much based on the conception of truth as correspondence to reality. For instance, they define testing competing theories as "a contest between competing explanations of a phenomenon" (p. 629). However, pragmatists have serious reservations about this notion of truth.

Specifying a philosophical perspective does not imply that the perspective is upheld by the authors. In fact, it may not be necessary for authors to adopt any perspective if their objective is to compare how several perspectives would tackle a methodological issue. A typical example is Brannick and Coghlan's (2007) defense of insider academic research, which they define as "research by complete members of organizational systems in and on their own organizations" (p. 59). To challenge the established tradition that academic research in organizations is best conducted by independent outsiders, they describe and contrast the positions of positivism, hermeneutics, and critical realism with respect to the legitimacy of insider research. Without favoring one position over another, they conclude that insider research is justifiable within each position and thus conforms to standards of intellectual rigor.

Another example is Welch et al.'s (2011) discussion of how case study researchers may theorize from their findings. They distinguish four methods – inductive theory building, natural experiment, interpretive sensemaking, and contextualized explanation – based on respectively four philosophical perspectives – positivism (empiricist version), positivism (falsificationist version), interpretivism, and critical realism. From a content analysis of case studies published in three leading management journals, they discover that inductive theory building has been the dominant method and argue for greater utilization of the other three methods, without stating their preference.

Methodological issues covered

The highly heterogeneous nature of the methodological issues covered by the 50 articles defies any meaningful classification. That said, these articles vary a great deal along the dimension of whether the methodological issue is specific or general. Godfrey and Hill's (1995) discussion of unobservable constructs is an excellent illustration of the specificity end of the continuum. They focus on a well-defined methodological problem faced by strategy researchers – how to deal with unobservable constructs, which lie at the core of such major theories as transaction cost economics, agency theory, and the resource-based view. Another example is Tsang and Kwan's (1999) elaboration of the role played by replication in theory development on which chapter 6 is based. They address the apparent inconsistency that replication research is seldom published by management journals although management is claimed to be a (social) science discipline (whereas replication is a cornerstone of the natural sciences).

At the general end, we have articles that discuss the application of a certain philosophical perspective to management research. For instance, Prasad (2002) traces the historical development of hermeneutics and proposes some methodological guidelines for using hermeneutics in organizational research. These guidelines are concerned with diverse issues in empirical research such as the significance of the context, critical self-reflexivity, and the goal of interpreting data. Chia's (1995) and Kilduff and Mehra's (1997) discussion of postmodernism, Hosking's (2011) discussion of relational constructionism, and Mir and

Watson's (2000) discussion of constructivism also belong to this category. By the same token, Everett's (2002) introduction of Bourdieu's research methodology to the management discipline is a member of the category. An obvious problem of articles at this end is that within the length of a journal article, the broad coverage implies that the discussion is likely to be shallow and may provide few useful guidelines to researchers who are interested in trying out the perspective.

Nature of contribution

In spite of the heterogeneity of the methodological issues covered by the articles, there are four main ways through which the authors have contributed to the literature: (1) problem solving, (2) presenting an alternative approach, (3) comparing two or more approaches, and (4) creating a new approach. Table A.1 lists only the most salient kind of contributions for each article and does not rule out the possibility that an article may have more than one kind of contributions. For example, Lorino et al. (2011) propose "dialogical mediated inquiry" as a new approach to investigating organizational complexity. Their approach represents an alternative to the existing ones. Therefore they contribute in the second and the fourth ways. Their article is classified under the latter rather than the former because the novelty of their approach carries more significance. Each of the four kinds of contributions is discussed below.

Problem solving

For this kind of contribution, authors employ one or more philosophical perspectives to solve or address an existing problem. A good example is Runde and de Rond's (2010) proposed method for evaluating causal explanations of specific events. The business world is full of specific events that need to be explained, such as: Why did the merger of Daimler-Benz and Chrysler fail? Why did Carrefour exit from Japan? Why did Lenovo acquire IBM's PC business? Although there is no shortage of single-case research, it is not clear how one should assess causal explanations of such events. That is, this is a problem awaiting a solution. Based on the perspective of critical realism, Runde and de Rond (2010) work out a solution by detailing three criteria that a good causal explanation should satisfy.

As another example, Cohen (2007) attempts to address the difficulties that have plagued researchers' efforts to understand organizational routines, especially the paradox of their stability and change (Feldman 2003). He brings in Dewey's view of the primacy of human habit and its interplay with emotion and cognition. Instead of arguing that Dewey's view represents a solution to the difficulties, he suggests that it may help researchers craft an effective response to the problems:

> Dewey gets us started down this new road. With his help we can say broadly that the patterning of action is recognizable as the same because of the powerful shaping forces of human habits and emotions. They seem to provide

2 Appendix

the action repertoires of individuals and organizations with a coherent character that underlies their perceived sameness. At the same time, he helps us to appreciate that our remarkable powers of thought let us reassemble our habit-rooted repertoires of action to cope with novel conditions.

(p. 782)

Presenting an alternative approach

Authors present an approach to tackling a specific methodological issue (or conducting research in general) that is different from the existing approach(s). This is the most popular kind of contributions among the four, with a total of 23 articles. A number of these articles present postmodernism or constructivism as an alternative to the dominant positivist or realist methodology of conducting research (e.g., Avenier 2010; Hassard 1994; Jeffcutt 1994; Kilduff and Mehra 1997; Mir and Watson 2000). Although Cox and Hassard (2005) also adopt postmodernism, their focus is different from that of this group in that they address a specific methodology issue – triangulation. They first discuss triangulation through the contrasting lenses of positivism and postpositivism/postmodernism as a metaphor for capturing the research subject. They then introduce the concept of metaphorization and "re-present" triangulation in terms of movement between researcher–subject positions. In other words, they not only present postmodernism as an alternative perspective but also further develop the postmodernist view of triangulation.

Another example is Watson's (2011) attempt to enhance the potential for ethnography to play a more mainstream role in management research. As a qualitative research method, ethnography is usually justified on the grounds of interpretivism or constructivism (Knorr-Cetina 1983). Drawing on pragmatism, Watson (2011) throws some new light on ethnography by stressing the investigation of "how things work" in field settings rather than trying to "get into the heads" of organizational members in order to capture and interpret their subjective experiences. This change of focus would produce work that is more relevant to human experience and practice. As a result, ethnographic work will be more appreciated and its status raised among management researchers.

Comparing approaches

Authors compare two or more approaches with or without specifying the one that they prefer. When authors express their preference, this kind of contribution is somewhat similar to "presenting an alternative approach" discussed earlier. The only difference is that the former focuses more on making a comparison between the preferred and the dominant approaches. Harris et al. (2013), for instance, compare two perspectives on how empirical findings contribute to theoretical knowledge accumulation. The more popular "law-statement" perspective interprets research contributions as empirically confirming or refuting general axioms of theory while the "model-theoretic" perspective recognizes contributions from testing and verifying different models that improve researchers' ability to represent the world of managers. Although Harris et al. (2013)

promote and further develop the latter perspective by identifying three ways of building representational models – grafting, contextualizing, and repurposing – a substantial portion of their discussion is concerned with comparing the two perspectives, as summarized by their Figure 1.

An example of authors taking a neutral position with respect to the approaches they compare is Johnson and Duberley's (2003) discussion of reflexivity in management research. They show how three distinctive combinations of ontological and epistemological assumptions form three generic types of reflexivity, namely methodological, deconstructive/hyper, and epistemic, which are respectively associated with the philosophical perspectives of positivism/neo-empiricism, postmodernism, and critical theory. Each type has distinctive implications for the role played by the researcher.

Creating a new approach

Authors develop a new approach to addressing a methodological issue based on one or more philosophical perspectives. A unique feature of this kind of contribution is its novelty, which extends beyond a direct application of the perspective(s) concerned. In order to create a new approach, authors often draw on more than one perspective. Probably owing to the novelty requirement, there are only five articles in this category, the fewest among the four kinds of contributions. This statement should be read with the usual caveat that novelty is not equivalent to quality. There is no indication that this group of articles are of higher quality than the other three.

An excellent illustration is the novel storytelling diamond model created by Rosile et al. (2013), who define storytelling as "the intraplay of grand (master) narratives (epistemic or empiric) with living stories (their ontological webs of relations)" (p. 558). A distinctive feature that separates this definition from other definitions in management research is its strong philosophical flavor – using terms like "empiric," "epistemic," and "ontological." To provide guidance to those interested in conducting storytelling research, they develop the storytelling diamond model with six facets (which they also call "paradigms"): narrativist, living story, materialist, interpretivist, abstractionist, and practice, as pictorially shown in their Figure 1. The model serves as the methodological toolbox of storytelling scholars. Some of the facets are clearly associated with certain philosophical perspectives. The interpretivist facet, for example, by its very nature is related to interpretivism and constructivism. Moreover, the facets can be combined to satisfy the philosophical orientation of a researcher. For instance, "for the positivist, an appropriate method in storytelling inquiry is an abstractionist perspective of a narrativist epistemology" (Rosile et al. 2013: 567).

Another example is Hoon's (2013) meta-synthesis of qualitative case studies, which corresponds to meta-analysis of quantitative studies. The objective of meta-synthesis is to extract, analyze, and synthesize qualitative evidence to build theory. She first compares the positivist, postpositivist, and constructivist views of research synthesis and then selects postpositivism as the perspective supporting her eight-step method of meta-synthesis. The method has sufficient novelty to be considered a new approach.

Style of presentation

Since management researchers generally receive little training in philosophy, it is important that philosophy-based articles published in management journals are written in a lucid style and calibrated at a level that is understandable to most readers. In particular this should be the case for articles discussing post-modernism, which is famous for having abstruse writing styles. Sokal and Bric-mont (1998) provide a detailed analysis of the misuses and abuses of science and scientific terminology committed by key figures of postmodernism.

Most authors with a postmodernist orientation in this review attempt to translate original postmodernist ideas into a readily understandable version. Yet there are exceptions. Consider, for example, the following passages extracted from Chia's (1995) argument for postmodernist organization studies:

> In other words, the postmodern *is* the modern in a *nascent* state. It is not located nor locatable through the framing of a simple succession of histori-cal periodizations, since this latter idea is itself a pivotal feature of modernist discourse. Rather, modernism is better construed as a consequence or outcome of the systematic suppression and consequent "forgetting" of its other term (i.e. the postmodern) through the cumulative effects of more than three centuries of privileging a dualistic mode of thought.
>
> (p. 580, emphasis in original)

> This example helps illustrate how concepts and ideas conceived within a different thought style can be easily assimilated into the dominant discourse in such a way as to neutralize claims which do not fit into the dominant order of things. A process of selective appropriation frequently occurs whereby concepts and ideas generated within a different set of ontological commitments and intellectual priorities are systematically appropriated and intellectually subdued to fit the underlying organizational logic of the dominant thought style.
>
> (p. 583)

> What is implied here is the violence done to this emergent and ephemeral reality when we attempt to impose our static organizing codes onto it. The apparent concreteness of the qualities we perceive in the social world are in reality attributes which we impute, through language, to that we apprehend as a way of ordering our experiences and organizing our understanding.
>
> (p. 590)

The ambiguous terms, convoluted logic, and figurative language used in these passages are not conducive to promoting postmodernist thinking among man-agement researchers.[2] As beautifully illustrated by Karl Popper's works, profound ideas do not have to be expressed in a pedantic manner.

As philosophical concepts and arguments are generally more abstract than those of management, the use of illustrative examples would improve clarity of exposition and enhance the readability of a philosophy-based article. There are two kinds of examples, namely theoretical and empirical, used by authors in this review. For the former kind of examples, Tsang (2006) uses transaction cost economics throughout to illustrate his argument that the core behavioral assumptions of a theory have to be realistic, although he maintains that his analysis is applicable to other management theories such as agency theory. Similarly, Durand and Vaara (2009) illustrate their counterfactual approach to causal analysis by the relationships between firm resources and performance. As to empirical examples, Prasad (2002) applies his proposed methodological guidelines for using hermeneutics to interpret the decision made by OPEC in 1973 to significantly raise the price of crude petroleum. Likewise, Sandberg (2005) proposes a set of criteria for justifying knowledge produced by interpretive research and then applies the criteria to his study of human competence at work published earlier (Sandberg 2000).

Pointers for future research

As mentioned, the publication of the 50 articles over the period 1984–2015 exhibits a significant upward trend. More management scholars seem to be interested in this stream of research, which is an encouraging situation. This section provides some practical suggestions to these scholars.

Have a sufficient understanding of philosophy

Those who have read both philosophy and the management literature probably would agree that the former is far more sophisticated and difficult to understand than the latter.[3] Moreover, philosophy is a broad discipline consisting of highly interrelated branches. For example, in order to understand philosophy of science, which is one of the most relevant branches for this research area, knowledge of metaphysics and epistemology is required. To acquire the latter knowledge, it is necessary to gain some knowledge of the history of Western philosophy. Thus, a huge investment of time and effort is needed in order to grasp a basic understanding of philosophy.

There are clear signs of insufficient understanding in some of the articles included in the current review. As mentioned in chapter 2, Welch et al. (2011) construct a typology of theorizing from case studies based on the trade-off between causal explanation and contextualization. Their argument regarding the trade-off is flawed, and the typology thus falls apart (Tsang 2013a). Moreover, footnote 5 of their article claims that Popper's falsificationism is a variant of positivism, and therefore the philosophical orientation of the "natural experiment" method of theorizing from case studies is stated as "positivist (falsificationist)" in their Table A. Obviously this is a factual error. Popper was a strong critic of positivism. In his *Unended Quest: An Intellectual Autobiography*, he famously claimed the responsibility for killing positivism:

> Everybody knows nowadays that logical positivism is dead. But nobody seems to suspect that there may be a question to be asked here – the

question "Who is responsible?" or, rather, the question "Who has done it?" . . . I fear that I must admit responsibility.

(Popper 2002 [1982]: 99)

Another example is Mir and Watson's (2000) comparison of constructivism and realism when they promote the former perspective. Kwan and Tsang (2001) point out that their version of constructivism is problematic and their understanding of realism is flawed.[4] These articles managed to pass through the review process despite the errors probably because there were, and still are, few qualified reviewers (Tsang 2013b).

Needless to say, errors should be avoided. Researchers should refrain from the temptation to convert their ideas into journal submissions immediately after reading several articles on a certain philosophical perspective or topic. A general understanding of philosophy as a subject is recommended before focusing on any specific perspective or topic. In addition, collaborating with professional philosophers not only enhances one's philosophical knowledge but also the quality of a publication.

Look out for philosophical insights

When management researchers have developed interest in a methodological issue, there is always no harm to search the literature of philosophy and see what insights it can provide. There may be positive surprises. A good example is the issue of HARKing (Hypothesizing After the Results are Known) discussed in chapter 4. Surprisingly, none of the three scholars who discuss the problem in the management or psychology literature (i.e., Bettis 2012; Kerr 1998; Leung 2011) refer to any references in philosophy despite the fact that this issue was discussed and debated in as early as the 1980s (e.g., Gardner 1982; Maher 1988; Schlesinger 1987). The debate continued until recent years (e.g., Douglas and Magnus 2013; Harker 2013; McCain 2012). There is a wealth of knowledge on which management researchers may be able draw to enhance the quality of their discussion. For instance, Bettis (2012) develops his argument against HARKing on statistical grounds. When formulating his argument, he would probably have benefited from reading Howson's (1990) statistical-cum-philosophical counter-argument, which is based on the so-called Personalist Bayesianism, that fitting theory to data may not be a bad thing after all.

A further example is Edwards and Berry's (2010) argument for making theories more precise. Specifically they propose several methods for increasing the precision of hypotheses (as summarized in their Table A), thereby putting the theory in question at greater risk of falsification. The discussion is heavily statistics-based and with only meager reference to philosophy. A stronger philosophical flavor would probably enhance their argument. For instance, the Duhem-Quine thesis covered in chapter 4 is germane to their discussion of theory testing. The thesis maintains that the presence of auxiliary hypotheses confounds the test of the principal hypothesis. Instead of focusing on the principal hypothesis only,

Edwards and Berry's (2010) discussion would be enriched by examining the effects of auxiliary hypotheses as well.

Revisit an old issue

As this stream of research develops, there may be opportunities for researchers to revisit some of the methodological issues discussed earlier based on the more recent literatures of philosophy, management, and other disciplines. For example, a core argument supporting Astley's (1985) view that administrative science knowledge is socially constructed is as follows:

> As administrative scientists, we formulate knowledge subjectively through biased, selected observations of everyday managerial practice. The world of practice has its own "objective" reality, but since, as scientists, our only recourse to that world is through what we see and do, our knowledge is unavoidably subjective in nature. The "facts" constituting our knowledge are necessarily theory-dependent, since we can perceive nothing except through the knowledge structure in which perception is embedded.
>
> (p. 498)

The argument is closely related to the "theory-ladenness of observation" problem discussed in chapter 6. The problem can be traced to the influential arguments of Hanson (1958) and Kuhn (1962) that theory does influence observation. It has been well discussed in philosophy (e.g., Brewer and Lambert 2001; Hunt 1994; Raftopoulos 2001; Schindler 2011). Astley's (1985) argument may be strengthened or revised based on this literature.

Another example is Tsoukas's (1989) defense of the external validity (or generalizability) of results obtained from idiographic studies based on critical realism. Since then there have been discussions of this methodological issue, especially in the context of case studies, which are the most popular form of idiographic studies in management research (e.g., Firestone 1993; Gobo 2004; Gomm et al. 2000; Schofield 1990; Tsang 2014a, b). Moreover, adopting the perspective of critical realism, Easton (2000, 2010), Harrison and Easton (2004), and Wynn and Williams (2012) justify case studies as a legitimate research method, discuss their functions, and offer guidelines to case study researchers.

Pick a fight

Critical thinking is a core element of the tradition of Western philosophy started by Socrates, Plato, and Aristotle. Philosophers like to argue and debate, and that is how the discipline moves forward. In fact, Nietzsche's critique of the various philosophical thoughts that came before him forms the foundation of postmodernism.

Management researchers have much to learn from philosophers in this respect. Unfortunately there are few debates or dialogues in this stream of research. The most prominent example is the critique of Powell's (2001) pragmatist treatment of the concept of competitive advantage by Arend (2003) and Durand (2002) and his responses (Powell 2002, 2003). A more recent example is Ellsaesser et al.'s (2014) critique of causal graph modeling introduced by Durand and Vaara (2009) as a tool for inferring causes in strategy research. They propose vector space modeling as an alternative. Presenting different or contradicting views on a methodological issue helps deepen and broaden the understanding of the issue. Management researchers are encouraged to read articles, especially philosophy-based articles, critically, identify problems, and present their critiques and solutions. Such intellectual dialogues will make the field stronger.

A concluding remark

The prior review shows how philosophy has contributed to tackling a set of fundamental methodological issues faced by management researchers. It reveals the flaw of a rather common association of research methodology with statistics alone. For example, improving the statistical techniques in discovering significant relationships among variables in a database will not shed any light on the epistemic difference between accommodation and prediction (see chapter 6). Similarly, enhancing the predictive power of a model does not address the issue of whether or not the assumptions of the model have to be realistic (see chapter 3). This is because these are intrinsically philosophical problems and have to be dealt with philosophically.

Notes

1 The terms "constructivism" and "constructionism" are often used in an interchangeable manner (*Cambridge Dictionary of Philosophy* 1999). Interested readers may refer to Al-Amoudi and Willmott (2011: endnote 2) for a discussion of their subtle differences.
2 This comment should by no means be interpreted as a personal attack on the author. Rather, it is used purely to illustrate the importance of intelligible writing.
3 Unconvinced readers may try to read Popper's (1959) *The Logic of Scientific Discovery* and compare it with Cyert and March's (1992) *A Behavioral Theory of the Firm*. Both are seminal works in their respective fields. A caveat is that it will not be a fair comparison for management researchers, who have received training that helps them understand the latter. That said, the much greater extent of background knowledge and intellectual capability required for understanding the former can still be appreciated. Moreover, note that Popper is among the few great philosophers who are well-known for lucid writing. There is a long list of philosophers, such as Hegel, Heidegger, and Nietzsche, whose works are hard to decipher.
4 A far more serious case happened outside the management field. Invoking Hume's problem of induction, Lee and Baskerville (2003) attempt to clarify the concept of generalization and classify it into four types for guiding information systems research. In spite of their good intention, the article contains numerous logical and philosophical errors (see chapter 5).

References

Al-Amoudi, I. and Willmott, H. 2011. Where constructionism and critical realism converge: Interrogating the domain of epistemological relativism. *Organization Studies*, 32: 27–46.

Amis, J. M. and Silk, M. L. 2008. The philosophy and politics of quality in qualitative organizational research. *Organizational Research Methods*, 11: 456–480.

Arend, R. J. 2003. Revisiting the logical and research considerations of competitive advantage. *Strategic Management Journal*, 24: 279–284.

Astley, W. G. 1985. Administrative science as socially constructed truth. *Administrative Science Quarterly*, 30: 497–513.

Avenier, M. J. 2010. Shaping a constructivist view of organizational design science. *Organization studies*, 31: 1229–1255.

Ayer, A. J. 1946. *Language, truth, and logic*. London: Gollancz.

Berger, P. L. and Luckmann, T. 1967. *The social construction of reality*. New York: Anchor Books.

Bettis, R. A. 2012. The search for asterisks: Compromised statistical tests and flawed theories. *Strategic Management Journal*, 33: 108–113.

Brannick, T. and Coghlan, D. 2007. In defense of being "native": The case for insider academic research. *Organizational Research Methods*, 10: 59–74.

Brewer, W. F. and Lambert, B. L. 2001. The theory-ladenness of observation and the theory-ladenness of the rest of the scientific process. *Philosophy of Science*, 68 (Proceedings): S176–S186.

Calás, M. B. and Smircich, L. 1999. Past postmodernism? Reflections and tentative directions. *Academy of Management Review*, 24: 649–672.

Cambridge dictionary of philosophy (2nd ed.). 1999. Cambridge, England: Cambridge University Press.

Cederström, C. and Spicer, A. 2014. Discourse of the real kind: A post-foundational approach to organizational discourse analysis. *Organization*, 21: 178–205.

Chia, R. 1995. From modern to postmodern organizational analysis. *Organization Studies*, 16: 579–604.

Chia, R. and Holt, R. 2006. Strategy as practical coping: A Heideggerian perspective. *Organization Studies*, 27: 635–655.

Cohen, M. D. 2007. Reading Dewey: Reflections on the study of routines. *Organization Studies*, 28: 773–786.

Cox, J. W. and Hassard, J. 2005. Triangulation in organizational research: A re-presentation. *Organization*, 12: 109–133.

Cyert, R. M. and March, J. G. 1992. *A behavioral theory of the firm* (2nd ed.). Malden, MA: Blackwell.

Daft, R. L. and Lewin, A. Y. 1990. Can organization studies begin to break out of the normal science straitjacket? An editorial essay. *Organization Science*, 1: 1–9.

Douglas, H. and Magnus, P. D. 2013. State of the field: Why novel prediction matters. *Studies in History and Philosophy of Science*, 44: 580–589.

Durand, R. 2002. Competitive advantages exist: A critique of Powell. *Strategic Management Journal*, 23: 867–872.

Durand, R. and Vaara, E. 2009. Causation, counterfactuals, and competitive advantage. *Strategic Management Journal*, 30: 1245–1264.

Easton, G. 2000. Case research as a method for industrial networks: A realist apologia. In S. Ackroyd and S. Fleetwood (Eds.), *Realist perspectives on management and organisations*: 205–219. London: Routledge.

Easton, G. 2010. Critical realism in case study research. *Industrial Marketing Management*, 39: 118–128.

Edwards, J. R. and Berry, J. W. 2010. The presence of something or the absence of nothing: Increasing theoretical precision in management research. *Organizational Research Methods*, 13: 668–689.

Elder-Vass, D. 2012. *The reality of social construction.* Cambridge, England: Cambridge University Press.

Ellsaesser, F., Tsang, E. W. K. and Runde, J. 2014. Models of causal inference: Imperfect but applicable is better than perfect but inapplicable. *Strategic Management Journal*, 35: 1541–1551.

Everett, J. 2002. Organizational research and the praxeology of Pierre Bourdieu. *Organizational Research Methods*, 5: 56–80.

Fairclough, N. 2005. Peripheral vision discourse analysis in organization studies: The case for critical realism. *Organization studies*, 26: 915–939.

Farjoun, M., Ansell, C. and Boin, A. 2015. Pragmatism in organization studies: Meeting the challenges of a dynamic and complex world. *Organization Science*, 26: 1787–1804.

Feldman, M. S. 2003. A performative perspective on stability and change in organizational routines. *Industrial and Corporate Change*, 12: 727–752.

Firestone, W. A. 1993. Alternative arguments for generalizing from data as applied to qualitative research. *Educational Researcher*, 22(4): 16–23.

Gardner, M. R. 1982. Predicting novel facts. *British Journal for the Philosophy of Science*, 33: 1–15.

Gephart Jr., R. P. 2004. Qualitative research and the *Academy of Management Journal*. *Academy of Management Journal*, 47: 454–462.

Gill, M. J. 2014. The possibilities of phenomenology for organizational research. *Organizational Research Methods*, 17: 118–137.

Gobo, G. 2004. Sampling, representativeness and generalizability. In C. Seale, G. Gobo, J. F. Gubrium and D. Silverman (Eds.), *Qualitative research practice*: 405–426. London: Sage.

Godfrey, P. C. and Hill, C. W. L. 1995. The problem of unobservables in strategic management research. *Strategic Management Journal*, 16: 519–533.

Gomm, R., Hammersley, M. and Foster, P. 2000. Case study and generalization. In R. Gomm, M. Hammersley and P. Foster (Eds.), *Case study: Key issues, key texts*: 98–115. London: Sage.

Gray, P. H. and Cooper, W. H. 2010. Pursuing failure. *Organizational Research Methods*, 13: 620–643.

Hanson, N. R. 1958. *Patterns of discovery.* Cambridge, England: University of Cambridge Press.

Harker, D. W. 2013. McCain on weak predictivism and external world scepticism. *Philosophia*, 41: 195–202.

Harris, J. D., Johnson, S. G. and Souder, D. 2013. Model-theoretic knowledge accumulation: The case of agency theory and incentive alignment. *Academy of Management Review*, 38: 442–454.

Harrison, D. and Easton, G. 2004. Temporally embedded case comparison in industrial marketing research. In S. Fleetwood and S. Ackroyd (Eds.), *Critical realist applications in organisation and management studies*: 194–210. London: Routledge.

Hassard, J. 1994. Postmodern organizational analysis: Toward a conceptual framework. *Journal of Management Studies*, 31: 303–324.

Herepath, A. 2014. In the loop: A realist approach to structure and agency in the practice of strategy. *Organization Studies*, 35: 857–879.

Holt, R. and Mueller, F. 2011. Wittgenstein, Heidegger and drawing lines in organization studies. *Organization Studies*, 32: 67–84.

Hoon, C. 2013. Meta-synthesis of qualitative case studies: An approach to theory building. *Organizational Research Methods*, 16: 522–556.

Hosking, D. M. 2011. Telling tales of relations: Appreciating relational constructionism. *Organization Studies*, 32: 47–65.

Howson, C. 1990. Fitting your theory to the facts: Probably not such a bad thing after all. In C. W. Savage (Ed.), *Scientific theories*, Vol. 14: 224–244. Minneapolis, MN: University of Minnesota Press.

Hunt, S. D. 1994. A realistic theory of empirical testing: Resolving the theory-ladenness/objectivity debate. *Philosophy of the Social Sciences*, 24: 133–158.

Jeffcutt, P. 1994. The interpretation of organization: A contemporary analysis and critique. *Journal of Management Studies*, 31: 225–250.

Johnson, P. and Duberley, J. 2000. *Understanding management research: An introduction to epistemology*. London: Sage.

Johnson, P. and Duberley, J. 2003. Reflexivity in management research. *Journal of Management Studies*, 40: 1279–1303.

Kerr, N. L. 1998. HARKing: Hypothesizing after the results are known. *Personality and Social Psychology Review*, 2: 196–217.

Ketokivi, M. and Mantere, S. 2010. Two strategies for inductive reasoning in organizational research. *Academy of Management Review*, 35: 315–333.

Kilduff, M. and Mehra, A. 1997. Postmodernism and organizational research. *Academy of Management Review*, 22: 453–481.

Knights, D. 1997. Organization theory in the age of deconstruction: Dualism, gender and postmodernism revisited. *Organization Studies*, 18: 1–19.

Knorr-Cetina, K. D. 1983. The ethnographic study of scientific work: Towards a constructivist interpretation of science. In K. D. Knorr-Cetina and M. Mulkay (Eds.), *Science observed: Perspectives on the social study of science*: 115–140. London: Sage.

Kuhn, T. S. 1962. *The structure of scientific revolutions*. Chicago, IL: University of Chicago Press.

Kwan, K.-M. and Tsang, E. W. K. 2001. Realism and constructivism in strategy research: A critical realist response to Mir and Watson. *Strategic Management Journal*, 22: 1163–1168.

Lakatos, I. 1970. Falsification and the methodology of scientific research programmes. In I. Lakatos and A. Musgrave (Eds.), *Criticism and the growth of knowledge*: 91–196. Cambridge, England: Cambridge University Press.

Lee, A. S. and Baskerville, R. L. 2003. Generalizing generalizability in information systems research. *Information Systems Research*, 14: 221–243.

Leitch, C. M., Hill, F. M. and Harrison, R. T. 2010. The philosophy and practice of interpretivist research in entrepreneurship: Quality, validation, and trust. *Organizational Research Methods*, 13: 67–84.

Leung, K. 2011. Presenting post hoc hypotheses as a priori: Ethical and theoretical issues. *Management and Organization Review*, 7: 471–479.

Lewis, M. W. 2000. Exploring paradox: Toward a more comprehensive guide. *Academy of Management Review*, 25: 760–776.

Locke, E. A. 2007. The case for inductive theory building. *Journal of Management*, 33: 867–890.

Lorino, P., Tricard, B. and Clot, Y. 2011. Research methods for non-representational approaches to organizational complexity: The dialogical mediated inquiry. *Organization Studies*, 32: 769–801.

Maher, P. 1988. Prediction, accommodation, and the logic of discovery. *PSA: Proceedings of the Biennial Meeting of the Philosophy of Science Association*: 273–285. Philosophy of Science Association.

Martela, F. 2015. Fallible inquiry with ethical ends-in-view: A pragmatist philosophy of science for organizational research. *Organization Studies*, 36: 537–563.

McCain, K. 2012. A predictivist argument against scepticism. *Analysis*, 72: 660–665.

McKelvey, B. 1997. Quasi-natural organization science. *Organization Science*, 8: 352–380.

Miller, K. D. 2009. Organizational risk after modernism. *Organization Studies*, 30: 157–180.

Miller, K. D. 2015a. Organizational research as practical theology. *Organizational Research Methods*, 18: 276–299.

Miller, K. D. 2015b. Agent-based modeling and organization studies: A critical realist perspective. *Organization Studies*, 36: 175–196.

Miller, K. D. and Tsang, E. W. K. 2011. Testing management theories: Critical realist philosophy and research methods. *Strategic Management Journal*, 32: 139–158.

Mir, R. and Watson, A. 2000. Strategic management and the philosophy of science: The case for a constructivist methodology. *Strategic Management Journal*, 21: 941–953.

Mir, R. and Watson, A. 2001. Critical realism and constructivism in strategy research: Toward a synthesis. *Strategic Management Journal*, 22: 1169–1173.

O'Brien, D. 2006. *An introduction to the theory of knowledge*. Cambridge, England: Polity Press.

Podsakoff, P. M., MacKenzie, S. B., Lee, J.-Y. and Podsakoff, N. P. 2003. Common method biases in behavioral research: A critical review of the literature and recommended remedies. *Journal of Applied Psychology*, 88: 879–903.

Popper, K. 1959. *The logic of scientific discovery*. London: Hutchinson.

Popper, K. 2002 [1982]. *Unended quest: An intellectual autobiography*. New York, NY: Routledge.

Powell, T. C. 2001. Competitive advantage: Logical and philosophical considerations. *Strategic Management Journal*, 22: 875–888.

Powell, T. C. 2002. The philosophy of strategy. *Strategic Management Journal*, 23: 873–880.

Powell, T. C. 2003. Strategy without ontology. *Strategic Management Journal*, 24: 285–291.

Prasad, A. 2002. The contest over meaning: Hermeneutics as an interpretive methodology for understanding texts. *Organizational Research Methods*, 5: 12–33.

Raftopoulos, A. 2001. Reentrant neural pathways and the theory-ladenness of perception. *Philosophy of Science*, 68(Proceedings): S187–S199.

Rosile, G. A., Boje, D. M., Carlon, D. M., Downs, A. and Saylors, R. 2013. Storytelling diamond: An antenarrative integration of the six facets of storytelling in organization research design. *Organizational Research Methods*, 16: 557–580.

Runde, J. and de Rond, M. 2010. Evaluating causal explanations of specific events. *Organization Studies*, 31: 431–450.

Sandberg, J. 2000. Understanding human competence at work: An interpretive approach, *Academy of Management Journal*, 43: 9–25.

Sandberg, J. 2005. How do we justify knowledge produced within interpretive approaches? *Organizational Research Methods*, 8: 41–68.

Schindler, S. 2011. Bogen and Woodward's data-phenomena distinction, forms of theory-ladenness, and the reliability of data. *Synthese*, 182: 39–55.

Schlesinger, G. N. 1987. Accommodation and prediction. *Australasian Journal of Philosophy*, 65: 33–42.

Schofield, J. W. 1990. Increasing the generalizability of qualitative research. In E. W. Eisner and A. Peshkin (Eds.), *Qualitative inquiry in education: The continuing debate*: 201–232. New York: Teachers College Press.

Shotter, J. 2005. "Inside the moment of managing": Wittgenstein and the everyday dynamics of our expressive-responsive activities. *Organization studies*, 26: 113–135.

Simpson, B. 2009. Pragmatism, Mead and the practice turn. *Organization Studies*, 30: 1329–1347.

Singh, K., Ang, S. H. and Leong, S. M. 2003. Increasing replication for knowledge accumulation in strategy research. *Journal of Management*, 29: 533–549.

Sokal, A. and Bricmont, J. 1998. *Intellectual impostures: Postmodern philosophers' abuse of science*. London: Profile Books.

Steffy, B. D. and Grimes, A. J. 1986. A critical theory of organization science. *Academy of Management Review*, 11: 322–336.

Tomkins, L. and Simpson, P. 2015. Caring leadership: A Heideggerian perspective. *Organization Studies*, 36: 1013–1031.

Tsang, E. W. K. 2006. Behavioral assumptions and theory development: The case of transaction cost economics. *Strategic Management Journal*, 27: 999–1011.

Tsang, E. W. K. 2013a. Case study methodology: Causal explanation, contextualization, and theorizing. *Journal of International Management*, 19: 195–202.

Tsang, E. W. K. 2013b. Is this referee really my peer? A challenge to the peer-review process. *Journal of Management Inquiry*, 22: 166–171.

Tsang, E. W. K. 2014a. Case studies and generalization in information systems research: A critical realist perspective. *Journal of Strategic Information Systems*, 23: 174–186.

Tsang, E. W. K. 2014b. Generalizing from research findings: The merits of case studies. *International Journal of Management Reviews*, 16: 369–383.

Tsang, E. W. K. and Ellsaesser, F. 2011. How contrastive explanation facilitates theory building. *Academy of Management Review*, 36: 404–419.

Tsang, E. W. K. and Kwan, K.-M. 1999. Replication and theory development in organizational science: A critical realist perspective. *Academy of Management Review*, 24: 759–780.

Tsoukas, H. 1989. The validity of idiographic research explanations. *Academy of Management Review*, 14: 551–561.

Watson, T. J. 2011. Ethnography, reality, and truth: The vital need for studies of "how things work" in organizations and management. *Journal of Management Studies*, 48: 202–217.

Welch, C., Piekkari, R., Plakoyiannaki, E. and Paavilainen-Mäntymäki, E. 2011. Theorising from case studies: Towards a pluralist future for international business research. *Journal of International Business Studies*, 42: 740–762.

Whitley, R. 1984. The scientific status of management research as a practically-oriented social science. *Journal of Management Studies*, 21: 369–390.

Wicks, A. C. and Freeman, R. E. 1998. Organization studies and the new pragmatism: Positivism, anti-positivism, and the search for ethics. *Organization Science*, 9: 123–140.

Wittgenstein, L. 1922. *Tractatus logico-philosophicus*. London: Kegan Paul, Trench, and Trübner.

Wynn Jr., D. and Williams, C. K. 2012. Principles for conducting critical realist case study research in information systems. *MIS Quarterly*, 36: 787–810.

Name Index

Subject Index

For Product Safety Concerns and Information please contact our EU
representative GPSR@taylorandfrancis.com
Taylor & Francis Verlag GmbH, Kaufingerstraße 24, 80331 München, Germany

www.ingramcontent.com/pod-product-compliance
Ingram Content Group UK Ltd.
Pitfield, Milton Keynes, MK11 3LW, UK
UKHW021615240425
457818UK00018B/571